'Assembling a team of leading scholars, Kai He and his colleagues have convincingly argued that "contested multilateralism 2.0" is the key to understanding the new security dynamics in Asia. A must read for all students who care about the future of Asia and multilateralism.'

Shiping Tang, *distinguished professor, Fudan University and author of* The Social Evolution of International Politics

'Regional and international institutions in East Asia have been changing their roles, functions and geographical scope along with radical power shifts in East Asian politics. Institutions have become more important tools for national foreign policies and for creating a new regional and international order. Professor He's new edited book contributes to our understanding of this new phenomenon both theoretically and empirically, by putting together different theoretical perspectives and national policy orientations of the major countries in the region. I recommend this book to both researchers and policy practitioners who are interested in, and deal with, this important region.'

Yoshinobu Yamamoto, *Professor Emeritus, University of Tokyo, Japan*

CONTESTED MULTILATERALISM 2.0 AND ASIAN SECURITY DYNAMICS

In the 1990s there was a wave of multilateralism in the Asia Pacific, led primarily by ASEAN. Since the Global Financial Crisis of 2008, however, many non-ASEAN states have attempted to seize the initiative, including the USA, Japan, China, South Korea, and Australia.

Kai He and his contributors debate the reasons for this contested multilateralism and the impacts it will have on the region's security and political challenges. Will the 'Indo-Pacific turn' be a blessing or a curse for regional stability and prosperity? Using a diverse range of theoretical and empirical perspectives, these leading scholars contribute views on this question and on the diverse strategies of the great and middle powers in the region.

This collection will be of great interest to scholars and students of international relations in the Asia Pacific and of great value to policy makers in the region and beyond.

Kai He is a Professor of International Relations in the Griffith Asia Institute and Centre for Governance and Public Policy at Griffith University in Brisbane, Australia. He is currently an Australian Research Council Future Fellow (2017–2020) and a Visiting Chair Professor of International Relations at Nankai University, China (2018–2021).

ROUTLEDGE ADVANCES IN INTERNATIONAL RELATIONS AND GLOBAL POLITICS

For information about the series: https://www.routledge.com/Routledge-Advances-in-International-Relations-and-Global-Politics/book-series/IRGP

CONTESTED MULTILATERALISM 2.0 AND ASIAN SECURITY DYNAMICS

Edited by Kai He

Routledge
Taylor & Francis Group

LONDON AND NEW YORK

First published 2020
by Routledge
2 Park Square, Milton Park, Abingdon, Oxon OX14 4RN

and by Routledge
52 Vanderbilt Avenue, New York, NY 10017

Routledge is an imprint of the Taylor & Francis Group, an informa business

British Library Cataloguing-in-Publication Data
A catalogue record for this book is available from the British Library

Library of Congress Cataloging-in-Publication Data
Names: He, Kai, 1973- editor.
Title: Contested multilateralism 2.0 and Asian security dynamics /
edited by Kai He.
Description: Abingdon, Oxon ; New York, NY : Routledge, 2020. |
Includes bibliographical references and index.
Identifiers: LCCN 2019058819 (print) | LCCN 2019058820 (ebook) |
ISBN 9780367893378 (hardback) | ISBN 9780367893385 (paperback) |
ISBN 9781003018650 (ebook)
Subjects: LCSH: Asian cooperation. | Regionalism--Asia. |
Asia--Foreign relations.
Classification: LCC JZ5333 .C665 2020 (print) | LCC JZ5333 (ebook) |
DDC 355/.03305--dc23
LC record available at https://lccn.loc.gov/2019058819
LC ebook record available at https://lccn.loc.gov/2019058820

ISBN: 978-0-367-89337-8 (hbk)
ISBN: 978-0-367-89338-5 (pbk)
ISBN: 978-1-003-01865-0 (ebk)

Typeset in Bembo
by Taylor & Francis Books

CONTENTS

ILLUSTRATIONS

Figures

Tables

ACKNOWLEDGMENTS

Since the 2008 global financial crisis (GFC), the strategic competition between the United States and China has occupied the media headlines on world politics. Scholars and pundits are fascinated by the question of whether the United States and China will fall into the Thucydides Trap, in which a ruling power will tragically fight against a rising power in order to overcome the fear generated by the power transition in the international system. One intriguing, but largely omitted, phenomenon is that the US–China strategic rivalry and competition is quite different from what the United States and the Soviet Union experienced during the Cold War. While there has been a prolonged trade war between the United States and China since President Donald Trump came to power in 2016, a trade war is much better than a Cold War. We cannot rule out the possibility that a new Cold War between the United States and China may take place. Nevertheless, it is clear that the international order transition accompanying US–China strategic competition will be different from previous power transitions in history.

Multilateralism is one of the factors that will contribute to a different international order transition in the 21st century. This is why we have witnessed the emergence of 'contested multilateralism 2.0' in the Asia Pacific since the 2008 GFC, in which all major players in the region, including the United States, China, Japan, Australia, South Korea, and ASEAN, have actively engaged in multilateralism to differing degrees. Although withdrawing from the Trans-Pacific Partnership, Trump emphasized the 'rules-based order in the Indo Pacific' by reviving the Quadrilateral Security Dialogue (the so-called 'Quad 2.0') with Japan, Australia, and India in 2017. The United States will continue its leadership contestation with China in the region through a variety of existing regional instrumentalities and institutions.

Will 'multilateralism 2.0' still matter for regional security and international order transition? If so, how? In particular, how will regional actors employ differing institutional strategies to maximize their respective national interests during the period of international order transition? Several of the leading international relations (IR) scholars on multilateralism and Asian security offer new perspectives in this edited volume and shed some light on these questions regarding multilateralism and the future regional order transition against a background of US–China strategic competition in the 21st century. This book is supported by the Australian Research Council [grant number FT160100355] and a policy-oriented research grant from the Korea Foundation, which have made this publication possible.

I appreciate also the institutional support from Griffith University and the efforts of their skillful staff in successfully organizing a two-day conference in Brisbane, Australia, in May 2017. I would also like to thank Stephen Walker, my mentor, friend and advisor, for his suggestions and advice on this project. I am indebted to each of the contributors in this volume as well as all of the participants in the conference for their sharp comments and constructive suggestions on the project. I thank *The Australian Journal of International Affairs* and *The Pacific Review* (both published by Taylor & Francis/Routledge) for granting permission to re-use some articles in this book. I am grateful to Daniela Di Piramo, who provided professional editorial assistance for this project. Finally, I want to acknowledge the encouragement and support at the publication stage of this project from Simon Bates, my editor at Routledge.

Kai He
Griffith University
Brisbane, Australia

CONTRIBUTORS

Mark Beeson is a Professor of International Politics at the University of Western Australia (UWA). Before joining UWA, he taught at Murdoch, Griffith, Queensland, York (UK) and Birmingham. He is the founding editor of *Critical Studies of the Asia Pacific* (Palgrave). His latest book is *Rethinking Global Governance* (Palgrave, 2019).

Nick Bisley is Dean of Humanities and Social Sciences and Professor of International Relations at La Trobe University, Australia. His research and teaching expertise is in Asia's international relations, globalization and the diplomacy of great powers. Nick is a Director of the Australian Institute of International Affairs, a member of the Council for Security and Cooperation in the Asia-Pacific and has been a Senior Research Associate of the International Institute of Strategic Studies and a Visiting Fellow at the East West-Center in Washington DC. Nick is the author of many works on international relations, including *Issues in 21st Century World Politics, 2nd Edition* (Palgrave, 2013), *Great Powers in the Changing International Order* (Lynne Rienner, 2012) and *Building Asia's Security* (IISS/Routledge, 2009, Adelphi No. 408). He regularly contributes and is quoted in national and international media, including *The Guardian*, *The Economist*, and *South China Morning Post*.

Melissa Conley Tyler is Director of Diplomacy, Asialink, University of Melbourne, Australia. She served as National Executive Director of the Australian Institute of International Affairs from January 2006 to March 2019. She is a lawyer and specialist in conflict resolution, including negotiation, mediation and peace education. She was previously Program Manager of the International Conflict Resolution Centre at the University of Melbourne and Senior Fellow of Melbourne Law School. She has an international profile in conflict resolution, including membership of the editorial board of the Conflict Resolution Quarterly.

Kai He is a Professor of International Relations in the Griffith Asia Institute and Centre for Governance and Public Policy at Griffith University in Brisbane, Australia. He is currently an Australian Research Council Future Fellow (2017–2020) and a Visiting Chair Professor of International Relations at Nankai University, China (2018–2021). He was a postdoctoral fellow in the Princeton–Harvard China and the World Program (2009–2010). He is the author of *Institutional Balancing in the Asia Pacific: Economic Interdependence and China's Rise* (Routledge, 2009) and *China's Crisis Behavior: Political Survival and Foreign Policy* (Cambridge, 2016). He is the co-author of *Prospect Theory and Foreign Policy Analysis in the Asia Pacific: Rational Leaders and Risky Behavior* (with Huiyun Feng, Routledge, 2013) and *How China Sees the World: Insights from China's International Relations Scholars* (with Huiyun Feng and Xiaojun Li, Palgrave, 2019).

William Kang graduated from the State University of New York at Binghamton, USA, with a Bachelor of Arts degree in Economics and Philosophy. In 2014, he graduated from the Graduate School of International Studies (GSIS) at Sogang University, South Korea, with a Master of International Studies in International Relations degree.

Jaechun Kim is a Professor of International Relations at the Graduate School of International Studies (GSIS) at Sogang University. He is a political scientist trained at Yale University (MA in International Relations; Ph.D. in Political Science). Before joining Sogang, he worked at Yale University as a lecturer in the Department of Political Science and Yale Center for the International and Area Studies (YCIAS). He is currently a member of the advisory board for the Ministry of Foreign Affairs in the Republic of Korea (ROK). He was a member of the Government Performance Evaluation Committee and a member of the Presidential Committee for Unification Preparation in ROK. He served as the Director of Sogang University's Institute of International and Area Studies (IIAS) and the Dean of Sogang GSIS. He was a Fulbright Visiting Fellow to the Sigur Center for Asian Studies at George Washington University and a visiting scholar to Denver University. Earlier in his career, he worked for the National Assembly of ROK as a Legislative Assistant. His research interests include International Security, US Foreign Policy, Northeast Asia Regional Affairs, and Inter-Korean Relations

T. J. Pempel is the Jack M. Forcey Professor of Political Science at the University of California, Berkeley, USA. He has been on the Berkeley faculty since 2001. He has also held positions at Cornell University, the University of Colorado, the University of Wisconsin and the University of Washington. From 2001 until 2006 he was the director of Berkeley's Institute of East Asian Studies. He is a presidential appointee to the Japan–US Friendship Commission. His research focuses on comparative politics, Japanese political economy, and Asian regional issues. He has published over 120 articles and 24 books.

See Seng Tan is President/CEO-elect of International Students Inc. (ISI), a faith-based non-profit organization based in the US, and concurrently Professor of International Relations at the S. Rajaratnam School of International Studies (RSIS), Nanyang Technological University, Singapore. His latest books include *The Legal Authority of ASEAN as a Security Institution* (co-authored with Hitoshi Nasu, Rob McLaughlin and Donald R. Rothwell, 2019) and *The Responsibility to Provide in Southeast Asia: Towards an Ethical Explanation* (2019).

William Tow is an Emeritus Professor of International Relations in the Department of International Relations, Coral Bell School for Asia and Pacific Affairs at Australian National University. He has authored or edited over 20 volumes and 100 journal/book articles on alliance politics, Asia-Pacific security issues and regional order-building. Tow has been principal investigator in two major projects for the MacArthur Foundation's Asia Security Initiative. He has also been the editor of the Australian Journal of International Affairs and has served on the Foreign Affairs Council, Australian Department of Foreign Affairs and Trade, and the National Board of Directors, Australian Fulbright Commission. He has been a Visiting Fellow at Stanford University, the International Institute for Strategic Studies (IISS) in London and both the ISEAS Yusof Ishak Institute and the Rajaratnam School of International Studies (ISIS) in Singapore.

Hidetaka Yoshimatsu is a Professor of Politics and International Relations at the Graduate School of Asia Pacific Studies, Ritsumeikan Asia Pacific University, Japan as well as a Visiting Research Fellow at the School of Social Sciences, University of Adelaide. His recent publications include *Comparing Institution-Building in East Asia: Power Politics, Governance, and Critical Junctures* (Palgrave Macmillan, 2014) and *The Political Economy of Regionalism in East Asia: Integrative Explanation for Dynamics and Challenges* (Palgrave Macmillan, 2008). His current research interests include regionalism in East Asia and the Asia-pacific.

Jingdong Yuan is Chair of Department of Government and International Relations and an Associate Professor from the Centre for International Security Studies, University of Sydney, Australia. He specializes in Indo-Pacific security, Chinese defense and foreign policy, and global and regional arms control and non-proliferation issues. He has held visiting appointments at National University of Singapore, University of Macau, East-West Centre, National Cheng-chi University, and worked at the James Martin Centre for Nonproliferation Studies, Middlebury Institute of International Studies between 1999 and 2010. He is co-author of *A Low-Visibility Force Multiplier* (2014) and *China and India: Cooperation or Conflict?* (2003) and co-editor of *Australia and China 40* (2012).

ABBREVIATIONS

ABMI	Asian Bond Market Initiative
ADB	Asian Development Bank
ADMM	ASEAN Defense Ministers' Meeting
ADMM+	ASEAN Defense Ministers' Meeting Plus
AFC	Asian Financial Crisis
AFTA	ASEAN Free Trade Area
AIIB	Asian Infrastructure Investment Bank
AMF	Asian Monetary Fund
AMRO	ASEAN + 3 Macroeconomic Research Office
APC	Asia Pacific Community
APEC	Asia-Pacific Economic Cooperation
APRSAF	Asia-Pacific Regional Space Agency Forum
APSCO	Asia-Pacific Space Cooperation Organization
APT	ASEAN Plus Three
ARF	ASEAN Regional Forum
ASEAN	Association of Southeast Asian Nations
ASEM	Asia-Europe Meeting
ASPAC	Asia Pacific Council
BRF	Belt and Road Forum
BRI	Belt and Road Initiative
CCAMLR	Convention for the Conservation of Antarctic Marine Living Resources
CCP	Chinese Communist Party
CD	Conference on Disarmament
CICA	Conference on Interaction and Confidence Building Measures in Asia
CMI	Chiang Mai Initiative
CMIM	Chiang Mai Initiative Multilateralization

CPTTP	Comprehensive and Progressive Agreement for Trans-Pacific Partnership
CSCAP	Council for Security Cooperation in the Asia-Pacific
CUES	Code of Unplanned Encounters at Sea
DPJ	Democratic Party of Japan
EAC	East Asian Community
EAS	East Asia Summit
EASG	East Asian Study Group
EAVG	East Asian Vision Group
EVSL	Early Voluntary Sector Liberalization
FDI	Foreign Direct Investment
FOIP	Free and Open Indo-Pacific
FTA	Free Trade Agreement
FTAAP	Free Trade Area of the Asia Pacific
GATT	General Agreement on Tariffs and Trade
GFC	Global Financial Crisis
GSOMIA	General Security of Military Information Agreement
IAEA	International Atomic Energy Agency
IBSA	India, Brazil and South Africa Dialogue Forum
ICNND	International Commission on Nuclear Non-proliferation and Disarmament
IEA	International Energy Agency
IMF	International Monetary Fund
INTERFET	International Force in East Timor
IORA	Indian Ocean Rim Association
KORUS	Korea–US Free Trade Pact
LDP	Liberal Democratic Party
MD	Missile Defense
MDB	Multilateral Development Bank
MPAC	Master Plan on ASEAN Connectivity
MSRI	Maritime Silk Road Initiative
NAPCI	Northeast Asia Peace and Cooperation Initiative
NAPCOR	Northeast Asia Plus Community of Responsibility
NDB	New Development Bank
NDRC	National Development and Reform Commission (China)
NRC	National Role Conception
NSS	National Security Statement
PECC	Pacific Economic Cooperation Council
PPP	Public–Private Partnership
PSI	Proliferation Security Initiative
RATS	Regional Anti-Terrorism Structure
RBIO	Rules-Based International Order
RCEP	Regional Comprehensive Economic Partnership
ROK	Republic of Korea

SAARC	South Asian Association for Regional Cooperation
SCO	Shanghai Cooperation Organization
SEACAT	Southeast Asia Cooperation and Training
SLD	Shangri-La Dialogue
SOE	State-Owned Enterprise
TAC	ASEAN Treaty of Amity and Cooperation
TCOG	Trilateral Coordination and Oversight Group
TCS	Trilateral Cooperation Secretariat
THAAD	Terminal High Altitude Area Defense
TPP	Trans-Pacific Partnership
TSD	Trilateral Security Dialogue
UNGA	United Nations General Assembly
UNSC	United Nations Security Council
WHO	World Health Organization
WTO	World Trade Organization

1

CONTESTED MULTILATERALISM 2.0 AND REGIONAL ORDER TRANSITION

Kai He[1]

The 2008 global financial crisis (GFC) introduced 'contested multilateralism 2.0' into the Asia-Pacific. Different from 'multilateralism 1.0' of the 1990s, which was mainly led by the Association of Southeast Asian Nations (ASEAN), this second wave of multilateralism was initiated by non-ASEAN members either by inaugurating new institutions or by reinvigorating existing establishments in the region. For example, Australian Prime Minister Kevin Rudd's 2009 proposal for an Asia Pacific Community (APC), which eventually morphed into the East Asia Summit (EAS), is illustrative, as is Japanese Prime Minister Yukio Hatoyama's advocacy for the building of an East Asian Community (EAC) in the same year. In 2013, South Korean President Park Geun-hye proposed the Northeast Asia Peace and Cooperation Initiative (NAPCI) to strengthen security cooperation in that sub-region. Chinese President Xi Jinping simultaneously advocated the building of a 'community of common destiny' in Asia in 2013, along with massive Chinese investments and financial initiatives, such as the 'One Belt, One Road' initiative (or Belt and Road Initiative—BRI). In December 2015, the Chinese-led Asian Infrastructure Investment Bank (AIIB) was successfully established with 57 prospective founding members despite US opposition.

As part of its 'pivot' or 'rebalancing' strategy toward Asia, the United States under the Barack Obama Administration also actively engaged in this wave of 'multilateralism 2.0' through formally joining the EAS in 2011. In addition, Obama proactively promoted the Trans-Pacific Partnership (TPP)—a multilateral trading bloc that excluded China, with the 12 TPP countries finally reaching an agreement in October 2015. The rise of Donald Trump's presidency in 2016 has seemingly killed the TPP in its infancy, but his determination to secure 'better trade deals' for the United States represents an obvious US competitive orientation and signals a continued US role to contest Chinese leadership in the Asia-Pacific through a variety of existing regional instrumentalities and institutions.

During his first trip to Asia in late 2017, Trump emphasized the 'rules-based order in the Indo Pacific' by reviving the Quadrilateral Security Dialogue (the so-called 'Quad 2.0') with Japan, Australia, and India. Although the 'Quad 2.0' may be just a strategic effort at 'minilateralism' instead of multilateralism, it still reflects a US institutional approach to dealing with the potential order transition in the region, especially against the background of China's rise (Tow 2019). On June 1, 2019, the United States released its 'Indo-Pacific Strategy Report.' Less than one month later, the 'ASEAN Outlook on the Indo Pacific' was published. It represents a possible 'Indo-Pacific' turn of multilateralism in the region in the future.

Why do we witness this 'contested multilateralism 2.0' after the GFC? Will multilateralism 2.0 make any difference in addressing regional security and political challenges? How did major powers perceive and engage this new wave of multilateralism in the region? Will the 'Indo-Pacific turn' of multilateralism be a blessing or a curse for regional stability and prosperity? It is time to seriously examine the nature, processes, and impact of this 'contested multilateralism' as well as the future of regional order.

This edited volume intends to address the above questions through diverse theoretical and empirical perspectives. By inviting the leading scholars to contribute their views on 'contested multilateralism 2.0' as well as distinctive institutional strategies of major powers, this book will shed some light on the study of multilateralism and regional security as well as offer policy insights to the policy making community in the region.

This rest of the chapter aims to assess the emergence of 'multilateralism 2.0' following the GFC in the region, with the aim of addressing two specific questions: Why did major powers engage in this wave of 'multilateralism 2.0' in the Asia-Pacific? What are the implications of contested multilateralism for the evolving regional order? I suggest that two systemic variables—higher strategic uncertainties in the region and deepening economic interdependence—prompted various Asia-Pacific powers to pursue institutional balancing to compete for advantage during what is clearly a time of order transition in the region. In addition, I briefly introduce a 'balance-of-roles' argument to explain how states have utilized various institutional balancing strategies to pursue power and influence in the era of international order transition (He 2018).

Institutional balancing is a new type of balance of power strategy through which states can use multilateral institutions instead of traditional military means to compete for power and influence in world politics (He 2008, 2009). There are three types of institutional balancing. Inclusive institutional balancing means to include a target state in an institution and relies on the rules and norms of institutions to constrain the target state's behavior. ASEAN Regional Forum (ARF) is an example of inclusive institutional balancing, through which the ASEAN members constrained China's behaviour in the South China Sea in the 1990s by ARF's cooperative security rules and norms (Foot 1998; He 2008; Katsumata 2009).

Exclusive institutional balancing refers to a strategy to exclude a target state from an institution and relies on the cohesion and cooperation inside the institution to exert pressure toward, or to neutralize threats from, the target state. An example of exclusive institutional balancing is the ASEAN Plus Three (APT) in the 'multi-lateralism 1.0' era. ASEAN and three major powers—China, Japan, and South Korea—used this grouping to promote economic cooperation among Asian countries after the 1997 Asian economic crisis in order to express resentment toward, as well as countervail pressures from, the United States and its control of the International Monetary Fund (IMF) (Stubbs 2002; Beeson 2003).

Inter-institutional balancing is an institutional strategy through which states can promote a new institution to reduce or dilute influences of existing institutions (He 2008, 2009). It is an extended form of both inclusive and exclusive institutional balancing. The target of inter-institutional balancing is not a state per se, but another institution that might or might not include the target state (Lee 2016). For example, the establishment of the East Asia Summit (EAS) has been seen as a rival institution to the APT because EAS stole the thunder of the APT in structuring regional cooperation in the 2000s (He 2008, 2009).

This chapter argues that non-ASEAN members conducted various institutional balancing strategies in the 'multilateralism 2.0' era after the GFC, suggesting that overlapping multilateral institutions could well become a 'new normal' in the Asia-Pacific as a result of intensified institutional balancing among major powers. The 'balance-of-roles' argument further suggests that the different role conception of states during the international order transition will shape their various institutional balancing strategies in the era of multilateralism 2.0. One unintended consequence of this process is that it may lead to a more peaceful transformation toward a new Asia-Pacific economic and political-security order.

It is worth noting that institutional balancing theory and the balance-of roles argument suggested by this chapter are by no means *the* consensual view of this edited volume. Instead, I intend to set a debating table for other scholars in this volume to engage with and challenge. The second section of this chapter introduces the structure of this edited volume. In conclusion, I discuss the policy implications of this new wave of multilateralism for regional security in particular and international order transition in general.

Contested multilateralism 2.0: conceptualization, causes, and implications

What is contested multilateralism 2.0?

Asian multilateralism is not new in world politics. Since the end of the Cold War, various multilateral institutions have proliferated in the Asia-Pacific, marking 'multi-lateralism 1.0' in the region. A remarkable feature of 'multilateralism 1.0' was that it centered on ASEAN. The establishment of ARF in 1994, which has now expanded to 27 members, was the apex of this process. The ARF is the only security forum and dialogue mechanism that includes all major powers in the world (the European Union also participates in the annual ARF meeting as an institutional member). The EAS is another example of multilateralism 1.0. This grouping is an extended version of APT, also driven by ASEAN. The United States and Russia formally joined the EAS in 2011. Although this ASEAN-centred multilateralism is widely criticized for its inefficiency or as talk-shops without teeth, ASEAN has firmly remained in the 'driver's seat' for more than two decades.[2]

The second wave of multilateralism in the Asia-Pacific was triggered by the GFC. It involves the reinvigoration of existing institutions and the initiation of new establishments in the region. It has three distinctive features. First, it is driven by major powers—the United States, China, Australia, Japan, and South Korea—not ASEAN. Second, it is comprehensive in addressing both traditional and non-traditional security and economic challenges with a geopolitical emphasis on East Asia in particular and the Asia-Pacific in general, instead of being mainly Southeast Asian-centric. Third, it coexists, competes, and interacts with 'multilateralism 1.0' and with other forms of security organizations, such as US-led bilateralism, as well as nascent, 'minilateral' arrangements in shaping the Asia-Pacific's future regional order.

Some scholars have proposed similar concepts to 'contested multilateralism' or 'multilateralism 2.0.' Morse and Keohane (2014, 385) define 'contested multilateralism' as a situation that 'results from the pursuit of strategies by states, multilateral organizations, and non-state actors to use multilateral institutions, existing or newly created, to challenge the rules, practices, or missions of existing multilateral institutions.' In a similar vein, Luk Van Langenhove (2010, 263) argues that a transformation of multilateralism mode 1.0 to mode 2.0 is taking place, the main characteristics being: '(1) the diversification of multilateral organizations; (2) the growing importance of nonstate actors such as substate regions and supranational regional organizations; (3) the increased interlinkages between policy domains; and (4) the growing space for citizen involvement.'

However, the idea of 'contested multilateralism 2.0' in the Asia-Pacific introduced here differs from Morse and Keohane (2014) and van Langenhove (2010) in two different and important ways. First, the nation-state remains the major actor of 'contested multilateralism 2.0,' superseding institutional, sub-state and non-state actors. Second, the 'contestation' aspect of the multilateralism 2.0 variant under review here refers to both intra-institutional and inter-institutional competition among state actors through multilateral means. The reason for coining 'multilateralism 2.0' in this context is to differentiate this second wave of multilateralism as it is now unfolding in Asia from the previous 'multilateralism 1.0' led by ASEAN soon after the Cold War. It does not imply that the changing nature of world politics is based on the primacy shifting from nation-states to non-state actors, as the other two conceptualizations cited above suggest (although it is clear that the roles of non-state actors are commanding increased importance in international relations).

Why is there contested multilateralism 2.0?

Different arguments have been offered to explain why 'contested multilateralism 2.0' has become more prominent. Neorealists and some others embracing a broader realist outlook suggest that institutions are just an epiphenomenon of power politics among great powers (Mearsheimer 1994). Therefore, so-called contested multilateralism is just another name for power politics among states. For example, Marc Lanteigne (2005) suggests that China used multilateral institutions such as the ARF as a diplomatic tool to pursue its great-power status after the Cold War.

At a time when observers are increasingly engrossed with China's (invariable) rise, America's (possible) decline and an increasingly multipolar international security environment, Gill and Green (2008, 3) point out that 'Asia's new multilateralism is still at a stage where it is best understood as an extension and intersection of national power and purpose rather than as an objective force in itself.' For example, China actively advocated the 'New Asian Security' concept—the 'Asia-for-Asians' idea—at the Conference on Interaction and Confidence-Building Measures in Asia (CICA) in 2014. This initiative was seen by outside observers as a countervailing effort against the United States, which started to 'pivot to Asia' in 2011 (Anderlini 2014).

Conversely, liberalism, especially neoliberalism, argues that the impact of institutions in contemporary world politics is significant because they reduce transaction costs and foster cooperation among states (Keohane and Martin 1995). This outlook likewise privileges the nation-state as the primary agent of concern, although in a markedly different way than its realist/neorealist counterpart. Liberals/neoliberals insist that multi-lateralism 2.0 is rooted in the *functional* imperative for states facing emerging regional security challenges in Asia to embrace targeted modes of cooperation which, if absent, could only lead to crisis escalation or worse. For example, Richard Stubbs (2002) praises the functional success of APT as a new regional institution in promoting economic cooperation between Southeast Asia and Northeast Asia after the 1997 Asian economic crisis. Similarly, the establishment of the AIIB led by China in 2015 is also intended to address the insufficient investments in infrastructure in Asian developing countries.

Last, but not least, a constructivist school of thought sees institutions and multi-lateralism as reflecting certain ideas and the norms emanating from them as under-writing world politics (Wendt 1995, 1999). In the case of the Asia–Pacific region, the ASEAN-dominated 'multilateralism 1.0' in the 1990s was built on a shared 'we-feeling' among ASEAN members about how their collective identity was nurtured relative to regional order building (Acharya 2001). For the 'contested multilateralism 2.0' phenomenon, constructivists suggest that it is a clash of different visions or ideas among major powers on how regional order building should evolve (He 2016).

For example, former Japanese Prime Minister Hatoyama proposed an EAC, which is based on a shared culture and civilization among Asian countries. A particularly unique aspect of Asians' approaches to order building is their emphasis on a distinct regional culture or civilization. As Hatoyama (2010) states,

> one characteristic of Asians is that we do not perceive ourselves and others or humans and the environment in a western dualistic manner, but rather attach importance to the sameness between the two … This will surely also serve as a launching point for a 'cultural community.'

Hatoyama's civilization-based EAC proposal is quite different from Rudd's more 'Western-centric' APC suggestion, which embodied a much broader geographical scope, including non-Asian countries (Australia and the United States) as well as normative and legalistic principles (Frost 2009; Rudd 2008). Arguably, these different visions and ideas of regional order led to the emergence of 'contested multilateral 2.0' in the Asia-Pacific.

Although these three contending approaches reveal some elements of truth, they fail to explain the timing, complicity among actors, and dynamics of 'contested multilateralism 2.0' after the GFC. Realists are correct to suggest that multilateralism and multilateral institutions are an extension of power politics among major powers. However, why and how did major powers instigate this new wave of multilateralism after the 2008 GFC? Power transition theorists would explain this development as a result of intensified competition between the United States and China (see, for example, Danilovic and Clare 2007; Allison 2017). However, they face difficulties in accounting for the active institutional involvement of other powers, such as Australia, Japan, and South Korea.

It is also true, as neoliberals have suggested, that some new institutions forged during the multilateralism 2.0 timeframe fit the functional needs of the region. Still, the EAC, the APC, and China's community of common destiny are examples of competitive approaches to linking preferred economic models to more comprehensive strategies for strengthening major powers' positionality. Accordingly, these initiatives seem to go beyond the mere functional boundary emphasized by neoliberals. For constructivists, ideas constitute the basic fundamental motivating agent behavior in international relations. However, purely ideational competition among states cannot really account for all the behavioral dynamics of states that have transpired under multilateralism 2.0 in the Asia-Pacific. Why did the United States continue to support such existing institutions as the EAS and the TPP while other major powers hedged against possible US retrenchment from the region by proposing various new institutions? Moreover, constructivists' ideational arguments cannot explain why these other powers proposed these multilateral institutions soon after the financial crisis, not significantly earlier or much later. The timing problem cannot be addressed by the contingent ideas and visions of political leaders alone.

Potential order transition and institutional balancing

As mentioned earlier, an 'institutional balancing' argument sheds additional light on the emergence of 'contested multilateralism 2.0.' Focusing on two systemic variables—the high level of uncertainties and high economic interdependence—is particularly useful for developing a greater understanding of the convergence of multilateral behavior among different states.

The 2008 GFC began in the United States and quickly spread to the rest of the world. The daunting and widespread impact of the crisis on the world economy revealed two new trends in world politics: the rapid decline of the US-led liberal order since the World War II, and the deepening economic interdependence among states. As G. John Ikenberry (2012, 4) points out, 'the 2008 financial crisis and subsequent world economic downturn—the most severe since the Great Depression—was an especially stark demonstration of the pressures on the American-led liberal system.' Compared to the relative decline of US power, the 'rise of the rest' became a new feature of world politics (Zakaria 2008). In the Asia-Pacific, China's sustained economic growth during the GFC triggered both a power transition between the United States and China as well as a regional order transformation from the old US-led order to an uncertain regional flux.

The GFC's widespread damage also reflected a core trend of globalization—a deepening economic interdependence among states. In the Asia-Pacific this interdependence featured increasing intra-regional trade and investment. As the Asian Development Bank (ADB) (ADB 2016, x, 18) has since observed, 'Asian economies traded with regional partners well beyond what geographical, cultural, or economic proximity can explain; with 57.1% of total trade intraregional.' Although it is still lower than the European Union (63 percent), it is much higher than the intra-regional trade in North America (25 percent). Moreover, the intra-regional foreign direct investment to and from Asia and the Pacific has increased over time and reached 52.5 percent of total foreign direct investment inflows in 2015 (ADB 2016, xi).

The GFC, therefore, marked the beginning of an Asia-Pacific regional order transition from the previous US-led hegemonic system and liberal order to a more uncertain condition of fluctuating multipolarity. This growing level of strategic uncertainty in the region, combined with deepening economic interdependence among Asia-Pacific states, encouraged those countries' policy elites to deem institutions as venues of competition for greater power and influence. This epitomized traditional balance of power behavior among states under anarchy. The potential order transition after the GFC, moreover, intensified the 'balancing' activities among states through institutions. Major powers and other states in the region perceived both risks and opportunities accompanying the power transition process, and the emergence of contested multilateralism 2.0 was an inevitable by-product of institutional balancing among these countries.

Here, I would like to highlight a balance-of-roles argument to explain how states have engaged in different institutional balancing strategies during the period of potential order transition (He 2018). It argues that during the order transition era, major powers will re-examine their respective role conceptions in the context of strategic uncertainties along with the order transition. The fundamental goal of states is still the same, i.e. to maximize their security first and then pursue more power and influence when it is possible. States will actively engage in institutional competitions during the order transition through various institutional balancing strategies in order to secure their advantageous positions in the future international order. How states will conduct institutional balancing is mainly shaped by their role conceptions in the order transition process.

There are three types of role conceptions in an international order: order defender, order challenger, and kingmaker. An order defender is a state that sees itself as part of the existing order and will try its best to keep the order intact. What it does not like is any possible changes in the existing order. Therefore, it is more likely to choose an *exclusive institutional balancing* strategy toward any institutional challenges from rising powers. It can keep rising powers out of its own institutions so that the influence of a rising power will be undermined. It can also decline to endorse and join any new institutions that are initiated by rising powers, i.e. excluding itself from institutions. The purpose of this self-exclusion strategy is to deny the legitimacy of any new institutions and institutional challenges from rising powers (He 2018).

An order challenger, by definition, is a state that pursues a transition of the current order. The major goal of an order challenger is to gain legitimacy and recognition from others. Therefore, it is more likely to adopt both *inclusive and exclusive institutional balancing* strategies as long as it can increase power and influence through institutional buildings and initiations. A rising power is more likely to create a new institution because the rules and principles of the existing institutions were set by the hegemon or ruling power when the rising state was still weak. Through setting up a new institution, the rising power can change the institutional arrangements of the international order. However, this new institution must be accepted and recognized as a legitimate alternate of the existing ones by majority of states. Therefore, a rising power will conduct inclusive institutional balancing to invite all countries, including the existing hegemon to join, so that the new institution can gain as much legitimacy as possible in the order transition era. The rising power might choose exclusive institutional balancing if it believes that it has enough followers for this new institution so that it does not need the endorsement from the hegemon.

The third type of role conception is to be a 'kingmaker.' It refers to the proactive role a second-tier state can play during the order transition. Due to its limited power capabilities, a 'kingmaker' state will not be able to compete for leadership in the future international order. However, it can play an important role in facilitating either the existing hegemon to defend the current order or a rising power to change the order. Being a kingmaker, a state will need to play an active and, more importantly, an independent role in institutional building during the order transition. Therefore, it is more likely to choose an *inter-institutional balancing* strategy to establish or support a new institution that is different from the existing one but embraces both the hegemon and rising powers. On the one hand, a kingmaker state will enjoy more leverage in an institution it creates. By including both the hegemon and rising powers, the kingmaker can create a balance between the two parties and make itself the center of attention. On the other hand, this new institution can ensure that it can reap all the benefits of the new international order when one inevitably emerges.

In the era of 'contested multilateralism 2.0,' China's role conception is an order challenger, which suggests that China is more likely to conduct both inclusive institutional balancing and exclusive institutional balancing in order to maximize its power and influence during the order transition period. China's AIIB and One Belt, One Road initiative (or Belt and Road Initiative—BRI) exemplify inclusive institutional balancing adopted by China to increase its regional power and influence through forming new rules and norms for financial and economic governance in the Asia-Pacific.

As the hegemon, the role conception of the United States is an order defender because the hegemon does not want the international order to be changed. Under the Obama Administration, the TPP was an exclusive institutional balancing strategy of the United States against China because the high trading and investment standards intentionally excluded China from the TPP. The success of the TPP would inevitably reduce China's power and influence in the region. In order to counter the TPP, China supported the establishment of the Regional Comprehensive Economic Partnership (RCEP) led by ASEAN, a rival trading bloc that is built on the APT framework. Therefore, the RCEP can be seen as an inter-institutional balancing effort of China against the US-led TPP (He 2018).

Besides the United States and China, other Asia-Pacific powers also devoted more attention to the future of a new regional order. It is worth noting that the 2008 GFC is just a direct trigger of the 'perceived order transition,' which accounts for the timing but not the emergence of this new wave of multilateralism in the Asia-Pacific. The fundamental driver of the order transition is the rapid rise of China and the relative decline of the United States in the post-Cold War era. The 2008 GFC, at the most, seems to further vindicate this inevitable trend of power transition between the United States and China as well as a potential order transition in the Asia-Pacific. The existing ASEAN-based multilateralism, supported by the ARF, the APT, and the EAS, was viewed as insufficient to address strategic uncertainties that would accompany order transition. Therefore, a new wave of multilateralism appeared in the Asia-Pacific, in which major powers started to compete for institutional leadership through either initiating new institutions or reviving existing ones.

Some active middle powers, therefore, are encouraged to play a 'kingmaker' role in shaping the international order transition through institutional balancing strategies. For example, South Korea proposed the establishment of the NAPCI in 2013 under the Park Administration to 'build trust and foster a spirit of cooperation in the region by accumulating a habit of cooperation among regional partners' (Korean Ministry of Foreign Affairs 2013, 13). As Lee (2014) points out, '[a] vacuum in leadership has perpetuated the absence of coordination towards the construction of a regional multilateral security framework' in Northeast Asia. And 'South Korea may be better poised to promote NAPCI, free from great power rivalry and competition, particularly among the United States, China, and Japan.' It is clear that the NAPCI was seen as an opportunity for South Korea to play a critical and 'kingmaker' role in building a new regional order in the future. Since the potential target of the NAPCI is the ASEAN-driven ARF, South Korea is conducting an inter-institutional balancing strategy as the balance-of-roles argument suggested.

In a similar vein, Japan under Hatoyama and Australia under Rudd also held a role conception of 'kingmaker' in this period of international order transition after the 2008 GFC. Both Hatoyama's EAC initiative and Rudd's APC proposal also exemplified the use of inter-institutional balancing strategy to at least complement if not outright supplant ASEAN's 'multilateralism 1.0.' They were both geared to maximize the potential influence of Japan and Australia respectively in any future Asia-Pacific regional order. Unlike the US or China, neither Japan nor Australia is able to become the next leader of the international order in the Asia-Pacific due to their limited power capabilities. However, both countries can potentially assist the existing hegemon to defend or the rising power to structure the future international order. It is a 'kingmaking' role that both Hatoyama and Rudd intended to play after the GFC.

Unfortunately for them, both the EAC and APC proposals became mere 'thought bubbles' due to their domestic political situations and naïveté about regional and alliance sensitivities overwhelming their visionary geopolitics. Hatoyama's adoption of 'muddle through' tactics for finessing his own political party's management of Japan's alliance with the United States, and Rudd's inability to control rival factions in the Australian Labor Party and ASEAN resentment over his failure to consult about his APC proposal before he publicly revealed it, simply eclipsed their foreign policy innovations (see Clausen 2012; Lee and Milner 2014). However, future political leaders in Japan and Australia may be more successful in implementing inter-institutional balancing with new ideas and initiatives if they intend to play a more active role in shaping the regional order toward their preferences and interests.

Structure of the book

It is worth noting that the main purpose of this chapter is to introduce the concept of 'contested multilateralism 2.0' in the Asian Pacific for other scholars to engage with and debate. Institutional balancing theory and the associated balance-of-roles argument are only one of the possible explanations for this new wave of multilateralism after the 2008 GFC. The rest of the book is divided into two parts. While the first part examines the multilateralism 2.0 phenomenon from a regional perspective, the second part takes a country-perspective view on how major players in the region have engaged in this new wave of multilateralism after the 2008 GFC.

Chapter 2 by Nick Bisley directly challenges the mere notion of 'multilateralism 2.0' and critiques the premise that there are two phases of regional multilateralism: pre- and post-global financial crisis. Instead it argues that there has been one long 25-year expansion phase. Initially, this was prompted by the risks and opportunities of globalization but eventually was adapted as a strategy to manage a changing regional order. More recently, regional multilateralism has taken on competitive characteristics reflecting Asia's more contested dynamics.

T. J. Pempel in Chapter 3 examines the interactions between the United States and the expanding ecosystem of East Asian and Asia-Pacific institutions. Concentrating on the period since the GFC of 2008–2009, this chapter analyzes the 'rival regionalisms' that are now mushrooming throughout the region. It concludes by exploring what looks to be a new American disengagement from Asia-Pacific regional institutions as a consequence of the presidency of Donald Trump.

Chapter 4 by William Tow focuses on the nexus of multilateralism and mini-lateralism in regional security architecture. It argues that both have emerged as two increasingly prominent forms of such cooperation. Minilateralism's informality and flexibility appeals to those who are sceptical about multilateralism's traditional focus on norm adherence and community building even as great power competition in the Indo-Pacific is sharply intensifying.

Chapter 5 by Mark Beeson examines the effectiveness of Asian multilateralism in general. It suggests that, despite a growing number of regional initiatives in East Asia, multilateral institutions are generally distinguished by their ineffectiveness. It suggests that not only is China very comfortable with the idea of a rather feeble and ineffective institutional architecture, but the United States is also unlikely to do anything to change this picture, especially under the Trump Administration which is highly skeptical about the efficacy of multilateral institutions at the best of times.

The second part of this book consists of five chapters (Chapters 6 thru 10), which take a country-specific approach in examining individual countries' institutional strategies in this new wave of multilateralism 2.0 after the GFC. From the CICA to the AIIB and the BRI, Jingdong Yuan in Chapter 6 discusses the rationales, approaches, and implications of China's institutional balancing strategies in the era of contested multilateralism after the GFC. Yuan argues that it would be overstating Beijing's intentions and capabilities if these China-sponsored initiatives are viewed as direct challenges to the existing international and regional orders.

Chapter 7 by Hidetaka Yoshimatsu examines Japan's role conception in its multilateral commitments to the Asia-Pacific after the GFC in 2008 from Hatoyama to Abe. It suggests that Abe's new multilateral initiative of the Free and Open Indo-Pacific represents Japan's kingmaker role in maintaining a free and open maritime regime, and in keeping a liberal and open economic regime under the emergence of the Trump Administration. In Chapter 8 Jaechun Kim and William Kang trace the evolution of South Korea's view toward multilateralism through a role theory perspective. They suggest that the political ideology of the government, diplomatic profiles of the nation, perceived North Korean threats, and order transition from the US to China are identified as factors shaping the 'role conception' of South Korea, which in turn led to different institutional balancing strategies of South Korean governments.

In Chapter 9, Melissa Conley Tyler examines Australia's approach to multilateralism with MIKTA as a case study. Challenging the balance-of-roles argument that suggests that Australia can play a kingmaker role in the era of multilateralism 2.0 after the GFC, this chapter argues that Australia is using multilateral diplomacy to increase its influence in line with a traditional 'middle power' role identity in MIKTA. Chapter 10 by See Seng Tan examines ASEAN's response to multilateralism 2.0. It contends that against an unsettled regional backdrop of strategic rivalry and rising tensions over trade and security concerns between the United States and China, ASEAN-led multilateralism continues to perform critical functions in maintaining the stability of the region.

Conclusion: peaceful order transition as an unintended consequence?

This book continues the long-standing debate among scholars on the implications of Asian multilateralism for regional order since the end of the Cold War (see, for example, Simon 1995; Leifer 1999; Acharya 2004; Jones and Smith 2007). In the 'multilateralism 1.0' era, some scholars assert that ASEAN-driven multilateral institutions were making process not progress; others suggest that the mere process of

ASEAN multilateralism signifies the success of ASEAN in mitigating regional rivalries and tensions. The rise of 'contested multilateralism 2.0' after the GFC has encouraged major powers to further engage in a new wave of institution building and competition in the Asia-Pacific. Although the overlap and redundancy of multilateral institutions seems inevitable, this 'contested multilateralism 2.0' phenomenon has at least three strategic implications for the regional order in the Asia-Pacific.

First, contested multilateralism 2.0 will reflect the power transformation in the regional system. The decline of US hegemony and the rise of the rest, especially China, will transfer the regional power configuration from unipolarity to either bi-multipolarity or multipolarity. In a bi-multipolar system the United States and China will dominate the institutional competition during the multilateralism 2.0 era, in which other states will have to pick sides between US-dominated institutions and China-centered ones. In a multipolar system, middle powers or second-tier powers, such as Australia, Japan, and South Korea, might rise up to become independent forces if they can seize the opportunity to build multilateral institutions and strengthen their voices in Asian affairs.

Second, the new and revived institutions in the 'multilateralism 2.0' era will compete with and complement the ASEAN-driven multilateral institutions in mitigating regional tensions. The rise of multilateralism 2.0 will, however, unavoidably threaten the relevance of ASEAN-driven institutions. For example, if the community of common destiny proposed by China succeeds, the role of the EAS and the APT in regional affairs will be eroded. As T. J. Pempel (2010) argues, institutional Darwinism will determine the rise and fall of multilateral institutions in the Asia-Pacific. However, it is not an automatic process because the sunk costs of abandoning an existing institution and the opportunity costs of establishing a new one are relatively high for states in world politics. We are more likely to see that 'multilateralism 2.0' will co-exist with 'multilateralism 1.0' into the foreseeable future.

Moreover, the future of multilateralism 2.0 will face more challenges from traditional power politics. The nuclear and missile crises on the Korean Peninsula and the territorial and maritime disputes in the East and South China Seas, as well as the border dispute between China and India, are all security hotpots that might encourage states to pursue unilateralism or traditional balance of power mechanisms for short-term gains in regional security. The relevance of multilateralism 2.0, together with the ASEAN-driven multilateralism 1.0, will be seriously questioned and also tested during military and diplomatic crises in the region. Given the complicated nature of these regional security issues, no country seems able to address these challenges alone. Multilateralism is by no means a panacea either. How to effectively integrate traditional military means and multilateralism in coping with security dynamics becomes an imperative task for policy makers in the region.

If managed appropriately, these new multilateral institutions can complement the existing ones in mitigating regional rivalries and tensions among states. For example, if South Korea's NAPCI proposal was successfully implemented, it would have complemented the role of the ARF in enhancing mutual trust and cooperation among Northeast Asian states. Unfortunately, the future of the NAPCI officially ended with the downfall of President Park in South Korea. Will South Korea's new

President Moon initiate a new multilateral framework to cope with the deteriorating situation on the Korean Peninsula? Will the United States and China resume the Six Party Talks or other similar security institutions to rein in North Korea? Or will Trump deal with Kim Jong-un alone? These questions are hard to answer right now. Things might get worse before they get better. Nevertheless, multilateralism remains a useful diplomatic tool for states to maintain regional security in the long run. More importantly, major powers, such as China and the United States, will need to offer leadership and public goods in the designated institutions if they further engage in the multilateralism 2.0 era. The Sino-American competition for providing public goods will generate positive externalities on the regional order.

Last, the emergence of multilateralism 2.0 could potentially facilitate a peaceful order transition in the region in the long run. Unlike power transition theory, which suggests that war or conflict is inevitable among great powers during a power transition, it has been argued here that the order transition based on institutional balancing might be more peaceful than is currently widely perceived. Although the purpose of institutional balancing is to compete for dominance and power in multilateral institutions as well as in the new regional order, the means of institutional balancing are different from traditional hard power strategies, such as alliance formation and arms build-ups. Rule-making and agenda-setting are the major features of institutional balancing. Although exclusive institutional balancing might be more hostile and antagonistic than inclusive institutional balancing, the overlapping nature of the 'contested multilateralism 2.0' regional order to a certain extent is, under certain conditions and circumstances, capable of mitigating potential tensions and rivalries among states (Yeo 2016).

In this context, there may be grounds for optimism. Although China was excluded from the TPP under the Obama Administration, both China and the United States are members of the Asia-Pacific Economic Cooperation (APEC) grouping and the proposed Asia-Pacific free trade agreement. In the same vein, although the United States is not a member of the CICA organization promoted and revived by China in 2014, both the United States and China are members of the ARF. Although the overlapping institutions in the era of multilateralism 2.0 may presently seem redundant and inefficient in solving regional disputes, it could be equally surmised that this overlapping multilateralism is inevitable due to intensified institutional balancing among major Asia-Pacific powers. An unintended consequence of this institutional overlap could therefore be a peaceful order transformation by default. This outcome, of course, would be more likely if major powers can find a new equilibrium among power, interests, and norms in whatever new regional architecture that does materialize, and if security hotspots in the region are managed appropriately.

Notes

1 This chapter is a revised version of He, Kai. 2019. "Contested Multilateralism 2.0 and Regional Order Transition: Causes and Implications." *The Pacific Review* 32 (2): 210–20.
2 For positive as well as negative evaluations on ASEAN and ASEAN-centered multilateralism, see Smith (2004); Severino (2007); Leifer (1999); Jones and Smith (2007); Emmerson (2007); Ravenhill (2009).

References

Acharya, Amitav. 2001. *Constructing a Security Community in Southeast Asia: ASEAN and the Problem of Regional Order.* London: Routledge.

Acharya, Amitav. 2004. "How Ideas Spread: Whose Norms Matter? Norm Localization and Institutional Change in Asian Regionalism." *International Organization* 58(2): 239–275.

ADB (Asian Development Bank). 2016. *Asian Economic Integration Report 2016: What Drives Foreign Direct Investment in Asia and the Pacific?* Manila: Asian Development Bank.

Allison, Graham T. 2017. *Destined for War: Can America and China Escape Thucydides's Trap?* Melbourne: Scribe.

Anderlini, Jamil. 2014. "China Reinvigorates Regional Clubs to Counter US Power." *Financial Times*, May 20, 2014.

Beeson, Mark. 2003. "ASEAN Plus Three and the Rise of Reactionary Regionalism." *Contemporary Southeast Asia* 25(2): 251–268.

Clausen, Daniel. 2012. "Examining Japanese Defense Policy and Politics through Failures of Leadership: The Case of Prime Minister Hatoyama Yukio." *Asian Politics & Policy* 4(4): 507–525.

Danilovic, Vesna, and Joe Clare. 2007. "Global Power Transitions and Regional Interests." *International Interactions* 33(3): 289–304.

Emmerson, Donald K. 2007. "Challenging ASEAN: A 'Topological' View." *Contemporary Southeast Asia* 29(3): 424–446.

Foot, Rosemary. 1998. "China in the ASEAN Regional Forum: Organizational Processes and Domestic Modes of Thought." *Asian Survey* 38(5): 425–440.

Frost, Frank. 2009. "Australia's Proposal for an 'Asia Pacific Community': Issues and Prospects." Parliamentary Library Research Paper, Department of Parliamentary Services, Canberra.

Gill, Bates, and Michael J. Green. 2008. "Unbundling Asia's New Multilateralism." In *Asia's New Multilateralism: Cooperation, Competition, and the Search for Community*, edited by Michael J. Green and Bates Gill, 1–29. New York: Columbia University Press.

Hatoyama, Yukio. 2010. "Speech by H. E. Dr Yukio Hatoyama Prime Minister of Japan on the Occasion of the Sixteenth International Conference on the Future of Asia Hosted by the Nihon Keizai Shimbun." May 20, 2010. See: http://japan.kantei.go.jp/hatoyama/statement/201005/20speech_e.html

He, Baogang. 2016. *Contested Ideas of Regionalism in Asia.* London: Routledge.

He, Kai. 2008. "Institutional Balancing and International Relations Theory: Economic Interdependence and Balance of Power Strategies in Southeast Asia." *European Journal of International Relations* 14(3): 489–518.

He, Kai. 2009. *Institutional Balancing in the Asia Pacific: Economic Interdependence and China's Rise.* London: Routledge.

He, Kai. 2018. "Role Conceptions, Order Transition and Institutional Balancing in the Asia-Pacific: A New Theoretical Framework." *Australian Journal of International Affairs* 72(2): 92–109.

Ikenberry, G.John. 2012. *Liberal Leviathan: The Origins, Crisis, and Transformation of the American World Order.* Princeton, NJ: Princeton University Press.

Jones, David Martin, and Michael L. R. Smith. 2007. "Making Process, Not Progress: ASEAN and the Evolving East Asian Regional Order." *International Security* 32(1): 148–184.

Katsumata, Hiro. 2009. *ASEAN's Cooperative Security Enterprise: Norms and Interests in the ASEAN Regional Forum.* New York: Palgrave Macmillan.

Keohane, Robert O., and Lisa L. Martin. 1995. "The Promise of Institutionalist Theory." *International Security* 20(1): 39–51.

Korean Ministry of Foreign Affairs. 2013. "Northeast Asia Peace and Cooperation Initiative." Korean Ministry of Foreign Affairs, Seoul.

Lanteigne, Marc. 2005. *China and International Institutions: Alternative Paths to Global Power.* London: Routledge.

Lee, Sang-Hyun. 2014. "The Northeast Asia Peace and Cooperation Initiative (NAPCI): A Vision Toward Sustainable Peace and Cooperation in Northeast Asia." *The ASAN Forum,* December 13.

Lee, Seungjoo. 2016. "Institutional Balancing and the Politics of Mega-FTAs in East Asia." *Asian Survey* 56(6): 1055–1076.

Lee, Sheryn, and Anthony Milner. 2014. "Practical vs. Identity Regionalism: Australia's APC Initiative, a Case Study." *Contemporary Politics* 20(2): 209–228.

Leifer, Michael. 1999. "The ASEAN Peace Process: A Category Mistake." *Pacific Review* 12(1): 25–39.

Mearsheimer, John J. 1994. "The False Promise of International Institutions." *International Security* 19(3): 5–49.

Morse, Julia C., and Robert O. Keohane. 2014. "Contested multilateralism." *Review of International Organizations* 9(4): 385–412.

Pempel, T. J. 2010. "Soft Balancing, Hedging, and Institutional Darwinism: The Economic-Security Nexus and East Asian Regionalism." *Journal of East Asian Studies* 10(2): 209–238.

Ravenhill, John. 2009. "East Asian Regionalism: Much Ado about Nothing?" *Review of International Studies* 35(S1): 215–235.

Rudd, Kevin. 2008. "Building on ASEAN's Success: Towards an Asia-Pacific Community." Institute of Southeast Asian Studies, Singapore.

Severino, Rodolfo C. 2007. "ASEAN Beyond Forty: Towards Political and Economic Integration." *Contemporary Southeast Asia* 29(3): 406–423.

Simon, Sheldon W. 1995. "Realism and Neoliberalism: International Relations Theory and Southeast Asian Security." *Pacific Review* 8(1): 5–24.

Smith, Anthony L. 2004. "ASEAN's Ninth Summit: Solidifying Regional Cohesion, Advancing External Linkages." *Contemporary Southeast Asia* 26(3): 416–433.

Stubbs, Richard. 2002. "ASEAN Plus Three: Emerging East Asian Regionalism?" *Asian Survey* 42(3): 440–455.

Tow, William T. 2019. "Minilateral Security's Relevance to US Strategy in the Indo-Pacific: Challenges and Prospects." *The Pacific Review* 32(2): 232–244.

van Langenhove, Luk. 2010. "The Transformation of Multilateralism Mode 1.0 to Mode 2.0." *Global Policy* 1(3): 263–270.

Wendt, Alexander. 1995. "Constructing International Politics." *International Security* 20(1): 71–81.

Wendt, Alexander. 1999. *Social Theory of International Politics.* Cambridge: Cambridge University Press.

Yeo, Andrew I. 2016. "Overlapping Regionalism in East Asia: Determinants and Potential Effects." *International Relations of the Asia-Pacific* 18(2): 161–191.

Zakaria, Fareed. 2008. "The Future of American Power: How America Can Survive the Rise of the Rest." *Foreign Affairs* 87(3): 18–43.

PART 1

Debating regional implications

2

MULTILATERALISM AND REGIONAL ORDER IN CONTESTED ASIA

Nick Bisley[1]

Unlike other key regions in the world East Asia was slow to establish multilateral institutions and mechanisms to advance shared regional interests. During the Cold War, as Europe began to develop the institutions that in time became the European Union, with the singular exception of Association of Southeast Asian Nations (ASEAN), the region did not have any multilateral institutions of substance. In their mutual dealings and in their security policies and economic ambitions, East Asian states opted for bilateral and unilateral approaches and arrangements. This was notable because, as many scholars have shown (Ruggie 1993), during that time multilateralism was playing an increasingly significant role in world politics. East Asian states kept their distance from collaborative interstate dealings.

However, in the late 1980s, the region began to change its collective mind. The easing of the Cold War's geopolitical tensions and growing trade and investment networks led the region's countries to recognize the need to develop multilateral policies and practices. This began with the creation of Asia-Pacific Economic Cooperation (APEC) forum in 1989. Originally, APEC met at ministerial level with a specific focus on trade liberalization. Its formation was spurred by concerns about how long the Uruguay Round of the General Agreement on Tariffs and Trade (GATT) negotiations were taking to conclude but was also prompted by a realization of the need for a framework to drive broader economic cooperation across the region (Ravenhill 2001). Within a few years it was upgraded to become a leaders' meeting in 1994. The year was also the first time that the ASEAN Regional Forum (ARF) convened. APEC was established with a strict focus on economic cooperation narrowly construed. In contrast, the ARF was created with a specific brief to address security concerns across the region and, indeed beyond it. This was followed shortly after by the establishment of the ASEAN Plus Three (APT) process (Stubbs 2002) with China, South Korea and Japan collaborating with the region's original institution to foster a more coordinated approach to regional economic concerns. This period also saw ASEAN create a range of 'plus one' processes, involving formal ties to key regional countries, established in short order as the grouping put a premium on trying to shape extra-Southeast Asian affairs. In the 1990s East Asia began to open its mind and bureaucratic resources to regional multilateralism (Wesley 2003).

As the new century dawned the region continued its enthusiasm with multi-lateralism, with new entities established by a range of different actors. Following an extensive consultation and development period by the East Asian Vision Group, ASEAN and six partners established the East Asia Summit (EAS) in 2005. Holding its first meeting in Kuala Lumpur, the Declaration it adopted at the conclusion of that meeting set out its vision of an ambitious process that sought to be a 'forum for dialogue on broad strategic, political and economic issues of common interest and concern with the aim of promoting peace, stability and economic prosperity in East Asia' (EAS 2005). Not content with this slate of programs in 2008 and 2009 both Japan and Australia, middle ranking powers with a particular zeal for multilateralism, began to advocate for yet more mechanisms in 2009 (Cook 2009).

Why did a region that had been so leery of multistate collaborative forms of sta-tecraft become so enamored by them in such a relatively short space of time? Why did a region that had but one small and relatively weak institution become endowed with so many that scholars and journalists regularly refer to the alphabet soup of regional mechanisms due to the profusion of acronyms? This book explores aspects of this broader trend with a particular focus on the trend toward more competitive forms of multilateralism that began to emerge in the 2010s. The intention of this chapter is to provide an account of the emergence of East Asia's interest in multi-lateralism and to develop a periodization of that process. In contrast to Kai He's chapter in this book (Chapter 1), which argues that regional multilateralism of the recent years is best understood as 'contested multilateralism 2.0,' this chapter argues that regional multilateralism should be understood as having one growth period which can be distinguished into three phases. The first phase entailed a growing interest in multilateralism prompted by the security and economic challenges of economic integration and globalization. In its second phase it became a means of responding to the shifts in the regional order as US primacy faded and growing Chinese power began to unsettle existing patterns of regional order. The third, and potentially terminal, phase is as a set of mechanisms through which great power rivalry is being played out. That is, multilateralism has become a means through which contestation about the region's future international order is being played out.

East Asian multilateralism

One of the most striking features of East Asia's recent international history is the speed with which it moved, in the late 1970s, from being a place beset with high intensity conflict to one of relative geopolitical tranquility. For the Cold War's first 30 years, East Asia was a war prone and violent place; during that time, it was the part of the world in which more people lost their lives to war than any other (Mack 2010). This was caused by the major conflict on the Korean Peninsula in the 1950s and the various wars in Indochina during the 1960s and 1970s. But from the late 1970s it became almost entirely peaceful (Kivimäki 2014). Resting on a foundation of great power amity—China and the US had struck a bargain under which both were comfortable with one another's respective regional roles—East Asia put aside its ideological and political differences and focused on domestic development. And as it did so the countries not only stopped fighting, they began to trade with and invest in each other's economies.

A further transformation in the form and function of the region's international relations occurred, starting in the late 1980s. Prior to that period the region had shown very little interest in multilateralism at the regional level. The only exception to this was ASEAN's establishment in 1967. In its first 30 years that organization remained a small and relatively limited entity. The five foundational members were not joined by Brunei until 1985 and the grouping remained as such until its expansion to a group of ten in the late 1990s. ASEAN was principally intended to promote inter-elite solidarity and had, beyond some broad rhetorical flourish, little interest in driving the kind of policy coordination and integration that multilateralism was being used to progress elsewhere in the world (Narine 2002). In 1989, this began to change, and accelerating through into the early 2000s, East Asian states began to experiment with multistate forms of cooperation and began to create a host of mechanisms and processes with often ambitious agendas.

The creation of APEC in 1989 started this period with the trade-focused forum rapidly capturing the policy imagination and expanding its membership to include economies from not only East Asia but also North and South America. In the same year that APEC established its leaders' summit, 1994, ASEAN created the ARF. Bringing together a wide array of participants from outside Southeast Asia it was ASEAN's first foray into extra-regional engagement. This continued with the foundation of APT in 1997. The grouping brought together the China, South Korea and Japan to meet with the ASEAN members in what seemed, for a few years at any rate, to be at the center of a broader form of regionalism. The first meeting of EAS was held in Kuala Lumpur in late 2005. In bringing together the APT members with India, New Zealand and Pakistan, East Asian multilateralism gained a structure with an ambitious and wide-ranging mandate and a geographically expansive 16-state membership. This was later expanded to 18 when, in 2011, Russia and the United States joined. The ASEAN Defense Ministers' Meeting (ADMM) first convened in 2006 and launched its 'ADMM Plus' process in 2010. With a membership identical to the EAS this ASEAN offshoot completed a significant expansion of mechanisms and processes that had ASEAN at their heart.

But that was by no means all. The Shanghai Five grouping that had first met in the mid-1990s was transformed into the Shanghai Cooperation Organization (SCO) in 2001 which has subsequently expanded to include not just the countries with a direct stake in the former-Soviet Central Asian lands but also India and Pakistan to be an organization of some heft. The Shangri-La Dialogue (SLD) was launched in 2002 and rapidly became a key part of the regional architecture, as the efflorescence of multilateralism came to be known (Tow and Taylor 2010). Multilateralism refers to any approach to interstate relations that brings together three or more states. While it is usually associated with large-scale programs, during this time East Asian states were not only creating grand mechanisms, they were also establishing smaller entities with a niche contribution to make, entities sometimes described as a process of minilateralism. This includes the Trilateral Security Dialogue established between the US, Japan and Australia in 2006, the Tripartite dialogue between China, South Korea and Japan started in 2008, the Six Party Talks established in 2003 to try to manage North Korea's nuclear ambitions and the Proliferation Security Initiative. As part of this expansion phase countries floated a number of ideas that ultimately failed to gain traction but nonetheless reflected the broader sense in the region that the economic, political and strategic circumstances in East Asia required a much higher level of institutionalized interstate cooperation than had previously been the case. Kevin Rudd's ill-fated Asia-Pacific Community idea was launched rather suddenly in 2008 but shelved by 2010 (Frost 2009) was one notable example. Japanese Prime Minister Hatoyama's East Asia Community (EAC) idea was a second gambit that never quite caught on. The region had caught the multilateral bug (Frost 2008; Green and Gill 2009).

How best to account for the dynamics of East Asian multilateralism? In his contribution to this collection Kai He argues that a distinction can be made between the opening phase of regional multilateralism in the late 1980s and 1990s, and the more recent initiatives. This rests on three observations. First, he argues that what he calls 'multilateralism 1.0' was ASEAN-centered, in contrast the more recent version is not. Second, he argues that the two periods of multilateral activity are distinguished by whether they occurred before or after the global financial crisis (GFC) of 2008. Those multilateral entities established before the crisis are, in his view, different from those that came after. Third, the initiatives that comprise the more recent phase, 'multilateralism 2.0,' are a result of growing economic interdependence and what he describes as a 'high level strategic uncertainty'; in contrast, the earlier efforts were prompted by more conventional understandings of the benefits of multilateralism.

There are a number of problems with He's depiction. The most obvious relates to his decision to distinguish between pre- and post- global financial crisis phases. With the exception of ASEAN, almost all of East Asia's multilateral bodies were established between 1989 and 2006. The ASEAN Defense Ministers' Meeting-Plus (ADMM+) held its first meeting in 2010 as did the Asian Infrastructure and Investment Bank (AIIB) and the EAS expanded in 2011 by two members. Otherwise, the creation and expansion were virtually all pre-2008. There is no clear burst after the GFC, indeed 2008 may well have marked the high-water mark of ambitious and expansive visions with both Japan and Australia's efforts to devise new entities in 2008–2010 having failed. While the GFC was a significant event in the global economy, it was primarily a North Atlantic problem in that its principal driver was poor regulation within the US economy and the really disastrous consequences were in the US and Western Europe. It did, of course, lead to an unprecedented economic stimulus program in China and it underscored the declining power and influence of the US globally and in the region, but it had little tangible impact on the ways in which East Asia's states approached their international policy generally or toward regional multilateral forms of statecraft more specifically. So rather than a clear grouping of developments in terms of time in which the GFC is a firm line, Asia's experience stands around two decades of growth in institutions that run from the late 1980s until the early 2010s.

ASEAN has for some time sought to be in what it describes as the 'driver's seat' of regionalism in East Asia. The reality is that during the 25-year period of multilateral expansion the process has been led by a range of different figures. Australia and Japan took the lead in establishing APEC while the decision to upgrade the annual ministerial meeting to a leaders' summit was driven from Washington. Equally, the SCO's formation in 2001 was the first glimpse of Chinese multilateral entrepreneurship of a kind that has become more visible in recent years with the establishment of AIIB and the forays to rejuvenate the Conference on Interaction and Confidence Building Measures in Asia (CICA). The EAS is rightly described as an ASEAN-centered body, yet for its entire existence it has struggled with the reality that the non-ASEAN members far outweigh the Southeast Asian states. In a grouping that includes the PRC, Russia, the US, India, Japan, the Southeast Asian ten, even with the best will in the world and extraordinary levels of solidarity, will inevitably be marginalized. Consequently, ASEAN keeps a tight rein on the process thus inhibiting the collaborative possibilities. ASEAN's efforts to bind EAS to its dictates and ensure that it remains at the center of EAS activity have put a handbrake on its activity as well as limitations on its future potential (Bisley and Cook 2014). From an analytical point of view, the entity that provides leadership or which sits at the center of nascent leadership does not actually tell us very much about the nature, character or implications either of a particular example of regional multilateralism or of the trend more broadly. The argument that He makes that earlier multilateralism was ASEAN-led while more recent efforts are non-ASEAN led is not just empirically not right, but also, who is at the center of the cooperative effort does not tell us very much on its own.

The third problem with his depiction relates to what might be described as the drivers of multilateralism. He emphasizes what he calls 'high levels of strategic uncertainty' as the key factor prompting the new form of regional multilateralism, one characterized by institutional balancing. It is instinctively appealing to describe the current period as one experiencing high levels of strategic uncertainty but as an explanation it lacks specificity. It is not clear what exactly it is that states might be uncertain about. In classical realist terms this ought to refer to the distribution of power and uncertainty about its nature and the direction of its movement. Yet in hard military terms, both conventional and nuclear, the balance has not changed decisively over the past ten years. It is clear that there has been, and will continue to be, a slow and steady decline in relative US power and a slow and steady increase in that of the PRC, but that is hardly the stuff of 'high level of strategic uncertainty.' More importantly, 'uncertainty' itself is a protean term. Just because someone is uncertain it does not follow that their uncertainty would prompt significant policy changes. Equally, uncertainty could be short-lived, and the condition rapidly resolved.

The other claim, that strategic uncertainty is at 'high levels' is equally imprecise. What exactly defines high levels and what is the dividing line between medium and high levels? Is it the fact of the height of uncertainty or is it the difference between what has been its past status and its current form? There can be no doubt that states across Asia are aware that the region's international order is changing from a stable and settled pattern of relations and is being reconfigured in ways as yet unresolved. But uncertainty on its own is not especially helpful as an explanation. States can be uncertain about, for example, the strategic balance without it leading them to take any active steps in response. Equally, as we saw in the lead up to World War II, just because there is a good degree of certainty about the international environment it does not follow that it will be stable. The issue is not uncertainty itself; it is about which states are uncertain and their actions in response to that specific uncertainty that matters and on that He does not tell us a great deal.

But on one aspect of regional multilateralism, above all, He has it exactly right. A form of international policy that is normally associated with cooperative approaches has become a site for and manifestation of increasing international competition. In what remains of this chapter I will lay out an alternate account of the enthusiasm for multilateralism in East Asia and its increasingly competitive qualities.

Why East Asia came to embrace multilateralism

If focusing on two periods, pre- and post- financial crisis and on the question of leadership is not compelling then how better to understand the emergence and dynamics of multilateral institutions and processes in Asia? To begin, East Asia's move to multilateralism occurred over a single, two-decade or so period which itself is marked by a number of phases. These phases are distinguished by the forces prompting states to create and attempt to enhance regional multilateralism. That is, what it is that they were trying to achieve by gathering in and trying to advance multilateral agendas has given shape to the distinct period within the two-decade expansion.

During its first phase the growth in regional efforts to improve policy coordination coincided with the acceleration of globalization. Growing economic interdependence among Asian states led them to begin to embrace collaborative efforts. One of the key reasons that, prior to the 1990s, these countries were not especially interested in multilateralism is that they lacked the incentives to pursue the complex, difficult and politically challenging game of multilateral economic governance. It was not until they began to trade and invest with one another, on the back of Japan-led regionalization, that there was a good reason to take that step. APEC was established to promote trade liberalization and drive economic growth and integration. Prior to the late 1980s, beyond a small number of countries, few perceived the need to collaborate in that way. Those countries that were moving up the development ladder due to export-led industrialization were doing so by attracting inbound foreign direct investment (FDI) from North America and Western Europe and then exporting goods to those same markets. There is no need to try to promote cooperation with neighbors with whom one has little to do economically speaking. On the back of growing economic integration East Asian states saw that there was a need to reduce barriers to trade to further drive economic growth and created APEC.

As we now know all too well, the integrative forces of globalization are not solely focused on questions of economic interdependence and the binding forces of trade and investment flows, important though these may be. The networks moving goods, services, people and capital that improve prosperity and bring together the states and societies of the region also bring with them vulnerabilities. The linkages which facilitate trade and capital flows created weaknesses which can be exploited, whether by those with malicious intent, by nature or indeed by chance. Examples of these new threats include terrorism, unregulated population movements, and the spread of infectious diseases among many others. The very transnational nature of these risks means that on their own states cannot mitigate them. Thus, Asian states turned to cooperative efforts to try to manage the security challenges of globalization (Bisley 2009). It should be recognized that this move entailed not just a sense that states and societies faced security threats from a much wider set of sources which globalization had opened up, it was also the result of states perceiving challenges which had hitherto not been subject to securitization being recognized as presenting the sort of existential challenge which demanded collective action.

In its first phase, multilateralism in Asia was driven by fairly conventional functional ambitions. On the back of growing intra-regional trade and investment, East Asian states began to get together to collaborate to improve their economic welfare. This included efforts to lower tariff barriers, reduce regulatory constraints to trade, and promote increased investment. They were also motivated by the recognition that the ties that were increasingly binding them together economically, and which were tying them to broader global trade and investment flows, were creating new sources and forms of insecurity. To combat the threats, for example, of transnational terrorism that took advantage of increased financial integration to plan and undertake attacks or to see off growing problems of rapid transmission of infectious diseases due to heightened movement of people they began to collaborate in multilateral bodies like the ARF.

This first phase occurred from 1989 through until the early 2000s. The second phase, commencing in the mid-2000s involved a subtle but important shift in the motivations for multilateralism. To the functional ambitions of improved economic outcomes and increased security from new threats was added the desire to contain and control changes to the structures of regional order.

After the Sino-American rapprochement, East Asia enjoyed a high level of geopolitical stability which enabled a remarkable period of prosperity. In the early years of the new millennium the fractures in the foundations of the regional arrangements that had fostered the conditions that had created such a remarkable period of economic expansion were becoming visible. The dramatic increase in wealth and influence by the PRC meant that the old balance of power and the old rules of the road would need to change to reflect the emerging dispensation. Indeed, some in the region recognized early on that the locus of power was changing with potentially profound effects and that the best way to sustain a stable and peaceful set of arrangements was to corral the major powers and multilateralism was seen as an important way of navigating that process.

East Asia is notable for being an international environment with a small number of very large and powerful states and a larger number of relatively small and weak states. Multilateral mechanisms have a particular appeal in the region because they provide as good an opportunity as is practical for that second group of states to shape both the preferences of the powerful as well as to shape the broader regional order. And it was this motive, to improve communication among Asian states, establish a foundation to discuss shared interests and limit the extent to which the great powers would be the sole authors of a new regional order, that led to the creation of the EAS as well as the failed APC and EAC. In these forums, so the theory went, states large and small would be enmeshed into a web of practices, norms and institutions that would limit the prospects of opting for highly dangerous policy choices and shape their preferences in ways that would drive a more cooperative approach. The aim was not explicitly to see off rivalry but instead to create an environment in which common interests could come to the surface through habits of cooperation, frequent communication and a complex array of diplomatic practices that would bind states into a peaceful mode of operation. Rather than let great power politics determine the fate of the region, multilateralism, it was hoped, would provide the framework through which the worst effects of an anarchic international system could be ameliorated.

During the first two phases of multilateral expansion the locus of leadership was less important to the dynamics than was the motive forces driving states together. It was less the 'who' of multilateralism rather it was the 'why' that provides greater insight into the emergence of this form of statecraft in the region. Indeed, what was perhaps most striking about the overall pattern of multilateral growth during this period was not its leadership but the uncoordinated and almost ad hoc manner in which it occurred. It is because of this that the region has a set of mechanisms and institutions that have a very similar membership with overlapping functional intent even among bodies that are, ostensibly at least, centered around the same major power or leadership body.

A lack of larger coordination has been a hallmark of institutional growth among the array of bodies, yet in spite of this one can still identify three broad families or groups of institutions. The first are the entities that are centered around ASEAN. The Southeast Asian club took the institutional lead to drive the creation of these bodies and the underlying work processes were shaped by or simply lifted wholly from the organization. These entities, unsurprisingly, reflect a distinctly ASEAN conception of the form and function of regional order. These include the ARF, APT, the set of ASEAN Plus One groups and the ADMM and its 'plus' process. The second group entails mechanisms and processes that are led by the PRC and which reflect Beijing's desire to reshape regional order in a manner more conducive to its interests. This includes the AIIB, the SCO, CICA and the nascent Belt and Road Initiative (BRI). Including BRI here may be considered a category error. The massive infrastructure project has a range of larger objectives including exporting surplus capacity in China, aligning the interests of recipient states with those of the PRC, developing China's hinterlands and advancing the PRC's broader geopolitical interests. As yet it lacks a multilateral structure of the conventional variety. But as an effort to bind states together into a common direction—what the PRC styles as a common destiny of peace and prosperity—it shares the overarching aims of multilateralism. The third group is less coherent than the first two and is more of a residual category. It is made up of mechanisms whose purposes are either directly related to the broader patterns established by American regional primacy, and Washington's conception of its economic and strategic interests, or are entities that tacitly support that broader dispensation. Forums and processes within this group include APEC, SLD, Trilateral Security Dialogue (TSD), Proliferation Security Initiative (PSI), and the Asian Development Bank (ADB).

The empirical fact that East Asia enjoyed a roughly four-decade long stable regional order is widely accepted, even if, as in all scholarly endeavors, there is some debate about both its origins and its nature (e.g. Goh 2013; Bisley 2016). The region had the good fortune to enjoy 40 years with a stable balance of power, which meant an absence of arms races, great power rivalry and security dilemmas creating instability cycles. This was predicated on US military predominance and its acceptance by the region as a whole. US power was credible and the commitment to use force was believed. However, as important as American primacy was, it was also the fact that it was accepted by virtually all in the region and there was an absence of contestation about either the basic geography or the purpose of the geopolitical settlement that ensured long-term stability. North Korea was the only country that did not accept the terms of the order and its peripheral position meant it was of marginal significance to the overall setting. Perhaps most importantly, these circumstances were reinforced by a widespread focus on domestic programs of state and nation building. Instead of resources and national energy being spent on dangerous and destabilizing international activity such as cross-border infiltration or support of uprisings and civil conflict, the region's countries got on with the business of domestic development.

Since around 2012 the East Asian pattern of international relations began to change. Defense expenditure is on the rise and the increasing allocation of national resources is being dedicated to offensive war fighting capacities (IISS 2017, 237–49). Great power competition has moved from a nascent phase into an increasingly open form and US power, credibility and commitment are openly questioned. In response to the shifting perceptions of power and risk and growing doubts about the long-term efficacy of America's regional strategy the priority that the domestic once enjoyed over international security concerns is beginning to shift. And it is this process that has led regional multilateralism into its third phase. As the old order begins to unravel states have begun to use traditional security-focused efforts to manage a more uncertain and more challenging international environment, but they have also begun to turn to the array of multilateral mechanisms to contest the content of the regional order.

In conventional international relations scholarship multilateralism promises to reduce the likelihood of competition and improve the prospects of cooperation because of the way it changes the incentive structures states face. Better communication, improved understanding about shared interests and greater levels of trust are created by multilateral endeavors and it is these that provide the key to shifting how states reconfigure the cost-benefit calculations of their foreign policy dealings. In its first phase, due to the stable regional order, regional multilateralism was not focused on those concerns. In its second phase, collaboration was intended to drive these more liberally inspired goals. Viewed from the second decade of the 21st century that phase singularly failed and in the third phase, rather than fostering cooperation, East Asia's multilateralism appears to be contributing to competition.

The dynamics of this competitiveness have played out in a number of ways to date. For example, there has been competition between regional institutions or initiatives such as the ASEAN-centered Regional Comprehensive Economic Partnership (RCEP) competing with the US-led Trans-Pacific Partnership (TPP) to become the prime trade agreement for the region. With President Trump's withdrawal from TPP and RCEP's conclusion in 2019 that competition has been decisively won. Another example was President Xi's articulation of a vision for an Asian-centric security architecture at the 2014 CICA summit. There he not especially subtly called for an end to regional security arrangements that were organized around US military dominance. Equally, contestation is visible about the membership and work programs of institutional structures. This first appeared during the lead up to the establishment of the EAS when China and some in ASEAN wanted a narrower membership while Japan, South Korea and other ASEAN members sought a broader participation in that forum. And most prominently contests themselves play out within these forums. The one with the highest profile of all, the South China Sea dispute, regularly disrupts the working of ASEAN meetings, its offshoots as well as many others such as the SLD. At the 2019 meeting of that latter grouping, the US and China each took their opportunity at plenary sessions to lay out their visions for the region and in differing ways critique the other's place. Not entirely in keeping with traditional liberal expectations of what ought to happen at these forums.

But it is not only that a more contested regional order has become manifest in multilateralism, states are also beginning to see multilateral endeavors as a means through which they can advance their strategy to shape the larger competition for order. For example, Australia sees multilateral mechanisms as a potential means to manage regional instability. In 2018 it hosted a special summit with ASEAN that was not only about re-engaging with Southeast Asia but explicitly an effort to try to galvanize that grouping as a force that could buttress the status quo in the region. But beyond managing the dynamics of insecurity that are attendant in any significant shift in the balance of power, the more important element of a country like Australia's approach to multilateralism is that it sees these institutions as a means to buttress or to make adjustments to the status quo to reflect China's growing influence without ending the broader international disposition which has been so advantageous to liberally inclined countries such as Australia. The logic behind this thinking reflects liberal beliefs about the opportunities of institutions: they increase information flows between the regional powers, provide China the opportunity to shape the regional environment and of course establish a framework for constraining Chinese behavior. This approach is informed by the view that China can achieve its potential and find international satisfaction within the contours of the prevailing order. Equally, it was at APEC 2017 that President Trump articulated his administration's regional strategy. Traveling under the label of a 'Free and Open Indo-Pacific' that plan is squarely aimed at containing PRC influence and sustaining a regional order centered around US power, interests and values (White House 2017).

Canberra is not alone in hoping that the status quo can be sustained by multilateral mechanisms. One of the most important elements of the Obama Administration's foreign policy was its pivot to Asia (Campbell 2016). While much of the pivot was focused on public diplomacy and messaging, and much of the substance of US policy remained as it had been under George W. Bush, the multilateral engagement side of the policy marked a clear break with the tepid approach of the Bush White House. Indeed, the full-throated support of regionalism from the US was one of the most important facets of Obama's approach to East Asia. And at the center of this was an active engagement with ASEAN and its various offshoots. This was informed by the belief that these bodies had a status quo bias and could help Washington's ambitions to slightly adjust the regional order to reflect changing power alignments while retaining the region's core setting. The US wanted to adjust the region to reflect the reality of the PRC's significantly enhanced power without either an overt contest or ceding the core elements of the status quo. Multilateral institutions appeared to provide an ideal opportunity to do this. In essence, Washington believed that ASEAN and its outgrowths, such as the EAS and ADMM+, not only had center-stage in regional cooperative endeavors, but also that if you wanted to corral collaborative approaches to order building you had to take them seriously. Most crucially, they believed that those organizations' broader orientation was in line with the status quo. In the same way that ASEAN believes that its institutional processes can socialize the major powers and bind them into behavior that is in keeping with the broader values and interests of the Southeast Asian club, the Obama Administration felt that these norms and interests reflected the long-standing order centered around American primacy. In particular, China's participation in these processes could be used to continue to advance the US notion that the prevailing order is inclusive and open to all. Whether Washington and its allies are right to think that ASEAN-centered bodies are necessarily aligned to supporting the status quo is an open question. Washington, like Canberra, saw multilateral mechanisms as a means to buttress or adjust somewhat the status quo vision for international order.

Of course, in the move to the Trump Administration, this aspect of US policy has dissipated. Initially, Trump sustained the previous administration's engagement with regional institutions but this rapidly waned. In 2017 Trump attended most of the key meetings at which the US president is expected, by 2019 the level of participation was so low—Commerce Secretary Wilbur Ross was the highest ranking US participant—that ASEAN saw fit to rebuke the US openly, something that the usually cautious and risk-averse entity normally takes pains to avoid.

If the US and its fellow travelers see multilateralism as a means to protect the old order, others and in particular China, see it as a means to develop alternatives to a US-centered region. The US has been openly hostile to a range of Chinese initiatives, such as the AIIB, suspicious of others, such as the SCO, and openly dubious about yet others, such as the efforts to rejuvenate CICA or to advance the BRI. While much of the criticism of these bodies has been framed as technical concerns, for example that the AIIB would dilute standards of development lending, the underlying concern is that through these collaborative endeavors China is expanding its influence and its values in ways with which Washington is not comfortable.

A further example of Asia's multilateralism being caught up in the larger contestatio about the form and function of Asia's regional order is ASEAN's 'Indo-Pacific Outlook' (ASEAN 2019). This was adopted by the grouping in mid-2019 in direct response to the rise of the Indo-Pacific strategic construct and its adoption by the US, its allies and a number of other countries openly uneasy about China's rise. The term is seen by China as designed to organize a policy of containment and ASEAN saw fit to devise an approach to this notion that tried to defuse the geostrategic heat associated with it by emphasizing an open and not exclusionary conception. That ASEAN felt the need to act in this way, in effect to be a conceptual mediator in an ideational contest between the US and China, reflects how far the region has come.

During the latter parts of the second phase of regional multilateralism, when attempts to shape regional order jostled alongside the functional ambitions, contestation was beginning to be evident albeit in a sublimated way. In the third phase competition is now explicit. The US national security strategy plainly states that great power politics is now the main organizational drive of US policy and that China is one of its central antagonists. Yet at the same time both China and the US present visions for the region that they both claim are open and inclusive. The broadly liberal American order is said by its advocates and defenders to be open to all. Its legal and technocratic qualities are held up as embodying a neutral and dispassionate means for arbitrating differences and reflecting the belief that the order does not serve any one set of interests and values. The US, Australia and others believe that China not only can be accommodated in the order—it can find satisfaction within it. But it is far from clear that China can be accommodated within an international order oriented around American primacy. Equally, Beijing does not accept the purported neutrality of the existing international arrangements. Nor is it evident that the region's multilateral structures can provide the shaping and constraining of Chinese policy preferences that many hope.

On the other hand, China also presents a vision of the region that is not exclusionary. It famously pursues what it describes as 'win–win' approaches to international issues, seeking to make mutually beneficial relationships the cornerstone of its foreign policy engagement. Although both espouse a language of positive sum relations, the contestation for influence in the changing region, at least as it is manifest through the indirect means of multilateral competition, is taking increasingly zero-sum terms. While it has been shelved by President Trump, the language used by President Obama to try to convince Congress and the US population more broadly to support the TPP is illustrative. The agreement was necessary, declared the then president, so that the US and not China would write the rules for trade in the Asia-Pacific (Obama 2016). And the Trump Administration's approach is not only increasingly disengaged from multilateral mechanisms but also sees China as a full spectrum threat to its interests and increasingly its values and sees a contest that is starkly zero-sum (Pence 2018).

While Asia's multilateral institutions may have been inspired by liberal ideas, as the region has become more contested these bodies have become part of and are not ameliorating East Asia's competitive dynamic. Beyond the obvious point that they are a further venue for competition and are not damping it down, there are a number of other consequences for multilateralism in contested Asia. First, it is likely to continue to undermine efforts to strengthen the policy impact of multilateral collaborations. While Asia has experimented with a wide number of mechanisms and processes most of these efforts have so far had a rather weak grip on their members' policies. Initially, this was seen as a necessary price to pay to get states interested in participating, but as the challenges of globalization became more evident the need to coordinate policies has become more clear-cut. A contested dynamic will not advance that cause. Indeed, as we have seen at the EAS, although many are keen for the grouping to begin to deliver on its potential to be a lead body for political and strategic concerns, the buffeting it is experiencing in contested Asia is badly limiting this ambition (Bisley and Cook 2016).

Second, it will contribute to zero sum thinking playing a larger role in the way states approach their international engagements in Asia. This is likely to contribute to cycles of competition in which states perceive specific interactions as part of a larger contested dynamic. A third consequence is that it will encourage more ad hoc collaboration on specific issues or problems. Larger structures and processes have obvious appeal in terms of their potential for long-term impact on large issues, but as these are frustrated states are likely to turn to smaller scale issue-specific forms of cooperation. This will further weaken and erode the larger scale mechanisms and bodies. Indeed, there is a strong possibility that the third period of the two-and-a-half-decade experiment with regional multilateralism will be its terminal phase. In contrast to the first decade of the 21st century, when institutions seemed to be created almost every year, nothing new has been established for many years. While it is unlikely that the existing institutions will disappear, there is a strong chance that in a region in which great power rivalry sets the rhythm of international relations, multilateralism will retreat to the wings, evident only as a curious reminder of a more liberal and optimistic past.

Note

1 This chapter is a revised version of Bisley, Nick. 2019. "Contested Asia's 'New' Multilateralism and Regional Order," *The Pacific Review* 32(2): 221–31.

References

ASEAN (Association of Southeast Asian Nations). 2019. "ASEAN Outlook on the Indo-Pacific." June 23. https://asean.org/storage/2019/06/ASEAN-Outlook-on-the-Indo-Pacific_FINAL_22062019.pdf

Bisley, Nick. 2009. *Building Asia's Security*. London: Routledge for IISS.

Bisley, Nick. 2016. "Australia and the Evolving International Order." In *Navigating the New International Disorder: Australia in World Affairs 2011–15*, edited by Mark Beeson and Shahar Hameiri, 39–55. Oxford: Oxford University Press.

Bisley, Nick, and Malcolm Cook. 2014. "How the East Asia Summit Can Achieve its Potential." *ISEAS Perspective* No. 56 (October 28): 1–8. https://www.iseas.edu.sg/images/pdf/ISEAS_Perspective_2014_56.pdf.

Bisley, Nick, and Malcolm Cook. 2016. "Contested Asia and the East Asia Summit." *ISEAS-Yusuf Ishak Institute Perspective*, No. 46 (August 18): 1–7. https://www.iseas.edu.sg/images/pdf/ISEAS_Perspective_2016_46.pdf.

Campbell, Kurt M. 2016. *The Pivot: The Future of American Statecraft in Asia.* New York: Twelve.

Cook, Malcolm. 2009. "Japan's East Asian Community." *The Interpreter*, Lowy Institute, September 25. https://www.lowyinstitute.org/the-interpreter/japans-east-asia-community.

EAS (East Asia Summit). 2005. "Kuala Lumpur Declaration on the East Asia Summit." Kuala Lumpur, December 14. http://www.mofa.go.jp/region/asia-paci/eas/joint0512.html.

Frost, Ellen L. 2008. *Asia's New Regionalism.* Boulder, CO: Lynne Rienner.

Frost, Ellen L. 2009. "Australia's Proposal for an 'Asia Pacific Community': Issues and Prospects." Australian Parliament Research Paper No. 13, December 1. https://www.aph.gov.au/binaries/library/pubs/rp/2009-10/10rp13.pdf.

Goh, Evelyn. 2013. *The Struggle for Order: Hegemony, Hierarchy and Transition in Post-Cold War East Asia.* Oxford: Oxford University Press.

Green, Michael J., and Bates Gill, eds. 2009. *Asia's New Multilateralism: Cooperation, Competition and the Search for Community.* New York: Columbia University Press.

IISS (International Institute for Strategic Studies). 2017. *The Military Balance.* London: Routledge for IISS.

Kivimäki, Timo. 2014. *The Long East Asian Peace.* London: Routledge.

Mack, Andrew. 2010. *Human Security Report 2009–10.* Oxford: Oxford University Press.

Narine, Shaun. 2002. *Explaining ASEAN: Regionalism in Southeast Asia.* Boulder, CO: Lynne Rienner.

Obama, Barack. 2016. "President Obama: The TPP Would Let America, not China, Lead the Way on Global Trade." *The Washington Post*, May 2. https://www.washingtonpost.com/opinions/president-obama-the-tpp-would-let-america-not-china-lead-the-way-on-global-trade/2016/05/02/680540e4-0fd0-11e6-93ae-50921721165d_story.html?utm_term=.7138081ef1e3.

Pence, Mike. 2018. "Vice President Mike Pence's Remarks on the Administration's Policy Towards China." Hudson Institute, October 4. https://www.hudson.org/events/1610-vice-president-mike-pence-s-remarks-on-the-administration-s-policy-towards-china102018.

Ravenhill, John. 2001. *APEC and the Construction of Pacific Rim Regionalism.* Cambridge: Cambridge University Press.

Ruggie, John G., ed. 1993. *Multilateralism Matters: The Theory and Praxis of an Institutional Form.* New York: Columbia University Press.

Stubbs, Richard. 2002. "ASEAN Plus Three: Emerging East Asian Regionalism." *Asian Survey* 42(3): 440–455.

Tow, William T., and Brendan Taylor. 2010. "What is Asian Security Architecture?" *Review of International Studies* 36(1): 95–116.

Wesley, Michael, ed. 2003. *The Regional Organisations of the Asia-Pacific: Explaining Institutional Change.* Basingstoke: Palgrave.

White House. 2017. "Remarks by President Trump at APEC CEO Summit." Da Nang, Vietnam, November 10. https://www.whitehouse.gov/briefings-statements/remarks-president-trump-apec-ceo-summit-da-nang-vietnam/.

3

DISCONNECTING FROM THE REGION

The Asia-Pacific minus the US?

T. J. Pempel[1]

This chapter addresses two puzzles central to research in international political economy. First, what is the relationship between economics and security? To what extent does economic interdependence temper security conflicts (e.g. Barbieri 1996; Goldstein and Mansfield 2012; Mansfield and Pollins 2009; Oneal and Russett 2015, inter alia)? Second, to what extent do multilateral institutions mitigate national differences and enhance the prospects for state-to-state cooperation on otherwise contentious issues (Acharya 2003; Mearsheimer 1994–1995; Ruggie 1993, inter alia)? The Asia-Pacific provides a tantalizing laboratory within which to examine these two puzzles, primarily because of the complex but sustained interactions within the region on both issues. Central to the interplay of Asia-Pacific relations in both areas has been the United States.

In the aftermath of World War II, the US created a web of institutions that forged a global international order that has largely prevailed until today (Ikenberry 2009). The bulk of the economic and financial institutions were, with the conspicuous exception of the communist bloc, *global* in nature. Key examples include the World Bank, the International Monetary Fund (IMF) and the General Agreement on Tariffs and Trade (GATT) along with its successor the World Trade Organization (WTO). In the security arena, by way of contrast, the US approach was *region-specific*. In some parts of the world, the US helped to forge regional security bodies; however, in East Asia it relied on a patchwork of bilateral hub-and-spokes alliances. When the Cold War ended, the most prominent security challenges that had originally justified American-led alliances had disappeared, leaving the US as the unquestioned global and regional hegemon. The US enjoyed what Barry Posen (2003) called unchallenged 'command of the commons.' From this powerful perch, the US had few incentives to alter the existing regional architecture. Instead, it strengthened, rather than scrapped, its bilateral alliances while continuing to bolster global economic institutions.

In the quarter century that followed, US policy makers watched, with varying degrees of encouragement, engagement and dismissal, as governments in East Asia cobbled together a multiplicity of multilateral institutions that Kai He has called 'multilateralism 1.0.' These reflected the widely divergent national interests prevailing across East Asia, the comparatively benign security environment, and the fact that most governments in East Asia prioritized economic development. Driven primarily by the Association of Southeast Asian Nations (ASEAN), Asia's most long-standing regional institution, these bodies sought to advance problem-specific cooperation while maintaining only thin layers of institutionalization. As such, these bodies fell far short of what Muthiah Alagappa (2003) has identified as normatively or solidaristically-driven bodies that embody a broad-based normative consensus and commitments to formally articulated rules and expansive enforcement mechanisms. With the exception of the Asian-Pacific Economic Cooperation (APEC) forum and the ASEAN Regional Forum (ARF), multilateralism 1.0 institutions were composed exclusively of Asian nations, and the bulk of them focused on economics and finance.

Following the global financial crisis (GFC) in 2008–2009 and the Asia-Pacific's increasingly contentious security situation, the region witnessed an explosion of competing regional visions promoted by numerous East Asian leaders, what Kai He has labelled 'multilateralism 2.0.' Altered regional conditions challenged US policy makers to recalibrate America's prior preference for global economic institutions combined with bilateral security alliances. Those recalibrations have been far from consistent.

Between the Asian Financial Crisis (AFC) and the GFC, the Bush Administration opted primarily for an Asian agenda marked by unilateralism (or what it called 'a la carte multilateralism'), and a heavy re-emphasis on security alliances. In contrast, the Obama Administration was broadly enthusiastic about deepening America's engagement with the region through participation in many of the new multilateral bodies. Yet such multilateralism-in-principle masked several distinct exceptions such as Obama's very public efforts to diminish China's proposed Asian Infrastructure Investment Bank (AIIB) and the BRICS's (i.e. Brazil, Russia, India, China, and South Africa) New Development Bank (NDB) as well as his administration's reluctance to embrace an unconditional resumption of the Six Party Talks over North Korea's nuclear and missile programs. Donald Trump, in a further swing in policy, advanced an atavistic nationalist agenda that promised, among other things, to jettison most of America's long-standing multilateral commitments, downplay bilateral alliance commitments, and concentrate policy-making energies through the narrowest of economic microscopes. The first three years of his administration saw an unqualified lambasting of numerous multilateral bodies, a drastic reduction in American influence in East Asian multilateral institutions, and a cascading decline in Asian trust in America's leadership (Wike et al. 2017).

The chapter proceeds in three sections. The first examines American engagement with regional multilateralism. An exploration of the development of 'rival regionalisms' and 'multilateralism 2.0' follows in section two. The analysis concludes with an assessment of the decoupling from prior US multilayered engagement with East Asia and Asian regionalism by the Trump Administration and an assessment of the consequences for the changing order in the Asia-Pacific.

The US and the expansion of regional multilateralism

When the Cold War ended, America's hub-and-spokes alliance system, combined with the widely divergent national interests across East Asia, left that region, unlike Western Europe, largely devoid of regional multilateral institutions with comprehensive memberships or robust agendas (e.g. Hemmer and Katzenstein 2002; Ravenhill 2009; Stubbs 2019). Since then, different American administrations have waxed hot and cold about how to best engage with regional Asia-Pacific institutions. The first serious US moves trace back to a 1989 proposal by Australia and Japan, both anxious to avoid any US disengagement from East Asia, to create the APEC forum and the subsequent proposal for the security-oriented ARF created in 1994. The Clinton Administration, facing a relatively benign security climate in East Asia, and with a heavy prioritization of geoeconomics, proved an enthusiastic proponent of APEC and an active participant in the ARF. However, initial American enthusiasm waned with the failure of APEC's Early Voluntary Sector Liberalization (EVSL) process and Japan's reluctance to open its forestry and agricultural markets to American exports (Krauss 2004; Tay 2006, 4). America further distanced itself from APEC, and multilateralism more broadly, following the 9/11 attacks. In their wake, the George W. Bush Administration downplayed global economic engagement while prioritizing its so-called Global War on Terror. Convinced that Southeast Asia threatened to become 'the second front in the Global War on Terror,' the Bush Administration sought unsuccessfully to 'securitize' APEC (Higgott 2004). Disengagement with APEC's economic priorities resonated with the Bush Administration's throaty embrace of 'a la carte multilateralism,' its withdrawal from a half dozen international agreements, and its unilateralist criterion of 'with us or against us.' Emblematic of American distancing from regional multilateral institutions was the sharp drop off in participation by high-level officials in East Asian regional multilateral meetings. This further widened the separation between the US and the burgeoning of East Asian multilateral institutions (for details see Pempel 2008).

While the US was prioritizing *hard military security* under Bush, East Asian countries, in contrast, concentrated on fostering multilaterally-based *economic security* arrangements. In the wake of the 1997–1998 AFC, Asian governments, spurred by ASEAN, created a bevy of financial institutions, as highlighted in Kai He's introductory analysis. These new bodies sought to buffer East Asian economies from any repeat of the overbearing demands from the US and the IMF, both widely perceived across East Asia as threatening the region's decades of economic development. These new institutions sought to provide a hedge, a firewall, or soft balancing against the worst excesses of unmediated globalization (Pempel 2010a). These new bodies included the ASEAN Plus Three (APT), the Chiang Mai Initiative (CMI, which was subsequently multilateralized as CMIM), the two Asian bond markets, and the East Asia Summit (EAS) (Beeson and Stubbs 2012; Dent 2016; Katzenstein and Shiraishi 2006; Pempel 2005, 2010b; Stubbs 2002). Many individual governments bolstered such multilateral actions with domestic 'self-insurance' in the form of expanded war chests of currency reserves. The US found itself even more outside-looking-in as a simultaneous cascade of bilateral free trade agreements (FTAs) also began to link the region's national economies. In combination, these new institutions and FTAs formalized, integrated, and facilitated the cross-border linkages among companies that had long been a part of the rising number of regional production networks.

The Obama Administration took office convinced that America's wars in Iraq and Afghanistan had mistakenly directed vast resources toward non-existential threats while simultaneously diverting both Treasury resources and senior policy-maker attention from the more strategically and economically critical Asia-Pacific. Obama moved to engage assertively with the Asia-Pacific and its multilateral institutions. That East Asia had emerged from the GFC far less scathed than the US or Europe offered added incentives for American engagement (Pempel and Tsunekawa 2015). The Obama Administration's initial articulation of this 'repositioning' came in a November 2011 speech by the president in Canberra, Australia. Secretary of State Hillary Clinton elaborated on the proposed shift in a November 2011 *Foreign Policy* article, 'America's Pacific Century' (Clinton 2011). America would take a new multipronged approach. Among other things, the Obama Administration expanded the frequency of visits to Asia by top US leaders; the US signed the ASEAN Treaty of Amity and Cooperation (TAC) and joined the EAS. It also appointed an American ambassador to ASEAN; carried out behind-the-scenes encouragement of regime change in Myanmar; and reinvigorated America's participation in the ARF, APEC, and the Shangri-La Dialogue (SLD). The US also increased its multilateral cooperation with regional bodies focused on specific areas such as crime, disaster relief, pandemics, and counter-terrorism. All became components of the US approach to the region's deepening multilateralism.

For the most part such actions involved the US joining Asia-initiated bodies rather than taking the initiative to create new regional bodies. In this regard, membership often meant adjusting prior US policy positions to demonstrate a willingness to accommodate existing institutional arrangements. Thus, joining the EAS in 2011 required a substantial reversal of America's prior opposition to the security limitations endemic in the TAC. The US, however, also played an instrumental role in forging certain multilateral 2.0 bodies such as the bilateral Strategic and Economic Dialogue with China, the Korea–US free trade pact (KORUS), and the Trans-Pacific Partnership (TPP). The prior Bush Administration's unilateral and bilateral predispositions by no means vanished but Obama's multilateralism layered in an additional and vital component to the country's pan-Pacific engagement, one warmly welcomed by most East Asian governments.

Even as multilateralism advanced, with its implicit promises of reduced tensions and enhanced cooperation, so did region-wide military security uncertainty and mistrust. China's rapid military modernization along with its growing assertiveness in the East and South China Seas, along with the growing nuclear and missile program of North Korea, combined to challenge long-held presuppositions that an emerging 'East Asian peace' would persist and that virtually all Asian governments would continue to focus centrally on national economic development. The US continually argued, for example, that China's economic success served the long-term interests of the United States and East Asia. Nevertheless, the Obama Administration simultaneously sought to hedge against increasing hard security uncertainties by tightening and in some cases multilateralizing its bilateral alliances with allies such as Australia, Japan and South Korea. In addition, despite its nominal prioritization of enhanced trade relations, strategic calculations were close to the surface in America's 2008 decision to enter negotiations on the TPP as they were for Japanese Prime Minister Abe, who joined TPP negotiations in 2012. As President Obama wrote in a *Washington Post* defense of TPP: 'The world has changed. The rules are changing with it. The United States, not countries like China, should write them. Let's seize this opportunity, pass the Trans-Pacific Partnership and make sure America isn't holding the bag, but holding the pen' (Obama 2016).

The Obama Administration's fulsome embrace of East Asian multilateralism and its consequent welcome by numerous East Asian governments, however, failed to carry over to the Trump Administration. Trump won office behind an unabashedly nationalistic and transactional approach to foreign affairs. He scorned long-standing alliances such as NATO as 'obsolete,' while allies such as South Korea and Japan, despite generous payments in support of American bases and troops in their countries, found themselves castigated as under-contributing free riders. Bilateral merchandise trade imbalances became a central target for rectification with little consideration of broader relationships or grand strategy. Within days of his inauguration, Trump pulled the US out of the TPP, a move followed by his removal of the US from the Global Climate Change agreement and a host of other multilateral agreements and bodies that put 'constraints' on US unilateralism and the xenophobia of 'America first.' A series of trade wars and unilateral tariff impositions, the most notable of which was with China, followed quickly in what became a sweeping effort to erase virtually all legacies of the Obama Administration, the Trump Administration opted for American disengagement from regional agreements, freer trade, multilateralism, and East Asian regional bodies. Even the long-standing military components of America's bilateral alliance structure came under attack.

Rival regionalisms and multilateralism 2.0?

Ellen Frost (2014, 1) advanced the term 'rival regionalisms' to highlight new Chinese and Russian-backed multilateral bodies designed, as she phrases it, 'to fragment Asia's institutional landscape, erode regional stability, and undermine Asian confidence in the legitimacy of the institutions and values underpinning the existing liberal economic order.' Here I appropriate her felicitous term for a different purpose, namely, to examine the ways in which several countries have been creating and using regional institutions as competitive forums aimed at advancing their particularistic national interests, rather than at advancing multilateral solidarity per se. He's discussion of 'multilateralism 2.0' highlights the most prominent of these competing architectural efforts, but unlike him I wish to focus as well on institutions that, even if they have not been 'created' by a single country, bear all the hallmarks of serving the national interest of one country (or group of countries) over another.

An easy starting point is the juxtaposition of the TPP with the Regional Comprehensive Economic Partnership (RCEP). As noted above, President Obama and Japanese Prime Minister Abe justified TPP not only for its integrative trade and economic benefits, but also for its geostrategic implications. For Abe, TPP had the twofold goal of bolstering his domestic economic agenda while buttressing Japan's security relations with the US, Australia and several Southeast Asian countries. Not at all marginally, TPP would also function as a corresponding counterweight to the rising influence of China, conspicuously not a participant in TPP negotiations.

The putative institutional alternative to TPP is RCEP. Although RCEP began as an ASEAN initiative, its less stringent agenda and its unwavering support from China led widely to its being characterized as the 'anti-TPP.' Interestingly however, China has advanced RCEP's appeal to Japan and other sophisticated economies by allowing the proposed pact to include non-trade issues such as investment and intellectual property. When Trump pulled the US out of TPP, RCEP looked to be East Asia's only regional trade alternative. Nevertheless, on January 28, 2018 representatives from 11 countries, following the strong leadership of Japan and Australia, agreed to a modified version of the TPP. This new pact—renamed the Comprehensive and Progressive Agreement for Trans-Pacific Partnership (CPTTP), or TPP 11—took effect in December 2018. The agreement represented a major recovery by the 11 countries following initial expectations that TPP was dead after the election of Donald Trump. Ironically, the TPP-11 and RCEP are advancing simultaneously with heavily overlapping memberships that mute their purported rivalry. At the same time, the TPP-11 has left the US outside the emerging, and potentially compatible, Asian trade pacts. In response, the Trump Administration threatened Japan with bilateral tariffs as a means to press Japan into a bilateral trade agreement. That agreement, made in fall 2019, gives the US most of the agricultural access to the Japanese market it would have achieved though TPP and thus provides Trump's farming voters with an offset to the markets they lost due to his trade war with China. The negative impact on US–Japan relations, not to mention the broader damage to America's alliances more generally, however, was palpable.

Tensions over regional multilateral leadership between Japan and China surfaced early in their respective advancement of the APT (by China) and the EAS (by Japan). China and Japan also support rival institutions to encourage regional cooperation concerning outer space with the Asia-Pacific Space Cooperation Organization (APSCO) organized by China and the Asia-Pacific Regional Space Agency Forum (APRSAF) driven by Japan (Pekkanen 2016). More recently, their competition played out around the China-initiated AIIB which the Obama Administration adamantly opposed and which it successfully convinced Japan to avoid. Such US–Japan collaboration left both countries marginalized as 57 countries including numerous Western European democracies, signed on as founding members. Several nation-states, including Japan, sought to offset the appeal of the China-led AIIB. Japan began a multi-billion-dollar 'Connectivity Initiative,' South Korea introduced the 'New Southern Policy' to focus on infrastructure development in key Southeast Asian countries, and Australia signed an investment agreement with the ASEAN to 'develop a pipeline of high-quality infrastructure projects, to attract private and public investment' (Heydarian 2018).

Such national competition between institutions reinforces the narrative that the region is 'ripe for rivalry' (Friedberg 1993) and that current institutional rivalries do little more than mirror the competition to shape the regional order by national antagonists. Driving that narrative is the perceived zero-sum competition between a rising China and a declining US. The two countries are, in this portrayal, the 21st century equivalents of Sparta and Athens, caught in a 'Thucydides Trap' and thus destined for inevitable conflict (e.g. Allison 2015; Pillsbury 2015). Indeed, the zero-sum competitive narrative began to worsen with the Trump Administration's public skepticism about both Paris and Iran, followed by the beginning of a trade war, and the US specification of China as an existential threat (e.g. Pence 2018).

Considerable evidence, however, challenges any presumption of inevitable conflict between the US and China. Not least is their mutual economic interdependence. As well, the two demonstrated before Trump that there were many areas in which they could cooperate such as the Paris Accord on global warming, the Iran nuclear deal, and their coordinated anti-piracy activities off the Horn of Africa (e.g. Christensen 2015; Pempel 2016 inter alia). This is not the place for that debate. Nevertheless, it is imperative to acknowledge that despite pervasive national rivalries that sometimes play out in regional institutions, other powers besides China and the US are taking increased agency in the shaping of the regional order.

Three insightful examples suggest that competition and cooperation are advancing simultaneously among the many new regional institutions and that middle powers are exerting important influence over regional developments. The first involves the AIIB. As noted above, the US and Japan feared that the new Chinese-led investment bank would threaten existing multilateral lenders where they dominated, notably the World Bank and the Asian Development Bank (ADB), and in the process serve not regional development so much as China's relative economic influence across the region. This catalyzed the Obama Administration's initial efforts to dissuade America's friends and allies from joining. However, the capital needed for infrastructural development in East Asia has been projected by the Japan-led ADB to be an astronomical US$26 trillion by 2030, an amount neither the ADB nor the IMF are positioned to provide.

To mitigate anxieties about the possible one-sided utilization of Chinese money to challenge existing institutions while also responding to the bottomless demand for development capital, Chinese officials made numerous compromises to their government's original plans for the AIIB. These involved reductions in China's voting rights, increased transparency in project selection, and eventually an enthusiastic collaboration in joint funding ventures with the ADB and the IMF. The central conclusion has to be that despite anxieties that AIIB would be a rigid rival devoted exclusively to advancing Chinese interests, the bank has evolved in ways that reflect substantial economic congruence with US and Japanese-led bodies as well as with the liberal global order.

The second example concerns CMIM. Its predecessor, the CMI, involved a complex web of bilateral currency swap arrangements created by the APT following the AFC. It sought to provide short-term relief to member countries facing future threats of the kind of liquidity problems that triggered the AFC. Ten years later the GFC spurred participants even further as they acknowledged certain weaknesses of CMI, most notably its convoluted web of bilateral swap arrangements, its limited funding and potentially constrictive conditionality clauses. All threatened rapid responses to any currency crisis. Thus, in 2009 at the APT meeting in Thailand, the member countries opted to multilateralize existing bilateral swap arrangements by creating a single pool of money. They also doubled and then tripled the amounts involved and permitted greater flexibility for emergency currency transfers. The APT leaders also established the ASEAN + 3 Macroeconomic Research Office (AMRO) as an independent regional financial surveillance organization (Grimes 2011). These moves involved a substantial deepening of the institutional commitments by the member countries. The compromise permitting the final agreement offers even more compelling evidence that national competitions are often manageable within institutions.

That compromise involved a deal among Japan, South Korea, and the PRC concerning their relative contributions to CMIM. Unsurprisingly, both Japan and China sought bragging rights as the 'largest' contributor. A compromise, engineered by Korean representatives, had Japan contributing 32 percent—the largest single national percentage of total funding while the PRC plus Hong Kong were allowed to contribute a combined 32 percent. Japan can claim it gives 'more' than China which in turn can retort that 'the Chinese' contribution equals that of Japan. South Korea, in turn, boosted its own position by securing the right to contribute one-half of the 32 percent maximum contribution at 16 percent. Such agreements underscore the fact that regional institutional commitments can serve to deflect erstwhile national competition into win–win compromises among putative rivals. This is particularly the case in areas like finance where fungible compromises are easier to reach in areas connected to hard security.

Still a third example of multilateralism bridging deep national rivalries is the trilateral leaders' summit and its related Trilateral Cooperation Secretariat (TCS). In 2008 the leaders of Japan, South Korea and China who had until then been meeting on the sidelines of the APT agreed that many issues incentivized them to meet trilaterally, independently of APT. The three countries agreed to hold an annual leaders' summit at locations rotated among the three countries. By 2017, 18 ministerial meetings addressing more than 20 functional areas—including economics, environment, energy, finance, science and technology, education and culture—had gone forward to supplement these leaders' meetings. Several of the summits have faced delays, usually for political reasons underscoring the fact that the TCS has hardly obliterated national rivalries. Nevertheless, the summits continue and the ministerial meetings have been less subject to political delays.

Anodyne post-conference announcements should not detract from the fact that the three countries have continued their institutional commitments. They have forged a common investment treaty and they continue to explore a trilateral FTA. Moreover, a fully-staffed TCS in Seoul now actively advances a variety of projects designed to enhance trilateral cooperation. Beyond that, the summits themselves and the efforts that go into their planning reveal an embryonic but energized trilateral institution that is reducing tensions and pursuing cross-border solutions to common problems. These trilateral developments resonate with Haftel's (2007) broader demonstration that a combination of economic interdependence and regular meetings among high-level officials often mitigate violent conflict among states.

The multilateral institutions that now span East Asia and the Asia-Pacific fall far short of having created a normative or solidaristic order. Within East Asia, and especially in Northeast Asia, national rivalries and mutual mistrust bedevil efforts at multinational collaboration, and make clear that, in themselves, neither enhanced economic interdependence nor institutional membership have obliterated national pursuit of competitive advantage. Yet, that is a particularly high bar to set. National governments remain the ultimate repositories of power and the primary building blocks for regional multilateralism, particularly multilateralism 2.0. Territoriality and national governmental priorities continue to challenge the potentially integrative forces of cross-border economic interdependence and new regional institutions, not to mention the presumably unifying pressures of common problems such as pandemics or pollution. In the critical area of hard security, all of the weapons in East Asia remain aimed at other East Asians. In numerous areas, governments continue to joust with one another for comparative advantage. Win-win solutions remain rare in most hard security issues where zero-sum calculations still predominate. At best, the emerging order in East Asia remains instrumental. Nevertheless, multilateral institutional cooperation has been expanding rapidly in numerous diverse non-military areas (Pekkanen 2017). Moreover, as the trilateral relationship among China, Japan, and South Korea suggests, even countries deeply suspicions of one another will often find institutional linkages that mitigate mistrust.

In contrast to recent discussions of 'great power transition' or 'rivalry of great powers,' (Mearsheimer 2001; Allison 2015) power and hierarchy in the Asia-Pacific are by no means monotonic. China may well appear to be rivaling the US in any Asia-Pacific economic pyramid but simultaneously the US retains substantial military supremacy over China. As well, numerous middle powers such as Japan, South Korea, Vietnam, or ASEAN in its collective capacity occupy quite influential positions in functionally different power hierarchies. For the most part none of these countries prefers to choose sides between the US and China; most seek positive and beneficial relations with both.

Increasingly, most governments in East Asia, as well as the United States pre-Trump showed sensitivity to the ways in which zero-sum calculations in one area (such as security) need not impede the search for win-win solutions in others (such as finance, pollution, or trade). As has long been recognized by analysts of multilateral institutions (Haas 1964), successful institutional solutions in one functional area often enhance tentative explorations about possible cooperation in others. To date, no single regional institution in East Asia has emerged that purports to address such complex calculations and trade-offs. Instead, multiple institutions with different memberships and alternative agendas are the logical outcome. East Asia's multilateralism 2.0 is thus a manifestation of such nuanced calculations. The result, as He argues, is that 'redundant and overlapping multilateral institutions will become a "new normal" in the Asia-Pacific as a result of intensified institutional balancing.'

The Trump challenge and Asia's options

The Trump Administration has shown little interest in engaging in East Asia's increasingly nuanced multilateralism. As a result, America's regional role, particularly in activities not subject to influence by the Seventh Fleet, has rapidly diminished. That is not an outcome welcomed by most governments in the region. Despite criticisms of the Obama repositioning, its multifaceted and multilateral approach to the region resonated well with most East Asian governments.

Far more problematic has been the Trump Administration's xenophobia, unilateralism, and economic transactional approach to allies. Economic ties among Japan, South Korea, and China, as well as China and Southeast Asia are deep and mutually interdependent. Within Asia, collective frustration with Trumpian isolationism, warming toward North Korea and disregard of its security threats, along with his tariff wars, has triggered a warming of relations between Japan and China as well as Japan and South Korea. As the US backed away from positive ties with East Asia, Japan signed up to cooperate in over 50 AIIB projects. It thus became a de facto, if not a de jure, participant. Previously sour China–South Korea relations took a major turn toward improvement in tourism and economic ties during 2018–2019. Most ASEAN countries have welcomed Chinese investments while becoming collectively silent on Chinese territorial expansions in the South China Seas, instead welcoming the agreement on a common Code of Maritime Conduct. In short, as the US has backed away from its prior commitments to allies and its engagements with East Asian institutions, many countries have moved to accommodate China's rise.

Yet with or without American participation, East Asian regionalism remains on an expanding and deepening trajectory. Nowhere has this been clearer than in the decision by the 11 remaining members of TPP to forge ahead without the US and to reconfigure the TPP, as noted above. The decision by the Trump Administration to opt out of participation is less likely to 'make America great again' than it is to 'make America marginal again.' China has long sought to achieve the weakening of America's bilateral alliances and a reduction of America's regional influence. It is sadly ironic that the Trump Administration has unilaterally begun to deliver China's aim *gratis*.

Throughout the post-war period, the US, for better or worse, has been a stabilizing force in the Asia-Pacific (Christensen 1999, 2003; Mastanduno 2003, inter alia). What is the likely outcome of American self-marginalization? Close allies and security partners of the US as well as many private companies across the Asia-Pacific are finding it in their self-interest, not only to try coaxing the US back into multilevel regional engagement, but also to continue building their own linkages with one another while exploring expanded hedging options. Within the economic and financial areas, intra-Asian ties could well begin to supplant those involving US companies, as has become clear by the conclusion of the TPP-11 and the reluctance of most of its members to accommodate Trump's demand for new bilateral trade agreements. Any constriction of access to the US market, meanwhile, is likely to stimulate Asian companies and governments to search for alternative markets and partners. Numerous US companies once dependent on components from East Asian partners have felt the pinch of

Trump's tariffs. As well, witness the Japan–European Union (EU) free trade agreement. Asian governments could also opt to bolster their defense budgets in turn spawning an escalation of security dilemmas throughout the region. The result is likely to be exacerbation of security problems that the US might ultimately be compelled to enter, but on terms less favorable than those that continued engagement would have prevented.

One possible upside involves intra-regional reactions to America's earlier regional marginalization following the 1997–1998 AFC. These show that when the US opts out, albeit temporarily, Asian governments have the capacity to turn more to one another in the search for solutions (Pempel 2010b). American abstention going forward is likely to result in a closer reliance on intra-Asian institutions to address common concerns such as pandemics, disaster relief, environmental pollution and other non-traditional security problems. It will be also far less likely to see Asian governments capitulating to unilateral US demands.

That said, the question remains one of the leadership of any such collective intra-Asian projects. Chinese president Xi Jinping certainly lost no time attempting to position his country as the stalwart promoter of free trade in his Davos speech in early 2017 and as a country deeply committed to the Paris Accord on climate and renewable energy. For this, he won global and regional plaudits. The first Xi-Trump meeting in April 2017 showed Xi looking by far the leader and Trump as the out-of-his-depth student. Trump's early dalliance with Taiwan gave way to a quick acknowledgement of the long-standing 'one China' principle. On his promise to brand China a currency manipulator, he has reversed course declaring: 'They're not currency manipulators.' Months of uninformed bluster about North Korea gave way to Trump's naïve astonishment: 'After listening [to President Xi] for 10 minutes, I realized it's not so easy.' He ultimately provided Kim and North Korea with an international platform and a globally televised embrace that ignored decades of human rights and international security violations. Trump's imposition of aluminum and steel tariffs proved only marginally effective against its alleged target, China, triggering a politically lacerating Chinese tit-for-tat raising of a host of US agricultural goods the primary impact of which fell on the US economy.

It is hard not to conclude that any American disconnect from the region will result in enhanced Chinese influence. Indeed, that was clearly in evidence as the above examples show. Yet, given the depth of security mistrust that prevails across East Asia, and in particular the mistrust of long-run Chinese intentions, institutionalized cooperation on 'easy' issues like finance, pandemics, and pollution are unlikely to prove sufficient to create a region devoid of conflict and coercive diplomacy. Absent the US as a vigorous participant, East Asian multilateralism 2.0 is likely to deepen while nevertheless raising China's regional influence and failing to resolve the testy national mistrust across East Asia that to date has often been suppressed or shelved in the face of America's previously prominent regional presence.

The other major possibility is that the complex functional hierarchies among Asian states, the strong interests of middle powers plus those of the numerous private companies throughout the region will blend with the proliferation of multilateral institutions to check unwarranted exertions of bullying, whether by Trump or Xi. This combination instead may well usher in a greater willingness by all parties to continue doing what they have done in the past: concentrate on domestic economic development, shelve the most contentious territorial disputes and back away from stark military conflicts. The US may well become a marginal observer of the process under Trump but intra-Asian cooperation may nonetheless be the result.

Note

1   This chapter is a revised version of Pempel, T. J. 2019. "Regional Decoupling: The Asia-Pacific Minus the USA?" *The Pacific Review*, 32(2): 256–65.

References

Acharya, Amitav. 2003. *Constructing a Security Community in Southeast Asia: ASEAN and the Problem of Regional Order*. London: Routledge.
Alagappa, Muthiah. 2003. "The Study of International Order: An Analytic Framework." In *Asian Security Order: Instrumental and Normative Features*, edited by Muthiah Alagappa, 33–69. Stanford, CA: Stanford University Press.
Allison, Graham. 2015. "The Thucydides Trap: Are the US and China Headed for War?" *The Atlantic*, September 24. https://www.theatlantic.com/international/archive/2015/09/united-states-china-war-thucydides-trap/406756/.
Barbieri, Katherine. 1996. "Economic Interdependence: A Path to Peace or a Source of Interstate Conflict?" *Journal of Peace Research* 33(1): 29–49.
Beeson, Mark, and Richard Stubbs, eds. 2012. *Routledge Handbook of Asian Regionalism*. London: Routledge.
Christensen, Thomas J. 1999. "China, the US–Japan Alliance, and the Security Dilemma in East Asia." *International Security* 23(4): 49–80.
Christensen, Thomas J. 2003. "China, the U.S.–Japan Alliance, and the Security Dilemma in East Asia." In *International Relations Theory and the Asia-Pacific*, edited by G. John Ikenberry and Michael Mastanduno, 25–56. New York: Columbia University Press.
Christensen, Thomas J. 2015. *The China Challenge: Shaping the Choices of a Rival Power*. New York, NY: W.W. Norton.
Clinton, Hillary. 2011. "America's Pacific Century." *Foreign Policy*, October 11. https://foreignpolicy.com/2011/10/11/americas-pacific-century/.
Dent, Christopher M. 2016. *East Asian Regionalism*. London: Routledge.
Friedberg, Aaron L. 1993. "Ripe for Rivalry: Prospects for Peace in a Multipolar Asia." *International Security* 18(3): 5–33.
Frost, Ellen L. 2014. *Rival Regionalisms and Regional Order: A Slow Crisis of Legitimacy*. Special Report No. 48. Seattle, WA: National Bureau of Asian Research.
Goldstein, Avery, and Edward D. Mansfield, eds. 2012. *The Nexus of Economics, Security and International Relations in East Asia*. Stanford, CA: Stanford University Press.
Grimes, William W. 2011. "The Asian Monetary Fund Reborn? Implications of Chiang Mai Initiative Multilateralization." *Asia Policy* 11(1): 79–104.
Haas, Ernst B. 1964. *Beyond the Nation State: Functionalism and International Organization*. Stanford, CA: Stanford University Press.
Haftel, Yoram Z. 2007. "Designing for Peace: Regional Integration Arrangements, Institutional Variation, and Militarized Interstate Disputes." *International Organization* 61(1): 217–237.

Hemmer, Christopher, and Peter J. Katzenstein. 2002. "Why is There no NATO in Asia? Collective Identity, Regionalism, and the Origins of Multilateralism." *International Organization* 56 (3): 575–607.

Heydarian, Richard J. 2018. "Middle Powers Step Up in Asia." *China Focus*, Foreign Policy, October 24. https://www.chinausfocus.com/article/2018/1024/17295.html.

Higgott, Richard A. 2004. "US Foreign Policy and the 'Securitization' of Economic Globalization." *International Politics* 41(2): 147–175.

Ikenberry, G. John. 2009*After Victory: Institutions, Strategic Restraint, and the Rebuilding of Order after Major Wars*. Princeton, NJ: Princeton University Press.

Katzenstein, Peter J., and Takashi Shiraishi, eds. 2006. *Beyond Japan: The Dynamics of East Asian Regionalism*. Ithaca, NY: Cornell University Press.

Krauss, Ellis S. 2004. "The United States and Japan in APEC's EVSL Negotiations: Regional Multilateralism and Trade." In *Beyond Bilateralism: US–Japan Relations in the New Asia-Pacific*, edited by Ellis S. Krauss and T. J. Pempel, 272–295. Stanford, CA: Stanford University Press.

Mansfield, Edward D., and Brian M. Pollins, eds. 2009. *Economic Interdependence and International Conflict: New Perspectives on an Enduring Debate*. Ann Arbor: University of Michigan Press.

Mastanduno, Michael. 2003. "Incomplete Hegemony: The United States and Security Order in Asia." In *Asian Security Order: Instrumental and Normative Features*, edited by Muthiah Alagappa, 141–170. Stanford, CA: Stanford University Press.

Mearsheimer, John J. 1994–1995. "The False Promise of International Institutions." *International Security* 19(3): 5–49.

Mearsheimer, John J. 2001. *The Tragedy of Great Powers*. New York: W.W. Norton.

Obama, Barack. 2016. "The TPP Would Let the United States, not China, Lead the Way on Global Trade." *Washington Post*, May 2. https://www.washingtonpost.com/opinions/president-obama-the-tpp-would-let-america-not-china-lead-the-way-on-global-trade/2016/05/02/680540e4-0fd0-11e6-93ae-50921721165d_story.html.

Oneal, John R., and Bruce M. Russett. 2015. "The Kantian Peace: The Pacific Benefits of Democracy, Interdependence, and International Organizations, 1885–1992." In *B. M. Russett: Pioneer in the Scientific and Normative Study of War, Peace, and Policy*, 74–108. Cham, Switzerland: Springer.

Pekkanen, Saadia M. 2016. "China and Japan Vie to Shape Asia's Approach to Outer Space." *Forbes*, October 31. https://www.forbes.com/sites/saadiampekkanen/2016/10/31/china-and-japan-vie-to-shape-asias-approach-to-outer-space/#3c2e80d32606.

Pekkanen, Saadia M. 2017. *Asian Designs: Governance in the Contemporary World Order*. Ithaca, NY: Cornell University Press.

Pempel, T. J. 2005. *Remapping East Asia: The Construction of a Region*. Ithaca, NY: Cornell University Press.

Pempel, T. J. 2008. "How Bush Bungled Asia: Militarism, Economic Indifference and Unilateralism Have Weakened the United States across Asia." *The Pacific Review* 21(5): 547–581.

Pempel, T. J. 2010a. "Soft Balancing, Hedging, and Institutional Darwinism: The Economic–Security Nexus and East Asian Regionalism." *Journal of East Asian Studies* 10(4): 209–238.

Pempel, T. J. 2010b. "More *Pax*, Less *Americana* in Asia." *International Relations of the Asia-Pacific* 10(3): 465–490.

Pempel, T. J. 2016. "Thucydides [Clap] Trap: U.S.–China Relations in a Changing Asia-Pacific." *Global Asia* 10(4): 88–93.

Pempel, T. J., and Keiichi Tsunekawa, eds. 2015. *Two Crises, Different Outcomes: East Asia and Global Finance*. Ithaca, NY: Cornell University Press.

Pence, Mike. 2018. "Vice President Mike Pence's Remarks on the Administration's Policy towards China." Hudson Institute, October 4. White House Briefing. https://www.white

house.gov/briefings-statements/remarks-vice-president-pence-administrations-policy-toward
-china.

Pillsbury, Michael. 2015. *The Hundred Year Marathon: China's Secret Strategy to Replace America as the Global Superpower*. New York: Henry Holt.

Posen, Barry R. 2003. "Command of the Commons: The Military Foundation of US Hegemony." *International Security* 28(1): 5–46.

Ravenhill, John. 2009. "East Asian Regionalism: Much Ado about Nothing." *Review of International Studies* 35(S1): 215–235.

Ruggie, John G., ed. 1993. *Multilateralism Matters: The Theory and praxis of an Institutional Form*. Ithaca, NY: Columbia University Press.

Stubbs, Richard. 2002. "ASEAN Plus Three: Emerging East Asian Regionalism?" *Asian Survey*, 42(3): 440–455.

Stubbs, Richard. 2019. "ASEAN Sceptics versus ASEAN Proponents: Evaluating Regional Institutions." *The Pacific Review* 32(6): 923–950.

Tay, Simon S. C. 2006. "An East Asia Community and the United States: A View from ASEAN." Paper for International Workshop organized by the Council on East Asian Community, Singapore, June 26.

Wike, Richard, Bruce Stokes, Jacob Poushter, and Janell Fetterolf. 2017. "US Image Suffers as Publics Around World Question Trump's Leadership." Pew Research Center, *Global Attitudes & Trends*, June 26. https://www.pewresearch.org/global/2017/06/26/u-s-image-suffers-as-publics-around-world-question-trumps-leadership/.

4

MINILATERAL SECURITY'S RELEVANCE TO US STRATEGY IN THE INDO-PACIFIC

Challenges and prospects

William Tow[1]

Introduction

Effectively managing Indo-Pacific security has arguably become the most pressing imperative for preserving contemporary global peace and stability. Acute tensions over traditional security issues such as the Korean Peninsula, security dilemmas in the East and South China Seas, and the broader strategic implications of 'China's rise' remain all too evident. Newer security concerns relating to migration, humanitarian assistance and disaster relief, terrorism, drug trafficking, cybercrime, climate change, and pandemics like COVID-19 are likewise commanding regional officials' attention and influencing their policy agendas. Uncertainties relating to US President Donald Trump's economic and security postures directed toward Asia form an uncertain, complex and potentially explosive strategic landscape within the world's wealthiest and most dynamic region.

This landscape is further complicated by changes throughout Asia in post-war alliances, alignments and unaffiliated actors. The post-war American 'hub-and-spokes' alliance network has yielded to a broader array of security coalitions targeted on specific threats and issues. Despite North Korean leader Kim Jong-un's recent warming of ties with Xi Jinping, the People's Republic of China's historic security ties with North Korea remain strained as the latter moves aggressively to establish strategic leverage in its own right. Traditionally, non-aligned actors such as India and various member states of the Association of Southeast Asian Nations (ASEAN) are exploring advanced economic and security collaboration with other large and small powers within the increasingly fluid Indo-Pacific geopolitical environment. Russia yearns to play a major role in Asia's evolving strategic landscape as part of its global quest to challenge and revise what it views as the United States' decreasing global hegemony. These trends conform with Kai He's 'multilateralism 2.0' paradigm developed earlier in the introduction chapter of this volume.

Order building and alliance transition

Within this broader context of regional security cooperation and competition, two overlapping and increasingly critical trends have surfaced. First, China is now assuming a more central role in the shaping of any future Indo-Pacific regional security order. The extent to which Beijing collaborates or competes with the region's maritime powers—the United States, Japan, India and (to a much lesser extent) Australia—on various issues and crises will determine to what extent the region languishes in a multipolar state of anarchy or eventually develops into a concrete regional security order. China's collaboration with the US and its allies is now clearly required to defuse the North Korean nuclear crisis, and the level of cooperation that China generates with Washington and its allies in doing so constitutes a crucial test for regional war avoidance. Realizing these objectives, however, does not necessarily constitute either the 'major power relations' model which has been advanced by various Chinese policy makers or a Sino-American 'grand bargain' on regional crisis management as the two countries remain at odds over other critical regional flashpoints.[2]

The second trend will be assessed in more detail in this chapter. The American post-war bilateral security alliance network—known as the 'San Francisco System' since its inception with the signing of the Japan Peace Treaty in September 1951—has morphed into a less hierarchical and more pliable basis for security collaboration. Gone are the days when separate member states of this alliance network operated relatively seamlessly under the direction of the Pentagon or US Pacific (now Indo-Pacific) Command to contain mutually perceived threats: international communism led by the Soviet Union and China making inroads throughout Asia during the Cold War.

At least two factors explain this transition. First is the intensifying North Korean challenge to the credibility of post-war US-extended deterrence strategy which rested on traditional assumptions about an adversary's 'rationality' to ensure reasonable levels of escalation control during regional crisis (Fitzpatrick 2016). The shrill (arguably even histrionic) North Korean rhetoric intensifying during 2017 threatening to engulf Seoul and much of the Republic of Korea (ROK) in a 'sea of fire' using weapons of mass destruction or to subject Washing- ton and New York to a nuclear attack may or may not be taken literally. It does, however, introduce a new and strident element of nuclear brinkmanship into the region. The summit diplomacy President Trump conducted with Kim during 2018 and 2019 ultimately failed to dissuade North Korea from relinquishing its nuclear force assets. Placing this rhetoric in perspective, debate has sharpened among Western experts over how soon Kim Jong-un's increasingly formidable nuclear and missile capabilities will credibly threaten targets on the US mainland (Pollack 2018; Ratner 2018).

A second, complex factor which largely flows from the first is that the national security agendas of US treaty allies in the Indo-Pacific have become diverse and often contradictory. Japan feels more threatened by China than does South Korea. Yet Seoul remains sufficiently wary of Tokyo to preclude substantive bilateral Japan–ROK collaboration, absent US intercession. South Korea's current government clearly favors a more conciliatory approach toward North Korea than does either the

Trump Administration or the current Japanese government. As a 'Western' country situated in Asia, Australia faces no immediate existential threat. However, that country's current government, like its predecessors, fears the prospect of a looming strategic abandonment by its 'great and powerful' American friend leaving it culturally and strategically isolated in the region at a time when China is expanding its military power on its northern doorstep and when North Korea is developing long-range ballistic missiles potentially capable of hitting Australian targets (Hartcher 2017). Policy elites now ruling the United States' other two post-war treaty allies, the Philippines and Thailand, challenge the relevance of Western liberal political values and processes. During President Barack Obama's administration, the US view was that authoritarian political trends in the two countries produced social chaos and undermined democracy. In response, both Bangkok and Manila developed closer relations with China, notwithstanding the potential loss of traditional American security guarantees, and the Philippines' continued de facto reliance on US military assistance to counter a rising jihadist threat in Mindanao (Flores 2017). The Trump Administration has done little to address Thai and Filipino policy makers' concerns that American foreign policy is increasingly isolationist and that Southeast Asia is an afterthought relative to Washington's preoccupation with the Chinese and North Korean strategic threats (Sheng 2017).

The urgency of 'traditional security' politics—succinctly defined as 'the protection of national security and sovereignty from external state-level threats and the management of the impact of major power competition'—is obviously increasing in the Asia-Pacific (Tsjeng 2017). This has left uncertainty as to where 'non-traditional security'—described by Mely Caballero-Anthony as 'challenges to the survival and well-being of peoples and states that arise primarily out of non-military sources'—is placed by Washington and its security allies in an era of deepening great power competition and nuclear and intensifying Indo-Pacific security dilemmas (Caballero-Anthony 2010, 1).

The Trump Administration's open disdain for the politics of climate change, its projected budget cuts supporting food aid and its reductions in the funding of international health programs has underscored the centrality of traditional geopolitics in its policy agenda (Busby, Grépin, and Youde 2017; Chemnick 2017; Lee 2017b). President Trump's December 2017 National Security Statement (NSS) briefly addressed other emerging security threats such as terrorism and cyberspace threats. It did so, however, within the broader context of US homeland security—a focus consistent with Trump's oft advertised 'America First' posture. Moreover, Trump's initial NSS offered only a brief (two-page) commentary on the 'Indo-Pacific' strategic situation, representing it as a 'geopolitical competition between free and repressive visions of world order' and best addressed by strengthening traditional defense relationships with allies and emerging security partners (White House 2017, 45).

The 2017 NSS emphasized the need for the United States to underpin its own economic growth as an Indo-Pacific power by pursuing new investment opportunities and reinvigorated bilateral trading arrangements (prioritizing them over pan-regional economic and diplomatic instrumentalities), and 'pro-growth' national energy agendas. It envisioned the US 'work[ing] with partners to build a network of states dedicated to free markets and protected from forces that would subvert their sovereignty' (White House 2017, 47).

Within this very broad framework, such an approach could well encompass both traditional and non-traditional security policy components and alternative security networks to address them. Various forms of qualified multilateralism, and especially minilateralism, are now vying with the San Francisco System in its contemporary form as instruments of order building in the Indo-Pacific. Understanding what these groupings are and evaluating their relative effectiveness will allow us to better assess the relevance of minilateral security politics in the region.

Definitions

Initially some brief definitions of the types of security groupings are essential. These are offered below.

Multilateralism and multilateral security politics can be viewed as a formal effort by three or more states to build trust and avoid conflict by identifying, institutionalizing, and observing rules and norms for a common vision of regional or international order. It is usually an inclusive process and is designed to encourage more states to endorse its core principles of security governance by becoming members of such institutions over time (Keohane 1990). For multilateral security politics to be effective, leading international relations theorists have asserted three preconditions that need to be met. *Indivisibility* needs to be realized by its member states based on 'socially constructed' public goods (Ruggie 1993, 11). *General organising principles* must be defined and implemented in ways that commit all member states to observe them. No exceptions are afforded for larger power members that otherwise may prefer to follow their own interests, even at the expense of explicit institutional rules (Weber 1991, viii). *Diffuse reciprocity* must be in play; there is no expectation by any of a multilateral institution's member states to derive immediate rewards to themselves specifically in return for participating in a collective organizational effort to defend or protect another member state (Keohane 1986, 21–2).

Minilateralism is, conversely, a narrower and usually informal initiative intended to address a specific threat, contingency or security issue with fewer states (usually three or four) sharing the same interest in resolving it within a finite period of time. No consensus has yet been reached on how to precisely define 'minilateralism' in the international security context. At the end of the Cold War, Miles Kahler assessed how 'large' forms of collective action often morphed into 'smaller,' more informal forms of post-war collective action initiated *within existing* multilateral institutions when the larger groupings became too unwieldy or too much at odds with domestic political interests. This revised variant of multilateralism—termed by Brad Glosserman and Scott Snyder as the 'minilateral solution'—often worked to increase the likelihood and strength of cooperation among participants (Kahler 1992, 684–5; Glosserman and Snyder 2015, 162; Oye 1986, 20–1).

Victor Cha has further argued that minilateral security's three predominant traits have been: (1) a small number of participants relative to multilateral security groupings;

(2) its ad hoc characteristics as such groupings are usually formed and disbanded without an institutional legacy; (3) a typical focus on mostly traditional security issues (Cha 2003, 116–17).

'Bilateralism,' 'trilateralism,' and 'quadrilateralism' are defined by the number(s) of state participants and may be components of either multilateral or minilateral security politics. Bilateralism occurs when two states cooperate on a preferential basis to realize exclusive benefits or gains in accordance with their mutual interests (Tago 2017). Such cooperation can be embodied in a formal treaty or pursued informally depending on the common threat to be addressed or the joint security interest to be pursued. A trilateral coalition is 'situated between bilateral relationships and broader multi-partner arrangements, mak[ing] it the most minimal form of multilateralism' (Kamphausen et al. 2018, 4). Quadrilateralism involves dialogue and intermittent material cooperation (e.g. military exercises or humanitarian and disaster relief operations) between four states. Quadrilateralism has often been linked to cooperation between 'like-minded' states such as those sharing democratic values coming together in ways to balance (tacitly) against an actual or potentially hostile power (Campbell, Patel, and Singh 2011).

The multilateral climate

Critics, particularly those from the realist school of international relations theory, have asserted that multilateral institutions such as ASEAN and the South Asian Association for Regional Cooperation (SAARC) which emerged during the 1970s and 1980s did not meet their objectives. More comprehensive multilateral security dialogues in the region followed with the inception of the ASEAN Regional Forum (ARF) in the early 1990s and the East Asia Summit (EAS) in 2005. Neither the ARF nor the EAS, however, have satisfied the three definition-cited preconditions for a viable collective security institution. The prospect of forging socially constructed public goods, for example, cannot withstand states' predominant tendency to pursue national self-interest if they are given a choice between adopting one of these two approaches. If states conclude they have little to gain from collaborating on regional or international security problems there is little prospect that they will play the 'long game' demanded by diffuse reciprocity or adhere to general organizing principles sufficiently binding to ensure their strategic restraint (Mearsheimer 1994–1995, 15, 31–3; Kratochwil 1993, 70–1).

In post-war Europe, past legacies of crumbling alliances and great wars strengthened regional leaders' incentive to establish multilateral norms and institutions designed to guarantee European economic prosperity and collective security. However, there has been no commensurate historical experience applicable to the Indo-Pacific. Many Asian sovereignties were the products of accelerated post-war decolonization and many of their territorial, irredentist and ideological differences generated profound security dilemmas. Under such conditions, the prospects for Indo-Pacific multilateral security politics were dim. As John Ruggie (perhaps somewhat ruefully) observed, a 'reasonably stable' balance of power underpinned by the superpowers' embrace of bilateral alliances became a predominant mode of Asian security politics (Ruggie 1992, 563).

In this context, minilateralism may come to be viewed by Washington's policy planners as a useful variant of multilateralism for realizing US security objectives. Minilateralism's viability as an Indo-Pacific security approach, however, will depend on how successful the United States ultimately will be in transforming the San Francisco System into a more fluid and complex regional security network. To test this argument's validity, the interrelationship between minilateralism and multi-lateralism in an Indo-Pacific security context will first be discussed. How successfully minilateralism has been applied as a US policy tool in the Indo-Pacific to date will then be considered.

Minilateralism as a multilateral security variant

Minilateralism's appeal relates to its inherent flexibility, relatively low transaction costs and voluntary rather than mandatory kinds of commitment ordained by major power affiliates. The appeal of minilateralism, as Moises Naim has observed, is that it is a 'smarter, more targeted approach ... bring[ing] to the table the smallest possible number of countries needed to have the largest possible impact on a particular problem' (Naim 2009). The characteristics and manageability of minilateralism can be viewed as a viable contemporary alternative to multilateralism and bilateralism at a time when US hegemony is arguably declining in the absence of any alternative Asian security order rising to take its place.

Minilateralism, as part of its appeal, is voluntary rather than contractual; dis-aggregated rather than comprehensive; usually regional rather than global; and 'bottom-up' rather than 'top-down' (Patrick 2015, 116).[3] Proponents of minilateral security dialogues and associations also argue that they have 'second order traditional security effects' by strengthening the resilience of existing bilateral security alliances. The confidence-building dynamics ingrained in joint American, Japanese and South Korean security consultations and coordination on the North Korean nuclear issue can potentially modify the historical Japan–ROK security via American adjudication of Tokyo's and Seoul's differences and are illustrative (Cha 2003, 117–18).

Critiques of minilateralism include the concern that a smaller or more streamlined grouping relative to multilateral ones does not automatically guarantee success in managing any given security issue. It is essential that the *right* participants engage in any minilateral security enterprise for it to have a greater chance of success.[4] Despite the United States' substantial efforts to coordinate security collaboration between Japan and South Korea in response to a growing North Korean nuclear and missile threat, the three countries' Trilateral Coordination and Oversight Group or TCOG (established in 1999) floundered over still powerful historical and politico-economic differences between Washington's two Northeast Asian allies. Ultimately, North Korea's reluctance to adopt the formulas postulated by its negotiating partners to achieve that end led to that grouping's de facto termination.

A second concern relates to external states' perceptions of a minilateral grouping's actual purpose. Recent minilateral groupings involving four or more parties that have been proposed but not successfully implemented are illustrative: the Quadrilateral

Initiative (2007–2008) involving Australia, India, Japan and the United States, and intermittent suggestions for a 'League of Democracies' involving NATO and non-communist Asian states (the most notable variant of which was proposed by US Republican Presidential candidate John McCain in 2008). In both of these cases, China argued forcefully and successfully that such associations were merely derivatives of NATO's traditional containment strategy and would be directed primarily against itself. The Quadrilateral Initiative has been lately revived but whether its fate will be more successful than its original counterpart given the ongoing escalation of Sino-American tensions in the South China Sea remains unclear.

Trilateralism has thus far seemed to be more adaptive than other minilateral variants in Asia in addressing specific issue areas. Michael Green, arguably the leading authority on this trend, has surmised that 'future historians will look back at this active trilateralism as characterizing an intermediate phase between regional orders, as diverse states sought to hedge and shape an immature architecture still resting uneasily on the stability provided by bilateral alliances and the hope of growing economic interdependence' (Green 2014, 770).

Will Green's observation prove to be prescient or premature as the Asia-Pacific security setting takes shape over the remainder of this decade and beyond? For it to be validated, US-led minilateral security groupings will need to move beyond their current and relatively modest functions of generating low-key dialogues (often on the 'sidelines' of multilateral summits and meetings) and conducting intermittent military exercises. They will have to navigate successfully between the shoals of great power competition and the hegemonic tendencies that Kai He has described in his aforementioned introduction as 'competitive multilateralism.' Minilaterals will also need to establish a credible reputation over time as increasingly appropriate channels apart from the Indo-Pacific's existing and arguably stale multilateral forums for coordinating or negotiating regional security questions.

Indeed, as noted above, realists and others have largely written off most forms of multilateralism as nothing more than a license for unwieldy and fruitless talking-shops when dealing with high security issues. Should minilateralism likewise be discounted due to their US-led membership composition or their tendency to be viewed as merely watered-down instruments of containment strategy directed by Washington?

To evaluate minilateralism's current and future viability in the Indo-Pacific region's security politics, a brief assessment will now be offered on minilateralism's potential to bridge the asymmetrical 'hub-and-spokes' arrangement underwriting the bilateral US alliance system in Asia with the rapidly evolving structural changes in the Indo-Pacific which are seriously challenging multilateralism's relevance as an order-building mechanism in the region.

Minilateralism's role in US security politics toward the Indo-Pacific

As early as the immediate post-Cold War timeframe in the late 1990s, US policy makers and their allied counterparts in Japan, South Korea and Australia recognized that rapid structural changes in the Indo-Pacific strategic environment compelled them to search for ways to adapt the San Francisco System's time-honored post-war 'hub-and-spokes' system. China presents a different form of security challenge than that previously confronting Washington and its regional security partners. 'China's rise,' with its trading and investment benefits, is transforming the Indo-Pacific balance of power. Other policy approaches are clearly required by the US and its allies to hedge against the intensifying Asian geopolitical transition.

Multilateralism 2.0 (as Kai He labels it) emerged in the late 1990s and again, more prominently, during the Obama Administration as a 'default strategy.' Informal bilateral security partnerships and minilateralism both surfaced as logical derivatives of this process and as a means to restore the San Francisco System's relevance. Bilateral 'partnerships' with selected countries in the region are being promoted by Washington in niche areas where such countries' interests coincided with those of the United States. The US and Singapore signed a 15-year memorandum of understanding in 1990 to grant the US Navy systematic access to Singaporean naval and logistical air facilities. The US and India signed a ten-year defense agreement in 2005 and subsequently catalyzed what is now a substantial defense relationship in terms of both arms sales and joint military exercises. Vietnamese–American security ties have recently accelerated, and significant US defense ties with Taiwan and New Zealand have been sustained (Tow and Limaye 2016, 13–8).

While these emerging bilateral defense ties remain nascent relative to US bilateral alliances, they nevertheless are 'deepen[ing] in response to economic and political integration in Asia, persistent security challenges and the potential for changing power balances in the region' (Cronin et al. 2013, 37). Therefore, an 'Asia power web' of intra-Asian bilateral security cooperation has emerged—'building on pre-viously existing foundations of economic and political integration' (Cronin et al. 2013, 5). In building such linkages, participants are not eschewing either their ongoing or developing security relations with the United States or China. They are instead hedging against either US strategic retrenchment in the region or China expanding its military power in the region as an aspiring hegemonic actor.

It is unclear to what extent the Trump Administration's early decision to cancel US membership in the Trans-Pacific Partnership (TPP) and its public rejection of the Barack Obama Administration's 'rebalancing' or 'pivot' strategy will affect the long-term momentum of Asia power-web politics.[5] It is evident, however, that this trend largely conforms with He's argument that middle or 'second-tier' powers such as Australia, Japan, and South Korea are searching for ways to strengthen their influence within and beyond existing multilateral regional institutions. Such a quest represents a hedge against either US strategic retrenchment from the region or a premature American military escalation against a nuclear North Korea that could render their own diplomatic and economic national interests irrelevant.

US alliance revitalization and security partnership cultivation at the bilateral level during the late 1990s was accompanied by Washington's investigation of how mini-lateral security approaches might be employed to address regional security issues. The United States' voluntary (non-binding) participation in minilateral initiatives was deemed to compare favorably to bilateral collective defense arrangements as the credibility of US commitments remained vulnerable to oscillating American global strategy shifting away from the Asia-Pacific to focus on the Middle East, international terrorism and other priorities. The flexibility inherent in such minilateral cooperation and directed toward region-specific threats and challenges, without facing such traditional collective defense problems as alliance entrapment or abandonment, was an appealing outlook (Tow and Limaye 2016, 18–19).

Minilateral alignments led by the United States have thus recently developed in the Indo-Pacific as a means of complementing the San Francisco System's bilateral alliance politics. 'Junior allies' in post-war bilateral security partnerships with the United States previously deferred to Washington on short-term issues in return for gaining longer-term alliance benefits. However, the scale and nature of those benefits or 'collective goods' such as deterrence guarantees and defense technology transfers have gradually become more tenuous as the region's balance of power and its threat environment have transformed. Japan's and South Korea's traditional faith in US-extended deterrence commitments relative to a growing North Korean nuclear threat, for example, is now being tested. Trump's 'America first' rhetoric during his presidential campaign, speculating about the need for greater Japanese and South Korean defense burden-sharing within an alliance context, has tested that faith (Haberman and Sanger 2016; Kamphausen et al. 2018; Townshend 2017, 5, 14–16).

The Philippines and Thailand, the United States' two formal treaty allies in Southeast Asia, distanced themselves from the San Francisco System due to their current leaderships' differences with the Obama Administration over governance and human rights. As ASEAN members, both countries are becoming increasingly concerned with such non-traditional security concerns as counter-terrorism, organized crime, climate change and forced peoples' movements. Minilateral coalitions addressing such non-traditional challenges with the US and other San Francisco System member states are one policy option that could be strongly considered to address such challenges. A successful precedent for this approach was the formation of a short-lived but highly effective 'Core Group' of Australia, India, Japan and the United States to provide timely human security assistance and disaster relief to countries affected by the December 2004 earthquake and tsunami in the Indian Ocean region.

Several experiments in US minilateral security politics instigated over the past decade or so now give us a basis of judgement as to their effectiveness. Arguably the most significant of these was Australia, Japan and the US entering into a 'Trilateral Security Dialogue' or TSD (in 2005) at the ministerial level. This initiative was in response to both the US–Japan and US–Australia bilateral defense alliances' evolution from national security-centric accords to arrangements that responded to an increasingly wide scope of international security threats by adopting order-building postures.

Another trilateral dialogue was launched by two US treaty allies (Australia and Japan) and an emerging US security partner (India) to coordinate these countries' interest on maritime security, counter-terrorism strategies, regional connectivity and other challenges mandating collective security collaboration. All three participants share a determination to promote the rule of law as the binding norm for regional order building and a concern that in its absence, China could eventually implement its own rules for regional security governance. This has been a low-key but successful venture, with the fourth session addressing key Indo-Pacific security issues convening in New Delhi during December 2017 (Government of India 2017).

It remains to be seen if fresh efforts to expand this trilateral arrangement during side-talks at the November 2017 ASEAN Summit in Manila, and to revisit the Quad-rilateral Dialogue Initiative which was originally suspended in 2008, will succeed (Wyeth 2017). However, a form of creative minilateralism (Nilsson-Wright 2017; Pant 2017) has been anticipated in 2017 when then Australian Foreign Minister Julie Bishop's carefully worded, speculation about the positive interrelationship between the TSD and the 'early stage of a trilateral strategic dialogue between Australia, Japan and India' was expounded (Bishop 2017; Lee 2017a).

Cross-comparing low-key multilateralism with minilateralism

Despite the presence of various multilateral security frameworks in the Indo-Pacific—mostly cultivated by ASEAN in its self-proclaimed role as the region's order-building 'locomotive' during what Kai He has deemed the 'multilateralism 1.0' era—the region lacks anything resembling the historical authority, common values and joint mechanisms underwriting the NATO framework. The ARF's agenda for realizing a 'comprehensive security' formula has not been realized and the actual role of the EAS as a community-building agent remains ambiguous and buried within the confines of ASEAN Ministerial Meetings. There is an apparent inability of Asia-Pacific multilateral groupings that adhere to the 'ASEAN way' principle of member-state parity to resolve core 'hard security' issues in the region (see Teo and Singh 2016).

Minilateralism, on the other hand, represents a potentially viable policy option for addressing tensions emanating from dependency and resource disparities that larger and smaller allies intermittently experience in asymmetrical 'hub-and-spokes' alliance politics, and for bargaining security issues between institutional member states. As Green has observed, 'US alliance-centred trilaterals often act like caucuses within a legislature rather than collective security arrangements aimed at a third party' (Green 2014, 761). They are united by common democratic political systems, the need to avoid hierarchical predominance by the rival and potentially hostile hegemon (i.e. China) in the Indo-Pacific region, and a shared aspiration to cultivate a stable and predictable regional order-building process. They attempt, by acting minilaterally, to 'get the balance right' between the US senior ally/partner and the gains accrued by other allies/ partners. This balance involving US allies and partners invariably falls short of deriving complete advantage in such associations, but is substantially beneficial relative to specific issue-areas. Ideally, achieving such a balance makes minilateralism more than merely a 'talking-shop' exercise—a sustained criticism levelled toward larger multilateral groupings in the region. Minilateralism facilitates the pursuit of a mutually agreed objective. In this sense, it can act (as Green asserts) as a bridging component between the Cold War driven 'hub-and-spokes' system of the past and an as yet undefined and imperfect but effective multilateral order-building architecture.

Conclusion

Ultimately, the US and its allies should identify five preconditions as a basis for strengthening and adopting minilateral security politics in the Indo-Pacific. First, minilateralism should never be viewed as completely replacing existing alliances and institutions but as complementing them. Second, it should allow policy planners to focus on niche areas where shared interests and values can be identified and pursued. In this context (as a third precondition), minilateralism should emphasize expanded and more effective 'spoke-to-spoke' relations among US allies.[6] Fourth, minilateral cooperation should be sufficiently durable to withstand changes in US and allied political leadership that could otherwise render such collaboration outdated or irrelevant. Fifth and finally, minilateral security cooperation should be viewed as more than just 'threat-centric' in character. It should be regarded as a 'bridge-building' tool that can be employed with the San Francisco System alliance network.

There remain at least two major impediments to the maturation of minilateral security politics in the Indo-Pacific as it relates to US and allied security interests. The first is that a security crisis in the Korean Peninsula, the South China Sea, or elsewhere will erupt in ways that will result in policy makers losing control to outcomes (nuclear and/or great power wars) that will stifle any pretence of order building. The second is that either formal or ad hoc minilateral initiatives will be overwhelmed and could default to classical power balancing.

Minilateralism is a relatively ephemeral means to achieve a specific policy end. It is often an intrinsically fragile process for security collaboration, subject to changes in the domestic politics of its affiliate participant states or in the overall regional environment that render it irrelevant as time passes. The TCOG 'morphed' into the Six Party Talks as North Korea's nuclear capabilities intensified and the George W. Bush Administration concluded it was best to 'lead from behind' by having China as the prime mover. The Quadrilateral Initiative died a quiet death once its major proponent—Abe Shinzo—stepped down from his first term as Japan's prime minister in September 2007 and as the new Australian Labor government at the time became increasingly susceptible to Chinese pressure against this initiative. Although Japanese and South Korean intelligence sharing and logistical coordination has been sustained against an intensified North Korean threat, it still remains susceptible to the vagaries of South Korean domestic politics. For example, in August 2019, South Korea announced that it would exit the intelligence-sharing pact with Japan (later reversed due to US pressure) because it did not meet Seoul's 'national interests' (Johnson and Murakami 2019). The main reason for South Korea's decision was the trade dispute between South Korea and Japan.[7] These domestic politics are more than capable of jettisoning the recent US deployment of the THAAD (Terminal High Altitude Area Defense) missile defense system in Seoul or constraining Japanese support of US military operations in the seas adjacent to South Korean territory.

The future role of the United States as an Indo-Pacific security actor directly affects the viability of any 'minilateral solution' in that region's geopolitics. President Trump's apparent determination to 'make allies (and partners) pay more' for sustained US strategic involvement in the region, and to rely on China to fulfill US and allied interests in leveraging Pyongyang (notwithstanding his two summits with Kim Jong-un), could erode traditional relative gains for US allies. The extent to which the US is still willing or capable of sustaining a viable geopolitical footprint in the Indo-Pacific beyond a largely unilateral (and many observers would assert 'impulsive') basis shrouds the future outlook for Indo-Pacific minilateral security politics. So too does the need for increasingly direct great power (Sino-American) negotiation and/or coordination on problems of Indo-Pacific crisis management. In this sense, expectations that future historians will recall minilateralism as only a prelude to whatever will be the next phase of Indo-Pacific order building may, unfortunately perhaps, be premature.

Notes

1 This chapter is a revised version of Tow, William T. 2019. "Minilateral Security's Relevance to US Strategy in the Indo-Pacific: Challenges and Prospects." *The Pacific Review* 32 (2): 232–44.
2 Background on China's major power relations initiative is provided by Chen (2015) and Kiracofe (2017). For a thorough explanation of the grand bargain scenario, see Glaser (2015).
3 Patrick (2015, 116) lists other qualities, including 'trans-governmental rather than just intergovernmental … multi-level and multi-stakeholder rather than state-centric.' For purposes of this analysis, however, minilateralism is applied only as it operates in a state-centric context.
4 This point is raised in an unpublished and undated draft paper written by Jeremy Malcolm which cannot be formally cited here.
5 In March 2017, Susan Thornton, Acting US Assistant Secretary of State for East Asian and Pacific Affairs, rejected the idea that the rebalancing posture adopted by the Obama Administration would be retained by its successor; see Gamel (2017).
6 That said, such cooperation may be mostly functional and conditional rather than enduring and unqualified. Japanese–South Korean intelligence and logistical collaboration intended to deter a North Korean threat, for example, will not necessarily 'spill over' to form a passionate and unreserved bond unfettered by long-standing historical tensions.
7 The latest development is that South Korea decided to stay in the pact with Japan under US pressure in late November 2019. However, South Korea stated that it could terminate the pact anytime (see Rich and Wong 2019).

References

Bishop, Julie. 2017. "Joint Press Conference, Australia–Japan Foreign and Defence Ministers' Meeting (2+2), Tokyo." April 20. https://www.foreignminister.gov.au/minister/julie-bishop/transcript-eoe/joint-press-conference-australia-japan-foreign-and-defence-ministers-meeting-22-tokyo.
Busby, Joshua, Karen Grépin, and Jeremy Youde. 2017. "The World Health Organization Just Picked a New Leader: These Are the Challenges he Faces." *Washington Post*, June 15.
Caballero-Anthony, Mely. 2010. "Non-traditional Security Challenges, Regional Governance and the ASEAN Politico-Security Community (APSC)." Asia Security Initiative Policy Series Working Paper No. 7. S. Rajaratnam School of International Studies, Singapore, September. http://www3.ntu.edu.sg/rsis/nts/resources/research_papers/MacArthur_working_paper_Mely_Caballero-Anthony.pdf.

Campbell, Kurt, Nirav Patel, and Vikram J. Singh. 2011. "The Power of Balance: America in Asia." Center for a New American Security, Washington DC, June 11. https://www.cnas.org/publications/reports/the-\h power-of-balance-america-in-iasia.

Cha, Victor D. 2003. "The Dilemma of Regional Security in East Asia: Multilateralism versus Bilateralism." In *Regional Conflict Management*, edited by Paul F. Diehl and Joseph Lepgold, 104–122. Lanham, MD: Rowman & Littlefield.

Chemnick, Jean. 2017. "Trump Drops Climate Threats from National Security Strategy. Scientific American." *Scientific American*, December 19. https://www.scientificamerican.com/article/trump-drops-climate-threats- from-national-security-strategy/.

Chen, Jimin. 2015. "China–US: Obstacles to a 'New Type of Major Power Relations'." *The Diplomat*, April 9. http://thediplomat.com/2015/04/china-us-obstacles-to-a-new-type-of-major-power-\h relations/.

Cronin, Patrick M., Richard Fontaine, Zachary M. Hosford, Oriana Skylar Mastro, Ely Ratner, and Alexander Sullivan. 2013. *The Emerging Asia Power Web: The Rise of Bilateral Intra-Asian Security Ties*. Washington DC: Center for a New American Security.

Fitzpatrick, Mark. 2016. *Asia's Latent Nuclear Powers: Japan, South Korea and Taiwan*. Adelphi Books217. London: Routledge for IISS.

Flores, Helen. 2017. "US Forces Assisting Philippines in Battle to End Siege." *The Philippine Star*, June 11.

Gamel, Kim. 2017. "Trump Administration Rejects 'Pivot' to Asia—at Least in Name." *Stars and Stripes*, 14 March.

Glaser, Charles L. 2015. "A US–China Grand Bargain? The Hard Choice Between Military Competition and Accommodation." *International Security* 39(4): 49–90.

Glosserman, Brad, and Scott A. Snyder. 2015. *The Japan–South Korea Identity Clash: East Asian Security and the United States*. New York: Columbia University Press.

Government of India. 2017. "4th India–Australia–Japan Trilateral Dialogue." December 13. http://mea.gov.in/pressreleases.htm?dtl/29176/4th_IndiaAustraliaJapan_Trilateral_Dialogue_Decem ber_13_2017.

Green, Michael J. 2014. "Strategic Asian Triangles." In *The Oxford Handbook of the International Relations of Asia*, edited by Saadia M. Pekkanen, John Ravenhill, and Rosemary Foot, 758–774. New York: Oxford University Press.

Haberman, Maggie, and David E. Sanger. 2016. "Highlights from Our Interview with Donald Trump on Foreign Policy." *New York Times*, March 26.

Hartcher, Peter. 2017. "North Korean Missiles Can Strike Australia and We Can't Stop Them." *Sydney Morning Herald*, July 8.

Johnson, Jesse, and Sakura Murakami. 2019. "South Korea Decides to Exit Intelligence-Sharing Pact with Japan." *Japan Times*, August 22.

Kahler, Miles. 1992. "Multilateralism with Small and Large Numbers." *International Organization* 46(3): 681–708.

Kamphausen, Roy D., John S. Park, Rio Sahashi, and Alison Szalwinski. 2018. *The Case for US–ROK–Japan Trilateralism: Strengths and Limitations*. NBR Special Report No. 70, February. Seattle, WA: National Bureau of Asian Research.

Keohane, Robert O. 1986. "Reciprocity in International Relations." *International Organization* 40(1): 1–27.

Keohane, Robert O. 1990. "Multilateralism: An Agenda for Research". *International Journal* 45(4): 731–764.

Kiracofe, Clifford A. 2017. "Major Power Relations at Crossroads." *Beijing Review*, No. 13, March 30.

Kratochwil, Friedrich. 1993. "The Embarrassment of Changes: Neo-Realism as the Science of Realpolitik without Politics." *Review of International Studies* 19(1): 63–80.

60 William Tow

Lee, Lavina. 2017a. "Turnbull's India Visit an Opportunity to Revive the Quad." *The Interpreter*, Lowy Institute, April 10. https://www.lowyinstitute.org/the-interpreter/turn bull-s-india-visit-opportunity-revive-quad.

Lee, Matthew. 2017b. "As Trump Announces Famine Aid, Relief Funds Face Big Cuts." *US News*, May 26. https://www.usnews.com/news/politics/articles/2017-05-26/as-trump-announces-famine-aid-relief-funds-face-big-cuts.

Mearsheimer, John J. 1994–1995. "The False Promise of International Institutions." *International Security* 19(3) (Winter): 5–49.

Naim, Moises. 2009. "Minilateralism: The Magic Number to Get Real International Action." *Foreign Policy*, June 21. http://foreignpolicy.com/2009/06/21/minilateralism/.

Nilsson-Wright, John. 2017. "Creative Minilateralism in a Changing Asia: Opportunities for Security Con-Vergence and Cooperation between Australia, India and Japan." Research Paper, Chatham House Asia Program, London, July. https://www.chathamhouse.org/sites/files/chathamhouse/images/2017–2007–28-Minilateralism.pdf.

Oye, Kenneth A. 1986. "Explaining Cooperation Under Anarchy: Hypotheses and Strategies". In *Cooperation Under Anarchy*, edited by Kenneth A. Oye, 1–24. Princeton, NJ: Princeton University Press.

Pant, Harsh V. 2017. "India, Japan, Australia, and the US: The Return of Asia's 'Quad'." *The Diplomat*, April 28. http://thediplomat.com/2017/04/india-japan-australia-and-the-us-the-return-of-asias-quad/.

Patrick, Stewart. 2015. "The New 'New Multilateralism': Minilateral Cooperation, But at What Cost?" *Global Summitry* 1(2): 115–134.

Pollack, Jonathan D. 2018. "North Korea's Nuclear and Missile Programs: Strategies, Directions, and Prospects." Paper presented at the 6th Brookings-Korea Research Institute for National Strategy (KRINS), Seoul, January 17. https://www.brookings.edu/research/north-koreas-nuclear-and-missile-programs-strategies-directions-and-prospects/.

Ratner, Paul. 2018. "Here's What Experts Think Are the True Capabilities of the North Korean Military." *Big Think*, January 1. http://bigthink.com/paul-ratner/heres-what-exp erts-think-are-the-true-\capabilities-of-the-north-korean-military.

Rich, Motoko, and Edward Wong. 2019. "Under US Pressure, South Korea Stays in Intelligence Pact with Japan." *New York Times*, November 22.

Ruggie, John G. 1992. "Multilateralism: The Anatomy of an Institution." *International Organization* 46(3): 561–598.

Ruggie, John G. 1993. *Multilateralism Matters: The Theory and Praxis of an International Form.* New York: Columbia University Press.

Sheng, Li Jie. 2017. "Donald Trump's National Security Strategy and Southeast Asia." *The Diplomat*, December 28. https://thediplomat.com/2017/12/donald-trumps-nationa l-security-strategy-and-southeast-asia/.

Tago, Atsushi. 2017. "Multilateralism, Bilateralism, and Unilateralism in Foreign Policy." *Oxford Research Encyclopedias*, August. http://politics.oxfordre.com/view/10.1093/acre fore/9780190228637.001.0001/acrefore-9780190228637-e-449.

Teo, Sarah, and Bhubhindar Singh, eds. 2016. *The Future of the ADMM/ADMM-Plus and Defence Diplomacy in the Asia Pacific*. Policy Report, February 23. Singapore: S. Rajaratnam School of International Studies.

Tow, William T., and Satu Limaye. 2016. "What's China Got to Do with It? US Alliances, Partnerships in the Asia- Pacific." *Asian Politics & Policy* 8(1): 7–26.

Townshend, Ashley. 2017. *America First: US Asia Policy under President Trump.* Report, March. Sydney: United States Studies Centre.

Tsjeng, Henrick Z. 2017. "Time for ASEAN's Defense Ministers Meeting to Put Traditional Security on the Agenda." *The Diplomat*, May 6. https://thediplomat.com/2017/05/time -for-aseans-defense-ministers-meeting-to-put-traditional-security-on-the-agenda/.

Weber, Steve. 1991. *Multilateralism in NATO: Shaping the Postwar Balance of Power, 1945–1961.* Berkeley: University of California.

White House. 2017. *National Security Strategy of the United States of America.* December. https:// www.whitehouse.gov/wp-content/uploads/2017/12/NSS-Final-12-18-2017-0905.pdf.

Wyeth, Grant. 2017. "Why Has Australia Shifted Back to the Quad?" *The Diplomat*, November 16. https://thediplomat.com/2017/11/why-has-australia-shifted-back-to-the-quad/.

5

ASIA'S COMPETING MULTILATERAL INITIATIVES

Quality versus quantity

Mark Beeson[1]

East Asia has many distinctive features that set it apart from other comparable regions. Indeed, for students of comparative politics and the growing field of comparative regionalism (Sbragia 2008; Acharya 2012), what we now think of as 'East Asia' offers a veritable treasure trove of different political forms, economic structures and strategic perspectives. Attitudes to regional, as opposed to national, development and cooperation are equally varied, and this helps to account for the distinctiveness of East Asian institutions, their multiplicity and ultimately, I shall suggest, their ineffectiveness. The simple underlying regional reality in East Asia is that despite—or perhaps *because of*—the surprisingly large number of regional initiatives, none of the resultant institutions are especially effective (Beeson 2016). In this regard it is entirely possible that 'institutional balancing,' like its more well-known power balancing counterpart, is designed not to facilitate but to prevent something from happening.

If we put East Asia's regional institutions in their specific and unique historical circumstances it becomes easier to understand their distinctive trajectories. The question posed by this symposium is especially important in this context: is there something about the nature of the internal and external dynamics of regional development that helps to account for the particular style and—I argue—ineffectiveness of regional institutions? The short answer this question, I shall suggest in what follows, is 'yes.' The sort of 'multilateralism 1.0' developed by the Association of Southeast Asian Nations (ASEAN) has a lot to answer for in this regard: having established its own pattern of institutional effectiveness ASEAN's leadership has caused it to be replicated under the new wave of 'multilateralism 2.0,' or the more comprehensive, great power-driven variety that exists in tandem with earlier initiatives. Unlike some of the other contributors to this collection, I remain skeptical about the difference that 'great powers' have made in redefining the way regional institutions operate. On the contrary, I suggest that not only is China very comfortable with the idea of a rather feeble and ineffective institutional architecture (Beeson 2015), but the US is also unlikely to do anything to change this picture, especially under a Trump administration that is highly skeptical about the efficacy of multilateral institutions at the best of times (Wagstyl et al. 2017). More than that, Trump has explicitly cast down on the importance of key Asian alliance partners such as Japan, which has long been seen as the cornerstone of the existing regional order (Baker 2019).

To develop this argument I initially make some brief observations about the conceptual and theoretical debates that have emerged around East Asian institutions, before providing a sketch of their historical development. The subsequent claims are twofold: first, some of theoretical literature underestimates historically-generated 'structural' obstacles to cooperation and simultaneously overestimates the importance of norms and ideas in transforming them. Second, both East Asia's distinctive institutions and their limited impact are best explained by the specific, contingent circumstances from which they emerged. This legacy continues to influence the course of institutional development in the region; effective institutions remain an unlikely prospect as a consequence.

Making sense of multilateralism at the regional level

Given East Asia's remarkable social, political and economic heterogeneity it is unsurprising, perhaps, that observers come to such very different conclusions about what is going on in the region. Adding to the complexity is the fact that the status of 'the region' itself is contested both ontologically, and as the basis of actual diplomatic, economic and strategic activity. The various regional initiatives considered in more detail below invariably have different memberships, goals, rationales and purposes. As a result, the status of East Asia, or alternatives such as the Asia-Pacific, the Indo-Pacific, Northeast Asia, and Southeast Asia, is a matter of debate and generally determined by the political and strategic actions of potential members—or even non-members—and their concomitant ability to actually *institutionalize* their potentially competing regional visions. Significantly, the institutional development of East Asia and associated regions has often been a consequence of *extra*-regional actors, rather than the exclusive efforts of indigenous states themselves (He, Chapter 1, this volume; Cumings 2009). In this regard, multilateralism 2.0 is not entirely novel, even if some of its specific organizational manifestations are.

The institutional architecture of Western Europe, against which other regional institutions are still frequently judged, emerged in a very different historical milieu and helps to illustrate and explain what is distinctive about Asia (Katzenstein 2005). Significantly, 'American hegemony' played a major role in encouraging a process of reconciliation, reconstruction and ultimately deep regional institutionalization in Western Europe that is unparalleled anywhere else in the world or in history, for that matter. The European experience may have been *sui generis* in many regards (Diez 2004), but for the purposes of the current discussion the key feature of Europe's post-war development was that the United States encouraged a process of multilateral cooperation that eventually led to the emergence of the European

Union (EU) (Milward 2003). Even if the EU were to succumb to its current crop of crises, it would still stand as an important exemplar of the possibility of highly effective, deeply institutionalized regional cooperation.

No such similar development has occurred in any other part of the world. By comparison, under Southeast Asia's 'multilateralism 1.0,' regional integration, cooperation and institutionalization has been shallow and limited in its impact. Effectiveness in this context is relatively easy to define: have the institutions in question made a decisive, discernible difference in achieving stated goals and influencing the behavior of members? The rather grandiose and underspecified objectives of the ASEAN grouping in particular make this somewhat challenging (see ASEAN 2007), but it is clear that it has had far less impact on its members than the EU has on its. This is unsurprising. From the outset, and despite similar geo-political pressures and drivers to those that obtained in Europe, EU-style levels of sovereignty-pooling and interstate coordination have been studiously avoided by ASEAN. The Southeast Asian political elites who oversaw the development of ASEAN may also have been concerned with an unforgiving, threatening and unpredictable geopolitical environment, but the imperatives of the Cold War were mediated differently in Southeast Asia (Narine 2002).

Multilateralism 1.0 of the sort pioneered by ASEAN was a pale imitation of the European variety and this was no accident. On the contrary, the establishment of a small, ineffective and unthreatening ASEAN secretariat was precisely the intention of ASEAN's architects (Beeson 2009). Likewise, the development of the so-called 'ASEAN Way' of voluntarism, consensus, and informality may have been influenced by some bygone regional cultural values, but it was also a rather accommodating vehicle in which the potentially conflicting and fractious goals of Southeast Asia's prickly state leaders could be accommodated (Jones and Smith 2001). The glue that united ASEAN's disparate elites was the perception that they were relative minnows in shark-infested waters.

Why is the scholarly debate so inconclusive?

One of the reasons that the scholarly debate about Southeast Asia in particular and East Asia more generally is inconclusive is that the subject matter is so heterogeneous. It is possible to find evidence to support a variety of, often competing, claims and theses, in the region's bewildering array of political practices, economic structures and strategic relations. There are consequently deep methodological, epistemological and even ontological divisions and differences in the way scholars approach the region (Huotari and Rüland 2014). On the one hand, the very region under discussion remains con-tested and unclear. On the other, the significance of some of the ideas and institutions that seemingly shape—if not actually bring into being—regionally-based patterns of interaction remains a subject of heated dispute.

For constructivists such as Amitav Acharya (2009), for example, the entire process of regional development in East Asia has been a social, discursively realized process in which particular norms, cultural legacies and 'cognitive priors' have played a key role in determining the specific form of regional diplomacy and institutionalization. The smaller states of ASEAN have, the argument goes, a surprising degree of autonomy and even an ability to influence the behavior of their more powerful neighbors and extra-regional powers. It is this sort of claim that has given theoretical support to the idea that ASEAN is 'in the driving seat' as far as regional leadership and institutional development are concerned.

Realists take a very different view. There is, of course, a well-known skepticism on the part of realists about the capacity of institutions to significantly impact on the calculations of autonomous states (Mearsheimer 1994–1995), especially powerful ones, under any circumstances. In an East Asian context, realists have drawn attention to the limited efficacy, and even the nullifying impact of the very diplomatic practices and norms that constructivists take to be so important. Exhibit A in this context is the so-called 'ASEAN Way' of consensus, voluntarism and face-saving agreement that distinguishes Southeast Asia, and which has been adopted by a range of other pan-Asian organizations, such as the Asia-Pacific Economic Cooperation (APEC) grouping, the ASEAN Regional Forum (ARF), and the East Asia Summit (EAS), among others. What constructivists take to be a vital set of facilitating practices in a region with little history of cooperation, realists take to be a convenient mechanism for 'issue avoidance' (Jones and Smith 2007).

These sorts of inconclusive debates are likely to continue given the fundamentally different assumptions observers make about what is actually happening in the region and the sorts of forces and dynamics that are actually likely to determine consequential diplomatic and strategic outcomes. Before trying to assess just how multilateral processes and institutions are likely to be affected by recent geopolitical developments in the region, and by the rise of the Trump regime, it is worth making a couple of general observations. First, both realists and constructivists have important points to make, and one potential step forward is to take a more 'eclectic' view of both the subject matter in question and of the best way to make sense of it (Sil and Katzenstein 2010).

In this context, as I have argued elsewhere in more detail (Beeson 2017), realists are too deterministic and neglectful of contingent circumstances, including the ideational and cultural contexts in which organizations develop and operate. Constructivists, by contrast, indulge in a good deal of wishful thinking about the impact and nature of norms, and are similarly neglectful of the importance of material reality and the pursuit of national interests, even if they are right to claim that such interests are ultimately discursively realized. What is needed, I suggest, is recognition of the constraining impact of inherited social structures and the possibilities such structures consequently both foreclose and permit. The possible relevance of this claim can be seen in the actual operation of East Asia's growing array of multilateral institutions.

Multilateralism with Asian characteristics

Regions have become a focus of scholarly attention because they remain an important and distinctive feature of what has long been seen as an otherwise increasingly 'global' system (Coe et al. 2004; Hurrell 2010). In reality, even in a supposedly global era economic processes—arguably the driver and principal manifestation of 'globalization'—remain highly uneven. Institutional development is even more marked in this regard, and there are consequently significant differences in the style, depth and impact of regional organizations in different parts of the world as a consequence. In Europe—until recently, at least—the EU has been distinguished by a deeply institutionalized, powerful, and effective intergovernmental capacity, and an ability to develop innovative responses to governance challenges (Sabel and Zeitlin 2010). Member states were not only willing to 'pool sovereignty' and trade off autonomy for collective gains, but such efforts were facilitated by a 'thick' layer of private sector organizations, intergovernmental agencies and a complex array of non-state actors.

This is a crucial consideration and important difference between Europe and Asia: Asian states are much more cautious about compromising national autonomy and there is nothing like the same number of non-state actors to help with the process of overall governance. In short, certain relationships and initiatives simply cannot be undertaken in quite the same way in Asia as they can (or could) in Europe. Some observers, such as Luk van Langenhove (2010, 267) think that in the current era, the increased political space afforded to non-governmental actors operating outside of state auspices 'is perhaps the most revolutionary aspect of Multilateralism 2.0 but also the most difficult one to organise.' If this claim is correct, which I think it is, this is plainly a major difference between regions and a potential problem for the states of Asia: the ability of states to cooperate and implement policy is constrained by the absence of a facilitating institutional architecture (Beeson 2001). As Gill and Green (2009, 3) argue, the overall implication of attitudes toward institutionalized cooperation in Asia is that 'multilateralism is still at a stage where it is best understood as an extension and intersection of national power and purpose rather than an objective force in itself.'

However, notwithstanding such important caveats, this has not stopped policy makers from coming up with a plethora of initiatives revolving around the idea of regional cooperation in some form or other. Paradoxically enough, for a region that is arguably synonymous with limited and/or ineffective multilateral cooperation, there is no shortage of regional bodies in existence, on the drawing board, or in the imagination of one prominent regional leader or another. Indeed, it seems to be almost de rigueur for regional elites to come up with their preferred 'vision' for the region. Among the various initiatives that are currently vying for the limelight and policy relevance are APEC, the EAS, the ARF, the ASEAN Free Trade Area (AFTA), ASEAN Plus Three (APT), the Chiang Mai Initiative (CMI)/Chiang Mai Initiative Multilateralization (CMIM), the Asian Bond Market Initiative (ABMI), the Asia-Europe Meeting (ASEM), the Indian Ocean Rim Association (IORA), the Regional Comprehensive Economic Partnership (RCEP), the Free Trade Area of the Asia Pacific (FTAAP), the Shanghai Cooperation Organization (SCO), ASEAN Defense Ministers' Meeting Plus (ADMM+), the Council for Security Cooperation in the Asia-Pacific (CSCAP), to name only some of the more prominent that have actually assumed some momentum (see Dent 2013).

It is also possible to cite a number of initiatives that have fallen by the wayside, such as Kevin Rudd's Asia Pacific Community (Lee and Milner 2014), not to mention others that trundle on with little evidence of influence, such as the Pacific Economic Cooperation Council (PECC). The point should be clear: despite a remarkable number of organizations and initiatives, their collective impact has arguably been remarkably small. Organizations seem to be neutralizing rather than 'balancing' each other as Kai He argues in Chapter 1. True, economic integration in East Asia has gathered pace, but this has generally been achieved as a consequence of the efforts of multinational corporations and their integrated transnational production networks, rather than because of the impact of regional trade agreements (Ravenhill 2008). The record of regional organizations in the security arena is even less impressive: despite being the geographical epicenter of some of the world's most pressing and combustible strategic challenges, regional organizations have had remarkably little direct influence on such problems.

The ARF is the most glaring and disappointing example of this possibility. Although there are equally divided opinions about whether the Asia-Pacific/East Asia regions are models of stability or about to tip into conflict at any moment (Kang 2007; Kaplan 2014), there is little question that however the region is defined it contains some long-standing, unresolved potential flashpoints. If any organization ought to be in exactly the right place at the right time, therefore, it is the ARF. The status of Taiwan, the destabilizing behavior of North Korea—which is actually a member of the ARF—and most important of all, perhaps, the growing friction between the US and China, are all things that the ARF looks well placed to consider, if not resolve. In reality, however, all of these issues are off the agenda as they might prove too discomforting for the member states concerned and violate the ASEAN principles of face saving and consensus. As Emmers and Tan (2011) suggest, it is difficult not to conclude that the ARF was 'built to fail.'

This claim is a telling indictment of Asian regionalism at the best of times. At a moment of growing rivalry between the world's two most consequential powers, it is a potentially fatal weakness. It has taken the so-called rise of China and the election of an American administration that sets little store by multilateralism to make this apparent even to those who might not wish to believe it. This situation has come about in part as a result of a misreading of the importance and limited impact of Asian institutions. According to one influential thesis about the growing likelihood of outright conflict between the US and China (Allison 2017), it is entirely possible that brute historical reality will provide a telling empirical verification of this possibility. If so, it will also be a major test of regional organizations' ability to influence the behavior of the great powers. History suggests it is a test they are very likely to fail.

Putting Asian regionalism to the test—and the sword?

There is a widely held belief that ASEAN and its numerous organizational offshoots have played a unique and decisive role in maintaining the 'long peace of Asia' (Kivimäki 2014). The argument is that Asian institutions are responsible for a process of socialization and confidence building that has led to a radical decline in the incidence of interstate war. There is one fundamental problem with this argument: interstate war has declined everywhere (Pinker 2012). If Asian institutions really have played such a decisive part in making Asia peaceful, how do we account for similar declines in interstate conflict elsewhere? By contrast, if the decline of interstate war is a universal phenomenon, as seems to be the case, why would we attribute special powers or influence to ASEAN or any other regional organization?

This was an important and generally neglected question even before the rise of China and its subsequent involvement in a series of territorial disputes with some of its East Asian neighbors. Now, when the possibility of outright conflict appears to be growing by the day (Freedland 2017), such claims are being put to a searching theoretical and—more importantly, of course—empirical examination. Although it is too soon to say quite how the growing rivalry and tension between China and the US will play out one thing is already abundantly clear: ASEAN is unlikely to play a major role in deciding its outcome. On the contrary, ASEAN as a grouping has been effectively divided and marginalized by China's skillful diplomacy, as it has simply bought off key ASEAN states such as Cambodia (Kynge, Haddou, and Peel 2016). The net result is that ASEAN has been unable to arrive at a coherent, much less a joint position toward what is arguably the most important security challenge in its history. If ASEAN cannot come up with a collective response to an issue that directly impinges on the sovereignty, security, and standing of its member states, one may be forgiven for asking what its continuing purpose actually is (Callick 2016).

The two countries that will actually play a decisive part in determining the course of geopolitical development in the East Asian or the more broadly conceived Asia-Pacific region are China and the US. This is what makes their respective attitudes toward multilateralism, contested or otherwise, so important. Their bilateral ties and potentially incompatible goals offer a telling test of multilateralism 2.0. At this stage it seems as if the Trump Administration does not have the sort of the principled commitment to multilateralism as an idea that former regimes have had, even Republican ones (Daalder and Kagan 2016). Given the wild fluctuations in rhetoric and the lack of policy coherence that have characterized the Trump Administration's first period in office (Erlanger 2017), it is unwise to try and predict what form American engagement with the region will take. One point has become clear, however: as the US has pulled back from former commitments to institutionalized regional and global engagement, China has rapidly moved to capitalize on this abrupt change in America's long-standing foreign policy consensus (Browne 2017a).

The long-term significance of this change in US policy cannot be overstated, not least because of its potential impact on the credibility of multilateral institutions generally. The so-called 'rules-based international order' (RBIO) has been the institutional centerpiece and ideological justification for the hegemonic position and influence of the US. It is precisely the intentional or inadvertent undermining of the US-based order that causes so much angst among prominent American commentators. The RBIO is frequently seen as 'a club that promotes a common set of beliefs to which its members adhere,' in which

So far, the benefits of U.S. leadership have been large enough that other countries are willing to ignore a certain amount of hypocrisy. But at some point, if the United States goes from occasional free-riding to ostentatiously violating the rules, the system itself will be imperilled. (Posen 2018, 29–30)

It is precisely the growing doubts about the Trump Administration's commitment to the very order American foreign policy did so much to create that has provided China's leaders with an opportunity to play a new and unprecedented global leadership role. It is, however, equally unclear at this stage whether Xi Jinping's suggestion that China may become the new champion of multilateralism, free trade, climate change mitigation and much else will be realized. To judge by the region's historical record, and the ambivalence of China's leaders about taking on open-ended commitments to provide the sorts of collective goods that hegemons traditionally have been supposed to do, a healthy degree of skepticism seems warranted. And yet, it is also clear that Xi in particular sees this as a potentially unique opportunity to reposition China and enhance its reputation and 'soft power' at America's expense (Browne 2017b). If this is to happen, though, China's leaders will have to find some way of simultaneously reconciling national goals with regional and possibly global obligations. It was a task that frequently proved beyond the Americans, especially at moments of crisis (Beeson and Broome 2010); there is even less reason to expect a still inexperienced Chinese diplomatic cadre will find it any easier.

Such caveats notwithstanding, it is already evident that China may have both the will and the wherewithal to at least stake out a claim for a greater leadership role at both the regional and global levels. On the one hand, China is beginning to establish organizations that reflect its preferences and over which it has greater influence. The SCO was something of a pioneer in this regard, and one that has been built upon by potentially even more important initiatives such as the Asian Infrastructure Investment Bank (AIIB) (Beeson and Xu 2019). On the other hand, the AIIB is likely to prove welcome in a region still short on infrastructure, especially if it plays a pivotal role in financing China's hugely ambitious Belt and Road Initative (BRI) project. The BRI may enhance China's economic leverage over its neighbors and reinforce its importance at the center of deeply integrated regional production structures (Miller 2017).

This material transformation may, in fact, ultimately prove more consequential than any institutional or ideational change. It is important to remember that China's rapid economic ascent and concomitant strategic importance has been the basis for its challenge to the extant order that the US helped create and over which it has enjoyed unquestioned ascendancy until recently. It is not necessary to be an unreconstructed realist to recognize that material power will be both an important source of influence and the means to underwrite different, potentially competing 'visions' for regional order. In the absence of war, geoeconomics is becoming as, if not more, important than conventional military power, especially for China (Norris 2016).

The striking feature about the Trump Administration in this context is that the primary expression of material power is still likely to be geopolitical rather than geoeconomic, at least as far as engagement with East Asia as a whole is concerned

(Shear and Steinhauer 2017). Although Trump's economic advisors seem to believe they can pressure China into behaving in ways that suit them, this belief seems predicated on an entirely inaccurate reading of the nature of the economic relationship and the level of economic interdependence that exists between China and the US (Mufson 2017). Equally significantly, Xi Jinping seems just as capable of misreading the Trump Administration's intentions, not least because American policy seems hostage to the entirely unpredictable whims of its mercurial leader (Buckley and Bradsher 2019).

Given the continually evolving nature of the unprecedented trade war between China and the US, a definitive analysis of this relationship is not possible (see Cohen and DeLong 2010), but a few simple points can be made that are germane to the present discussion. First, however the relationship plays out between the US and China, multilateral institutions look likely to play a less, rather than a more important role. The G20, which many saw as the quintessential expression of a more effectively governed global economy (see Beeson 2019), has been unable to exert any meaningful influence over the conduct of the world's most important bilateral economic relationship (Boyes 2019). In the meantime, China continues to roll out the BRI, which has the potential to transform the material basis and connectivity of the larger Asian region and reinforce its growing geoeconomic leverage over its smaller, economically dependent neighbors. While there has been some pushback against the prospect of Chinese domination from some Southeast Asian states (Perlez 2019), at this point, the BRI retains much of its transformative material and even ideational potential (Rolland 2019; Winter 2019).

Second, regional security organizations are not capable of, and seemingly not seriously interested in, trying to influence the behavior of the two great powers. The shortcomings of the ARF have already been noted, but ASEAN's inability to influence the behavior of China is becoming clear, even to Southeast Asian leaders (Le Thu 2018). Similarly, the Trump Administration's emphasis on bilateralism and 'America first' does not suggest that they are willing to be voluntarily constrained by the very institutions they built, as so many liberals believe and/or hope. On the contrary, historically neither China nor the US has been willing to be bound by institutionalized rules and norms unless it suited them to do so. Failing to recognize this historical reality has caused generations of liberals and especially constructivists to overestimate the influence of institutions as a consequence. More immediately for the less powerful states of Southeast Asia in particular, there is no guarantee that the much invoked RBIO will insulate them from the actions of great powers when they pursue their own perceived national interests, rather than any notion of the collective good (Pham 2019).

Concluding remarks

The great question about East Asian institutionalism is this: how can so many organizations and so much diplomatic effort achieve so little? ASEAN is the quintessential embodiment of this paradox. Despite holding more than 1,500 meetings in some years on ASEAN-related affairs, the organization's actual impact on key economic, political, and strategic issues has arguably been very modest. The limited number of officials and diplomats from some of the region's more impoverished states means that there are fundamental questions about the ability of states to participate meaningfully and effectively, much less actually implement any initiatives that might emerge. While this limited, omnipresent group of officials may be good for regional 'confidence building,' it is less impressive when it comes to actually dealing with specific problems.

This counter-intuitive outcome, in which much effort and energy is expended for seemingly little return is unlikely to change for three principal reasons. First, once established organizations are very difficult to kill off. 'Stakeholders' develop a vested interested in keeping such organizations going long after their original purposes have been overtaken by events or—more likely in an Asian context—a competing body emerges with a similar purpose. In a situation where different organizations vie for authority and responsibility in similar issue areas, it is all too likely that none will act decisively—with or without the additional handicap of the ASEAN Way.

The second reason for being pessimistic about the capacity for regional organizations to address key problems is the nature of some of the problems themselves and the powerful vested and different interests that are likely to stymie even genuine (rather than rhetorical) efforts at cooperation. Southeast Asia's inability to address the 'haze problem' that afflicts the region every year with calamitous impacts on its population is perhaps the clearest example of this possibility (Varkkey 2012; Sim 2019). There are fundamental capacity constraints and conflicting interests that make agreement, much less effective cooperation, all but impossible.

The final reason for being skeptical about the impact of regional institutions is the competing aims and agendas of the region's—in this case the Asia-Pacific region—two great powers. True, China and the US may support the development of regional organizations, but they will inevitably be different organizations and the principal motivation is likely to be the pursuit of *national* rather than regional interests. China's support of APT which it hopes to dominate, and the US's support of the EAS, which it hopes to use to nullify Chinese influence, are important examples of this possibility. This may be an example of institutional balancing, but it is not one that is likely to lead to a productive outcome or anything to solve the region's growing problems, especially in the security arena. It is noteworthy that the US has shown more interest in the security-oriented Quadrilateral Dialogue—which includes itself, Japan Australia and India, and which is designed to keep China in its 'proper place'—than it has in any of Asia's more established and institutionalized organizations (Henry 2019).

The point to emphasize, therefore, is that institutional development in East Asia, the Asia-Pacific or even the more fashionable and potentially problematic—from the perspective of 'ASEAN centrality,' at least—Indo-Pacific (Sukma 2019), has always been constrained, or even driven by, wider geopolitical concerns that invariably have *national* rather than regional origins. China's recent initiatives and its determination to pursue a nationalist agenda of territorial expansion and assertion is a potentially destabilizing example of this possibility, and one the region looks incapable of addressing collectively. Nor can we derive any confidence or optimism from the behavior of the Trump Administration. On the contrary, the dominant discourse from Washington is one that continues to put 'America first' in a way that augurs badly for the future of multilateralism everywhere. In a region where institutionalized cooperation has always been viewed with a degree of nervousness and/or skepticism, the unreliable Trump Administration, the rise of nationalism worldwide, and the apparent demise of the EU as a cornerstone of the US-led RBIO (Erlanger and Bennhold 2019), may result in regional cooperation going backward rather than forward.

Note

1 This chapter is a revised version of Beeson, Mark. 2019. "Asia's Competing Multilateral Initiatives: Quality Versus Quantity." *The Pacific Review* 32(2): 245–55.

References

Acharya, Amitav. 2009. *Whose Ideas Matter? Agency and Power in Asian Regionalism.* Ithaca, NY: Cornell University Press.
Acharya, Amitav. 2012. "Comparative Regionalism: A Field Whose Time Has Come?" *The International Spectator* 47(1): 3–15.
Allison, Graham. 2017. *Destined for War: Can America and China Escape Thucydides's Trap?* Boston, MA: Houghton Mifflin Harcourt.
ASEAN (The Association of Southeast Asian Nations). 2007. "The ASEAN Charter." http://asean.org/wp-content/uploads/images/archive/publications/ASEAN-Charter.pdf.
Baker, Peter. 2019. "Trump Once Again Assails America's Friends as he Opens Overseas Visit." *New York Times*, June 27.
Beeson, Mark. 2001. "Globalization, Governance, and the Political-Economy of Public Policy Reform in East Asia." *Governance: An International Journal of Policy and Administration* 14(4): 481–502.
Beeson, Mark. 2009. *Institutions of the Asia-Pacific: ASEAN, APEC and Beyond.* London: Routledge.
Beeson, Mark. 2015. "Can ASEAN Cope with China?" *Journal of Current Southeast Asian Affairs* 35(1): 5–28.
Beeson, Mark. 2016. "Multilateralism in East Asia: Less Than the Sum of its Parts?" *Global Summitry* 2(1): 54–70.
Beeson, Mark. 2017. "Alternative Realities: Explaining Security in the Asia-Pacific." *Review of International Studies* 43(3): 516–533.
Beeson, Mark. 2019. *Rethinking Global Governance.* Basingstoke: Palgrave.
Beeson, Mark, and André Broome. 2010. "Hegemonic Instability and East Asia: Contradictions, Crises and US Power." *Globalizations* 7(4): 479–495.
Beeson, Mark, and Shaomin Xu. 2019. "China's Evolving Role in Global Governance: The AIIB and the Limits of an Alternative International Order." In *Handbook of the International Political Economy of China*, edited by Ka Zeng, 345–360. Cheltenham, UK: Edward Elgar.
Boyes, Roger. 2019. "G20 Club of Smug Can't Control US and China." *The Australian*, June 26.

Browne, Andrew. 2017a. "A U.S.–China Role Switch: Who's the Globalist Now?" *Wall Street Journal*, January 24.

Browne, Andrew. 2017b. "China Gloats as Trump Squanders US Soft Power." *Wall Street Journal*, February 28.

Buckley, Chris, and Keith Bradsher. 2019. "How Xi's Last-Minute Switch on US–China Trade Deal Upended It." *New York Times*, May 16.

Callick, Rowan. 2016. "ASEAN's Future Dim after Weak Statements on China Sea Ruling." *The Australian*, July 27.

Coe, Neil M., Martin Hess, Henry Wai-Chung Yeung, Peter Dicken, and Jeffrey Henderson. 2004. "'Globalizing' Regional Development: A Global Production Networks Perspective." *Transactions of the Institute of British Geographers* 29(4): 468–484.

Cohen, Stephen S., and J. Bradford DeLong. 2010. *The End of Influence: What Happens When Other Countries Have the Money.* New York: Basic Books.

Cumings, Bruce. 2009. *Dominion from Sea to Sea: Pacific Ascendancy and American Power.* New Haven, NJ: Yale University Press.

Daalder, Ivo, and Robert Kagan. 2016. "The US Can't Afford to End Its Global Leadership Role." Foreign Policy in the U.S. Presidential Debates series, Brookings, April 25.

Dent, Christopher M. 2013. "Paths Ahead for East Asia and Asia: Pacific Regionalism." *International Affairs* 89(4): 963–985.

Diez, Thomas. 2004. "Europe's Others and the Return of Geopolitics." *Cambridge Review of International Affairs* 17(2): 319–335.

Emmers, Ralf, and See Seng Tan. 2011. "The ASEAN Regional Forum and Preventive Diplomacy: Built to Fail?" *Asian Security* 7(1): 44–60.

Erlanger, Steven. 2017. "As Trump Era Arrives, a Sense of Uncertainty Grips the World." *New York Times*, January 16.

Erlanger, Steven, and Katrin Bennhold. 2019. "Rift Between Trump and Europe Is Now Open and Angry." *New York Times*, February 17.

Freedland, Jonathan. 2017. "First on the White House Agenda: The Collapse of the Global Order. Next, War?" *The Guardian*, February 4.

Gill, Bates, and Michael J. Green. 2009. "Unbundling Asia's New Multilateralism." In *Asia's New Multilateralism: Cooperation, Competition, and the Search for Community*, edited by M. Green and B. Gill, 1–29. New York: Columbia University Press.

Henry, Iain. 2019. "Finally, Some Plain Talk on the Quad." *The Interpreter*, October 25.

Huotari, Mikko, and Jürgen Rüland. 2014. "Introduction: Context, Concepts and Comparison in Southeast Asian Studies." *Pacific Affairs* 87(3): 415–439.

Hurrell, Andrew. 2010. "Regional Powers and the Global System from a Historical Perspective." In *Regional Leadership in the Global System: Ideas, Interests, and Strategies of Regional Powers*, edited by Daniel Flemes, 15–27. Farnham, UK: Ashgate.

Jones, David M., and Mike L. Smith. 2001. "The Changing Security Agenda in Southeast Asia: Globalization, New Terror, and the Delusions of Regionalism." *Studies in Conflict and Terrorism* 24(4): 271–288.

Jones, David M., and Mike L. Smith. 2007. "Making Process, not Progress: ASEAN and the Evolving East Asian Regional Order." *International Security* 32(1): 148–184.

Kang, David C. 2007. *China Rising: Peace, Power, and Order in East Asia.* New York: Columbia University.

Kaplan, Robert D. 2014. *Asia's Cauldron: The South China Sea and the End of a Stable Pacific.* New York: Random House.

Katzenstein, Peter J. 2005. *A World of Regions: Asia and Europe in the American Imperium.* Ithaca, NY: Cornell University Press.

Kivimäki, Timo. 2014. *The Long Peace of East Asia.* Aldershot, UK: Ashgate.

Kynge, James, Leila Haddou, and Michael Peel. 2016. "FT Investigation: How China Bought its Way into Cambodia." *Financial Times*, September 8.

Le Thu, Huong. 2018. "Why the Region Has Given up on 'Shaping China'." *Asia Society*, December 19. https://asiasociety.org/australia/why-region-has-given-shaping-china.

Lee, Sheryn, and Anthony Milner. 2014. "Practical vs. Identity Regionalism: Australia's APC Initiative, a Case Study." *Contemporary Politics* 20(2): 209–228.

Mearsheimer, John J. 1994–1995. "The False Promise of International Institutions." *International Security* 19(3): 5–49.

Miller, Tom. 2017. *China's Asian Dream: Empire Building along the New Silk Road*. London: Zed Books.

Milward, Alan S. 2003. *The Reconstruction of Western Europe, 1945–51*. London: Routledge.

Mufson, Steven. 2017. "Trump Unleashes his Trade Warrior." *Australian Financial Review*, February 22.

Narine, Shaun. 2002. *Explaining ASEAN: Regionalism in Southeast Asia*. Boulder, CO: Lynne Rienner.

Norris, William J. 2016. *Chinese Economic Statecraft: Commercial Actors, Grand Strategy, and State Control*. Ithaca, NY: Cornell University Press.

Perlez, Jane. 2019. "China Retools Vast Global Building Push Criticized as Bloated and Predatory." *New York Times*, April 25.

Pham Ngoc Minh Trang. 2019. "South China Sea: The Disputes and Southeast Asia's Culture of International Law." *The Diplomat*, October 22.

Pinker, Steven. 2012*The Better Angels of Our Nature: Why Violence Has Declined*. New York: Viking Press.

Posen, Adam S. 2018. "The Post-American World Economy: Globalization in the Trump Era." *Foreign Affairs* 97(2): 28–38.

Ravenhill, John. 2008. "Fighting Irrelevance: An Economic Community with ASEAN Characteristics." *The Pacific Review* 21(4): 469–488.

Rolland, Nadège. 2019. "Reports of Belt and Road's Death Are Greatly Exaggerated." *Foreign Affairs*, January 29.

Sabel, Charles F., and Jonathan Zeitlin, eds. 2010. *Experimentalist Governance in the European Union: Towards a New Architecture*. Oxford: Oxford University Press.

Sbragia, Alberta. 2008. "Comparative Regionalism: What Might It Be?" *Journal of Common Market Studies* 46(s1): 29–49.

Shear, Michael D., and Jennifer Steinhauer. 2017. "Trump to Seek $54 Billion Increase in Military Spending." *New York Times*, February 27.

Sil, Rudra, and Peter J. Katzenstein. 2010. *Beyond Paradigms: Analytical Eclecticism in the Study of World Politics*. Basingstoke: Palgrave.

Sim, Dewey. 2019. "Why Can't Southeast Asia Snuff Out Its Haze Problem for Good?", *South China Morning Post*, September 20.

Sukma, Rizal. 2019. "Indonesia, ASEAN and Shaping the Indo-Pacific Idea." *East Asia Forum*, November 19.

van Langenhove, Luk. 2010. "The Transformation of Multilateralism Mode 1.0 to Mode 2.0." *Global Policy* 1(3): 263–270.

Varkkey, Helena. 2012. "Patronage Politics as a Driver of Economic Regionalisation: The Indonesian Oil Palm Sector and Transboundary Haze." *Asia Pacific Viewpoint* 53(3): 314–329.

Wagstyl, Stefan, Arthur Beesley, Alex Barker, and James Politi. 2017. "Trump Flexes Muscle Against Pillars of Postwar Order." *Financial Times*, January 17.

Winter, Tim. 2019. *Geocultural Power: China's Quest to Revive the Silk Roads for the Twenty-First Century*. Chicago: University of Chicago Press.

PART 2

Regional actors and institutional behavior

6

CHINA AND THE NEW INSTITUTIONAL BALANCING IN THE INDO-PACIFIC

Challenging or conforming to the international order?

Jingdong Yuan[1]

Introduction

China's rise has been greeted with both expectation and trepidation. With its growing economic and military power and diplomatic influence, on the one hand, Beijing can and indeed has contributed to international order and regional stability, e.g. with its participation in international peacekeeping operations, anti-piracy expeditions, and its involvement in international financial reform and economic recovery. On the other hand, China's increasingly assertive foreign policy, especially where territorial disputes are concerned, and its diplomatic activism in advocating and promoting its preferred economic and security arrangements raise important questions about Beijing's fundamental attitudes and approaches to the existing international and regional orders that emerged largely as a result of the post-World War II settlement and the continuous US leadership and primacy over the past seven decades.

To date, most discussions and debates on China focus on whether it is a revisionist power and therefore likely to pose challenges to the liberal international order or whether the latter remains sufficiently resilient to withstand these challenges and can socialize and incorporate China into the system as a responsible stakeholder (Mearsheimer 2014; Allison 2017; Ikenberry 2008; Johnston 2008). Yet others contend that China does not have either the capability or the intention to challenge the existing order. At most, Beijing seeks to reform within this order rather than replace it with its own (Shambaugh 2013; deLisle and Goldstein 2017). However, an important but understudied question is how and in what ways China responds to both the challenges and opportunities of the post-GFC world to promote, protect, and advance its interests, and to become a more active participant in global and regional governance. More specifically, how Beijing engages in institutional balancing to protect and advance its interests could help highlight both its rationales and strategies as a rising power operating in a predominantly liberal but increasingly contested international order (Acharya 2018; Zürn 2018; Jones 2018). Indeed, while Beijing may continue as a member of the constituent institutions of the existing liberal international order and behave like a status quo power, it also seeks reforms in some and directly challenges other established norms and rules in international institutions or even sets up its own (Jones 2019; Johnston 2003; He 2015; He and Feng 2019). One way or another, a rising China will strive to have its voice heard and be properly represented in the corridors of power, where 'Chinese solutions' will be offered regarding the many emerging international and regional issues and challenges (Newman and Zala 2017). In other words, the apparent lack of willingness to directly challenge the international order, especially the US' position as its leader, says less about Beijing's desires and intentions than its tactics (Mastro 2019). In this context, understanding China's institutional balancing strategies, and how its perceived role informs these strategies, will be critical.

This chapter provides some preliminary analysis of China's perspectives on and approaches to multilateralism and how Beijing views multilateralism and/or international institutions and uses them to advance its national interests: prosperity and security in an international system still dominated by the United States, as well as socio-economic stability and the legitimacy of the Chinese Communist Party (CCP). I examine the rationale behind China's institutional balancing strategies over the past decade, and assess their implementation, efficacy, and limitations. The next section briefly recounts China's gradual embrace of multilateralism since the 1990s. This is followed by an examination of what can be described as Chinese institutional balancing strategies and practices: the Conference on Interaction and Confidence Building Measures in Asia (CICA); the Asian Infrastructure Investment Bank (AIIB), and the Belt and Road Initiative (BRI). Beijing has been most active in initiating and promoting its preferred concepts and institutions in the security arena at the regional level (CICA) while it has by and large embraced and followed existing institutional norms and practices in economic and financial areas. BRI to some extent can be construed as a response initially to the US Pivot to Asia strategy but was also informed by its domestic needs and imperatives (Clarke 2019). However, it has now evolved into a more integrated geopolitical strategy aimed at setting the economic and diplomatic agendas affecting many countries in Eurasia and beyond, and could affect norms governing development financing and economic development. I argue that the rationale behind these Chinese initiatives has much to do with Beijing's domestic agendas and shifting priorities, hence the need to address them, as it reflects a degree of dissatisfaction with some of the existing multilateral arrangements. But China's rise and its growing capacity as a great power do make it more confident in actively promoting its interests and extending its influence in regions and on issues in which it has major geopolitical and geoeconomic stakes. However, it would be overstating Beijing's intentions and capabilities if these China-sponsored initiatives and institutions were viewed as direct and intentional challenges to the existing international and regional orders, either security or economic ones.

China and institutional balancing: conceptual issues

China's rise raises important questions about the future of the liberal international order but there is no consensus on either the nature or the extent of challenges that China will pose to the existing order, on the one hand, and the latter's resilience during a period of power transition, on the other (Layne 2018; de Graaff and van Apeldoorn 2018; Ikenberry 2018). There is a growing literature on why rising powers would want to challenge the existing international order given the changing power distribution, divergent interests, and differences in agenda-setting in collective-action environments (Patrick 2016; Newman and Zala 2017; Stephen 2017). The issue of how rising powers challenge the existing order remains under-researched. Specifically, this chapter examines how Beijing has been using its growing power and influence to protect and promote its interests since the 2007–2008 global financial crisis (GFC), and analyzes both the implications and limitation of Chinese strategies.

For the better part of the two decades since the end of the Cold War, Beijing kept a low-profile in its foreign policy and avoided major conflicts with Washington given its priorities in economic development, for which the US market, capital, and technologies remained crucial. Granted, China confronted the US over issues vital to its national interests, such as sovereignty and Taiwan, but otherwise sought to respond to the 'unipolar moment' and check US unilateralism through soft balancing, including the use of international institutions such as the United Nations Security Council (UNSC) (Pape 2005; Paul 2005; Wang 2006). The GFC of 2007–2008 dealt a severe blow to the US and other Western industrialized countries, whereas China has emerged in a much stronger position. Beijing's growing economic and military power has enabled it to exercise and extend more diplomatic influence than it was able to do in the past and it remains an active participant in global governance even as its economy has experienced a slowdown over the past few years (Womack 2017; Loke 2018).

Indeed, departing from the decades-old 'taoguang yanghui' [韬光养晦] low-profile diplomacy, China under Xi Jinping is pursuing a more proactive—and at times assertive foreign policy to advance its national interests. Beijing has adopted a spectrum of strategies, including institutional balancing to gain power and exercise influence (Lake 2017). While calling for reform in existing institutions, Beijing is not seeking to fundamentally challenge the overall post-war international order. In fact, Beijing continues to see its role as a participant, a contributor, and a constructive facilitator, rather than a revisionist power seeking its overthrow (Wang 2015). As a rising power, Beijing's strategies have also been informed by a growing awareness of its changing role in international politics, and have been adopted to address various needs and challenges the country faces in its ascendance to great power status (Jones 2013).

The theory of institutional balancing seeks to explain how emerging powers can resort to a broad range of strategies to protect and advance their interests with manageable costs. It is based on the premise that overthrowing the existing liberal international order (itself a rather contested concept) may be neither necessary nor possible, not only because emerging powers have benefited from the existing order and still find it valuable—but also because of the enormous costs involved and the uncertainty of success (Kastner, Pearson and Rector 2016; Brooks and Wohlforth 2008, 2016). However, they also are not contented with the power structure, rules and procedures, and the distribution of benefits that continue to favor established powers despite the changing power distribution (Acharya 2018; Caffarena 2017; Parmar 2018). In other words, emerging powers contend that unless reforms are adopted within existing institutions, their interests will not be better served at best, and could be undermined at worst. As a result, conflicts become inevitable between emerging powers, which demand institutional reforms and adaptation but face institutional inertia or stickiness where existing structures, rules, and procedures continue to favor established powers (Stephen 2017; Lim 2015).

The emerging gap between existing institutional structures and changing power distribution can result in contested multilateralism, which describes strategies pursued by states or, increasingly also non-state actors, designed either to seek changes within institutions or set up alternative institutions to address specific issues (Morse and Keohane 2014; Zürn 2018). One key motivation in engaging in contested multilateralism is the dissatisfaction with the presence or the lack thereof, the ability, and the willingness of existing institutional arrangements to address an issue of serious concern to a particular party. For instance, the majority of the non-nuclear weapons states have in recent years become increasingly disillusioned and dissatisfied with the pace of nuclear disarmament within the existing institutional architecture—the Nuclear Nonproliferation Treaty of 1968. As a result, they called for and negotiated a new Treaty on the Prohibition of Nuclear Weapons to address this issue (Thakur 2018; Müller 2017). Another is that control or influence over institutions is crucial, even in circumstances where inclusive institutional balancing is applied, since defining rules and setting agendas can affect important outcomes and therefore can determine winners and losers in geopolitical games (Dai 2015).

Whereas contested multilateralism reflects the fragmentation of power and hence competing regime creation and regime complexes, institutional balancing theory offers a conceptual framework to describe strategies rising powers can adopt to advance their broader foreign policy objectives. It distinguishes between inclusive and exclusive balancing. The former seeks to include a target state in an institution and use the rules and norms to constrain its behavior. The latter, on the other hand, excludes a target state from an institution while mobilizing the resources within the said institution to counter perceived or real threats from the excluded target state (He 2015; He 2018). Whether a state chooses inclusive or exclusive balancing strategies depends on the gain-loss calculation and on the specific issues in question, and the extent of its existential influence or lack thereof. Where a state values more legitimacy and seeks broader support and recognition of what it seeks to achieve, and where it does not possess enough power and influence over issue areas it cares about the most, it is more likely to favor inclusive institutional balancing. In contrast, where the state faces perceived or real threats, when existing institutions and balance of power are not favorable, and where it exercises limited power or influence, it tends to adopt exclusive institutional balancing strategies to counter or at least minimize such threats. It should also be pointed out that the existing literature on institutional balancing predominantly takes the point of departure from the perspective of the initiating state but largely ignores the fact that the rationales and efficacy of any specific institutional balancing strategy is also affected by other major powers' policies and behaviors, especially when these can be and are influenced by their role as the leader, the challenger, or the follower (He and Feng 2019). This should be seen in relational rather than unidirectional terms. Another critique of the institutional balancing concept is that it carries a connotation of balancing against something, typically conceived as a threat, while institutions themselves are often created to carry particular functions, so the functional aspects should also be recognized (Haas 1965). In this sense, institutional statecraft is also used to describe the complexity of state policies and behaviors in international institutions (Ikenberry and Lim 2017; Kastner, Pearson and Rector 2016).

Multilateralism *à la carte*: China and institutional balancing

China returned to the international community when it was reinstated in the UNSC as a permanent member in 1971. However, it was not until the early 1990s that China began to more actively participate in multilateral institutions at both the global and regional level (Abbott and Snidal 1998). It needs to be pointed out though that China's concept of multilateralism refers by and large to multilateral diplomacy where it engages in institutions with more than two members, not the ideal type as defined by John Ruggie and others, where its organizing principles are indivisibility, generalized principles of conduct, and diffused reciprocity (Ruggie 1992; Caporaso 1992). Among these are the UN Security Council and various UN-affiliated organizations such as the International Atomic Energy Agency (IAEA), the Conference on Disarmament (CD), the World Bank, the International Monetary Fund (IMF), and World Health Organization (WHO), among others. Not only did China join most international treaties and conventions, it has also been gradually 'socialized' to accept the existing norms and practices of the international system, and increasingly become more active in global governance, albeit in selected areas given its capacities and specific interests (Economy and Oksenberg 1998; Wuthnow 2012; Chan, Lee, and Chan 2011; Johnston 2008; Kent 2007). In the Asia-Pacific, Beijing gradually became more comfortable with the ASEAN-led regional organizations as the latter typically reflect an Asian way of multilateral institutions that are less legalistic and formal in organizational structure, gradual and consensus-based in their approach to regional issues, and in fact can offer alternatives to US-led alliance systems (Acharya 2001; Leifer 1996; Wu and Lansdowne 2007).

ASEAN's efforts to engage China aside, Beijing also was motivated to participate in regional arrangements as a way to dispel concerns over the 'China threat,' especially by its smaller neighboring states which also have territorial disputes with China. At the same time, the Chinese leadership found it useful to advocate its own new security concept that very much aligned with ASEAN's promotion of common, comprehensive, and cooperative security (Acharya 1998; Emmers 2003).

However, Beijing resisted calls for greater institutionalization of the ASEAN Regional Forum (ARF) for fear that such developments could impose constraints on its freedom of action. It also sought to develop a great-power relationship with Washington to manage potential conflicts with the latter (Yuan 2000).

If China was largely a passive participant in multilateral institutions in the 1990s, Beijing has since become much more active, confident, and creative in both embracing and initiating multilateral arrangements since the new millennium (Wu and Lansdowne 2007; Nathan 2016). The 2008 GFC and the incoming Xi Jinping Administration in 2012–2013, which pursues a more active diplomatic agenda than its predecessors, provide the backdrop against which Beijing's institutional balancing strategies can be observed and assessed. Beijing's growing power and confidence is also affecting the identity and role it sees for itself, which in turn influences the priorities, direction and degree of its institutional balancing behaviors (He and Walker 2015). Three cases will be used to describe and analyze China's institutional strategies: AIIB, CICA, and BRI. They have been selected due to the fact that Beijing has played an important part in their initiation and development, and given that these cases represent what could at first easily be identified as instances of institutional balancing. We ask the following questions about Beijing's institutional balancing strategies: What are China's interests and role in initiating and pursuing these institutional balancing strategies in the Indo-Pacific region and beyond? What are the implications of Chinese policies and actions in the larger contexts of its goals, domestic as well as external, and the ways in which it seeks to achieve them? To what extent does the theory of institutional balancing appropriately capture the foreign policy approach of a rising power such as China?

The Asian Infrastructure Investment Bank

Chinese President Xi Jinping announced the creation of AIIB in late 2013. One of the motivating factors behind the initiative was, as Beijing would emphasize, that Asia's infrastructure needs, a critical ingredient for connectivity and economic development, were not being adequately addressed because of lack of attention and sufficient funding. The existing international funding agencies such as the World Bank and the Asian Development Bank (ADB) were either not interested or incapable of addressing this deficiency. A recent report by the ADB estimates that Asia's total infrastructural needs would require US$1.7 trillion until 2030 (ADB 2017). It was also conceived as meeting one of China's major initiatives that Beijing launched during 2013–2014: the so-called Belt and Road Initiative, which seeks to revitalize the ancient Silk Road through Central Asia, and a maritime route, to connect China with Central Asia, Southeast Asia, South Asia, part of Africa, and Europe to facilitate the flows of trade, investment, and people.

The launch of the AIIB reflects both Beijing's dissatisfaction with the existing international institutions that either do not properly reflect China's growing power or fail to address issues that are considered as its priorities, and also Beijing's willingness to become an active reformer and institution builder (Ren 2016). It represents a more fundamental departure from a cautious and low-profile Chinese foreign policy of *tao-guang yanghui* [韬光养晦] to one that harbors more ambitious goals [*fenfa youwei* 奋发有为] under the new Xi leadership (Blackwill and Campbell 2016; He and Feng 2013). That confidence is further underpinned by China's ability to weather the 2007–2008 GFC with continued high growth rate and huge accumulated foreign exchange reserves (at the peak amounting to US$4 trillion). China is now able and willing to set priorities if not yet the rules in investing in infrastructural projects that are critical for BRI (Dollar 2015; Chin and Thakur 2010).

Understandably, the Obama Administration was concerned that the AIIB initiative was a deliberate Chinese effort to undercut global norms and rules in international development financing and the general accepted practices of multilateral development banks (MDBs). Washington served notice to its allies and friends to not join the AIIB. Together with the promotion of the Trans-Pacific Partnership (TPP) and the US Pivot to Asia, the Obama Administration made it clear that the US, not China, would remain the dominant power and rule setter in the Indo-Pacific. However, with the UK breaking rank with the US, some of the key European countries such as Germany and Italy, and the majority of Asia states, including Australia and South Korea, ignored the US plea and joined the AIIB as founding members, spelling a major diplomatic setback for Washington (He and Feng 2019; Roach, Zha, Kennedy and Chovanek 2015; Perlez 2015).

The creation of the AIIB is an example of Beijing's institutional balancing strategy albeit an inclusive one in that the institution is open to all who want to join (Chan 2017). With its growing economic and financial power, China was frustrated at the slow pace of reform in existing MDBs such as the World Bank, the IMF, and the ADB. At the same time, there was growing recognition that Asia's massive infrastructural needs—critical for China's BRI that places connectivity in trade and investment at the front and center—could not be met by the ADB. Launched in 2013, the AIIB was initially envisioned as an alternative lending institution with a focus on Asia and on infrastructure projects. The Western media largely depicted it as Beijing's effort to challenge US dominance, especially in the contexts of the TPP and US pivot to Asia that characterized the emerging strategic rivalry between the two powers. Given the constraints imposed on China within the existing multilateral institutions and China's priorities in funding infrastructure projects to address what it considers to be serious bottlenecks in economic development and connectivity, setting up alternative or even competing institutions would be the natural course of action (Ikenberry and Lim 2017; Pilling and Noble 2015; Perlez 2015).

Beijing might have entertained the idea of introducing alternative norms and rules governing international lending practices in what could be perceived as a 'potentially disruptive institution in the previously rather settled landscape of international development finance' (de Jonge 2017, 1061). It certainly was motivated by such consideration; but the subsequent development was that with a large number of states joining the bank as founding members, including some of the key Western countries, China's contributing share to the AIIB has decreased from the original 50 percent to about 26 percent. This has meant that Beijing has retained the power of veto but does not have sweeping powers to set the norms and dictate the terms of the bank with regard to loan reviews and granting decisions. In fact, instead of introducing alternative or competing norms and rules, the AIIB has actually aligned itself with the prevailing norms and rules of existing MDBs. This may be because, while in bilateral contexts China as a lender may exercise greater power over the terms of the financial arrangements vis-à-vis the recipient states, its ability and willingness to challenge the prevailing international norms and rules may be mitigated against its interest in presenting AIIB as an open and inclusive multilateral development financing institution. In fact, the participation of the Western advanced economies in the bank's initial setup has transformed it from one that was viewed as a challenge to the existing system of multilateral development banks to one that is part of that system. Its senior management and governance structure is more diverse, drawing from multiple nationalities and based on their experiences (Knoerich and Urdinez 2019). One of the critiques that the AIIB would serve as the bank for BRI has not transpired so far; instead, most BRI projects have been funded by other major MDBs, with AIIB as the supplementary lender. It is too early to tell if the AIIB would be operating differently from other MDBs and whether, in due time, it will or could pose serious challenges to the latter (Wilson 2019; Callaghan and Hubbard 2016; Chin 2016).

Proponents of the 'new kid on the bloc' praise its functional utility in addressing one pressuring development issue, and the AIIB's efficiency in making loan decisions compared to the long (averaging seven years) assessment and feasibility study process of other traditional MDBs. Critics, however, do point out that emphasizing the separation of economics from politics, non-interference, and infrastructural projects over other economic priorities could over time create an alternative model of development, which is often state-led and with strong state intervention and participation, lack of transparency and accountability, and absence of or little emphasis on conditionality upon recipient states. Whether viewed as institutional balancing or statecraft, the establishment of the AIIB has far-reaching implications for existing norms and rules as their new and alternative counterparts have been introduced. It is not a question of whether this represents a direct challenge to the current liberal international order; it is how and to what extent the order itself is being changed from within, with emerging norms and rules eventually being accepted to coexist with or even replace the existing ones. AIIB, like other Chinese practices and preferences since it re-joined the global political economy, may be a harbinger of such a development to come (Mazower 2012; McNally, 2012).

CICA and China's new security concept

The CICA idea was first proposed in 1992 by then Kazakhstan President Nazarbayev at the UN and the first CICA foreign ministers meeting was held in September 1999. CICA today has 27 members states, eight observer states, and seven observer organizations (CICA 2019). The revival of the CICA since China assumed its chairmanship in 2014 represents a clear exclusive institutional balancing strategy on its part that aims to introduce a new discourse on international security very much reflective of Chinese interests and preferences. Framed as a New Asian Security Concept at the 2014 CICA Summit in Shanghai, President Xi Jinping put forth the idea that Asia's matters should be handled by Asians themselves, a not-so-subtle dig at the US-centered alliance system as the post-war Asian security architecture. Xi further elaborated on the substance of this concept as cooperative security, common security, comprehensive security, and sustained development and security. Beijing's confidence and interest in reviving the CICA and promoting a discourse is a stark contrast to what the Chinese dub as the 'Cold War mentality and relics' (Liff 2018). China clearly assumes an identity as a contributor to the development of a more equal and democratic (other than the US-dominated unipolar) international order. The CICA covers Central Asia but is much more expansive in its geographical reach (into Eurasia, South Asia and parts of East Asia) and membership.

CICA provides the platform for Beijing to advocate its concept of Asian security: common, cooperative, and comprehensive security and sustainable development. Recognizing the diversity of security architectures and institutions in the region—ASEAN-led initiatives such as ARF, East Asia Summit (EAS), and the ADMM+ (ASEAN Defence Ministers' Meeting Plus), the US-led alliance system, and multilateral security dialogues such as the International Institute for Strategic Studies (IISS)-Shangri-La Dialogue (SLD), the Xiangshan Forum, Beijing argues that future Asian security architecture requires the participation of all concerned, and must be one that is based on consensus, and providing security for all. It emphasizes the importance of economic cooperation and economic integration as conducive to the development of security architecture. It advocates multilateralism and calls for dialogues in addressing security issues and non-traditional security challenges. It promotes a new Asian security architecture that is inclusive, cooperative, and win-win, with states in the region encouraged to pursue partnerships rather than military alliances (China State Council Information Office 2017).

CICA represents Beijing's effort to revive and transform a little-known and dormant loose arrangement of largely small and medium-sized states in Eurasia and the sub-continent, as well as parts of Asia, into a recognized platform to introduce a 'new' and alternative security concept. Under Xi Jinping, China is to take the lead in advocating an alternative discourse on security that can chart a different course to the traditional security architecture built around military alliances and collective security. By promoting a different security discourse that places less emphasis on military alliances and security against potential adversaries, the new 'Asian security concept' delegitimizes military alliances as a relic of the Cold War era, and promotes a new security concept that is both more comprehensive in its content (economic development as well as security) and its format (cooperative and common security; security with rather than against someone). Xi's not-so-subtle admonition that Asians are capable of managing Asia's affairs, including security, is clearly aimed at the US-led alliance systems, the foundation of the post-war San Francisco security arrangement of hub-and-spokes lending legitimacy to the US' dominant position and military presence in the region. Should the CICA be turned into a well-developed regional security institution with Beijing's new security concept as the accepted guideline and principle, then it would represent an alternative and indeed a major challenge to the US and the current security architecture, especially considering the geographical reach covered by CICA members.

But significant challenges remain for China to turn CICA into an effective alternative security arrangement, in addition to promoting a discourse that is easy for rhetoric purposes but hard to implement given the diverse national interests held by member states, let alone Asia's other major powers not in the CICA framework. In fact, many of the latter would view the arrangement (and its ideational parallel) as China's attempt to establish hegemonic dominance in contestation with the established US primacy in the region for the better part of the last 70 years (Pollack 2017). Given Beijing's unresolved conflicts with a number of Asian states, and a growing rivalry between itself and the US, it remains to be seen if and whether the CICA will become a viable platform to fulfill China's institutional balancing agenda. Furthermore, compared to other institutions China is either a part of, or has in recent years helped develop, the CICA's institutional framework remains underdeveloped, unclear, and largely dependent on the rotating chair state and the types of agendas and preferences it promotes.

The Belt and Road Initiative

China's BRI is an ambitious project aiming to transform the economic landscape along its route in the areas of trade, investment, and energy supplies. It makes as its focal point the connectivity between China and Eurasia, South and Southeast Asia, parts of Africa, and Europe. During his visit to Kazakhstan in September 2013, Chinese President Xi Jinping announced the Silk Road Economic Belt. A month later, speaking at the Indonesian parliament, Xi proposed the idea of the 21st-Century Maritime Silk Road Initiative, or MSRI for short. The first captures and seeks to rekindle in the public imagination the ancient Silk Road that connected China to the Eurasian landmass, while the second replicates the overland trade routes in maritime terms to reflect the importance of modern seaborne commerce. Beijing often hastens to remind the world of ancient China's maritime interests and prowess, as represented by Admiral Zheng He's great maritime expeditions more than six hundred years ago.

BRI is a massive and ambitious geoeconomic and geostrategic initiative conceptualized, rationalized, and now being operationalized and implemented by Beijing. It combines multiple goals (economic, energy security, and diplomatic) with various stakeholders (government, enterprises, and financial institutions) to forge a coordinated, systematic, and phased development program on a grand scale with an extensive reach (Wuthnow 2017; Rolland 2017). Since its inception in 2013, 136 countries covering Central Asia, South Asia, ASEAN, Central and Eastern Europe, West Asia, and North Africa, over 900 projects, and 30 international organizations have signed BRI cooperation documents, receiving over US

$900 billion as of late 2019 (AEPF 2019). Two BRI summit meetings have been held (2017 and 2019). According to a forecast by the McKinsey Global Institute, these countries will be contributing to 80 percent of total global GDP growth by 2050 (Wang 2017; Zhang 2017).

In March 2015, the Chinese government issued a white paper titled, 'Vision and Actions on Jointly Building Silk Road Economic Belt and 21st-Century Maritime Silk Road' (NDRC et al. 2015), which emphasizes openness and inclusiveness, and advocates for consultation, cooperation, and coordination. In May 2017, the first BRI summit meeting was held in Beijing, attracting more than 20 heads of states and governments and hundreds of diplomats, businesspeople, and the media. President Xi called it the 'project of the century,' and it signified the onset of a multipolar international order, one in which China is beginning to play a more active role. In this context, it is much more than an economic project, it is a tectonic geopolitical one as well (Xi 2017; Pethiyagoda 2017). Not only has BRI been integrated into China's 13th Five-Year Plan (2016–2020), it has also been written into the CCP Constitution at the recently concluded 19th CCP National Congress. Beijing's commitment has been demonstrated by the announcement at the 2014 APEC Summit of a US$40 billion Silk Road Fund and the launch of the AIIB in 2016 (Chan 2014; Wilson 2019).

BRI is a multi-phase development project, moving from the proposal of the concept, feasibility study, to top-level design and partnership formation. The top-level design is reflected in the two important speeches by Xi in 2013 and various subsequent official documents, as well as the set-up of a core leadership group for implementation. Led by the executive vice-premier, Zhang Gaoli, with four deputies and the involvement of 13 government ministries and commissions, it demonstrates Beijing's seriousness and commitment to seeing it a success given the high stakes. According to Vice Premier Zhang, 'Promoting the Belt and Road Initiative is one of China's priorities for the next five years' (*Xinhua* 2016). BRI implementation also becomes an all-government effort through effective inter-agency coordination. The public–private partnership (PPP) model also enlists and encourages the participation of China's (and for that matter foreign firms' and partners') major state-owned enterprises (SOEs), financial institutions, and privately-owned businesses in BRI projects.

Beijing often emphasizes BRI's win-win potential and flatly dismisses allegations that the initiative is a cover for its hidden agendas of re-establishing China as the preeminent power in Eurasia, challenging existing international institutions, exporting its excess capacities and creating asymmetrical dependence relationships with developing countries, and extending political and diplomatic influence along the BRI routes. But that view has been contested, especially as China under Xi Jinping is clearly moving away from its hitherto 'hiding ambitions and keeping low-profile' diplomacy and becoming ever more proactive (if not assertive as some analysts suggest) in its pursuit of national interests. This is captured in Xi's call for China to make greater efforts in shaping the international environment ('The world is so big and faces so many problems, and the international community expects to hear China's voice and see China's solution'), even as it continues to place economic development at the top of its policy agenda (Xi 2015; Blanchard and Flint 2017; Blanchard 2017; Clarke 2019).

It is true that when BRI was first proposed in 2013, it was just a vision rather than a well-calculated strategy. However, seven years on, it has passed through the phases of conceptualization and top-level policy design to a coordinated strategy that aims to address several challenges China faces: its economy entering a 'new normal' period of slower growth rate; its energy security concerns; the development needs of its vast north-western and south-western regions; and the growing non-traditional security threats such as terrorism and ethnic separatism (Rolland 2017). The injection of capital for infrastructure development could stimulate economic growth and provide local employment; an improved economic environment in turn could mitigate some of the socio-economic problems; closer economic cooperation with the region extends China's influence; and the construction of ports and roads helps shorten the distance Chinese energy imports are transported and thus lower costs (Chung 2018).

BRI at the moment remains more of an ensemble of minilateral arrangements between China and countries along the ancient silk roads, land as well as maritime—it has yet to evolve into a multilateral institution. Nevertheless, the high-profile BRI summits and ongoing projects are beginning to reveal the institutional norms and practices preferred by Beijing. These are state-centric (between governments), infra-structure-focused in countries where connectivity is crucial to China's resource security and access to new markets for Chinese goods, and loan-repayment/debt-servicing arrangements that allow Chinese entities the right to control infrastructures (e.g. ports) in recipient countries should the latter fail to meet their financial obligations. This practice represents a different model from that held by the US and other Western countries, which often comes with conditionality with regard to human rights, cor-ruption, transparency, poverty reduction, social responsibility, local employment, among others (Hillman 2018). This represents an exclusive institution-balancing strat-egy on Beijing's part as it seeks to use BRI to gain influence and establish its dominant position in BRI-linked regions with norms and practices in ways that reflect its values, interests, and status as a rising power, while preventing or, at minimum, limiting those of the US. At the same time, the consolidation of Chinese influence in greater Eurasia and beyond would also serve to break the perceived US 'encirclement' effort in the Indo-Pacific and, over time, introduce geostrategic and economic alternatives to the US-led international order (Benabdallah 2019; Clarke 2019; Zhou and Esteban 2018).

Conclusion

Several observations can be drawn from the discussion. First, China has definitely come a long way in becoming an active participant and supporter of multilateralism since the mid-1990s. In both scope and depth, Chinese engagement in multilateral institutions has been encouraging in that Beijing recognizes and complies with generally accepted norms and rules rather than contesting them. Second, with growing power come changing interests, priorities, and preferences, and the need to promote and protect them. However, for historical reasons, China has either not been accorded the respect and influence within existing multilateral institutions commensurate with its growing economic, military and diplomatic weight; or, simply because of the weakness or non-existence of institutional arrangements in place to address issues of serious concern, Beijing has a significant incentive to develop alternative institutions as a result. Third, while Beijing's institutional balancing behaviors, especially those that can be viewed as exclusive in nature (e.g. CICA), have served its interests to some extent, it remains inconclusive as to whether these place China in the category of order challenger. If anything, Beijing has sought to establish some institutional forms, organizational as well as conceptual, to better serve its growing interests. Finally, the record of Chinese-sponsored institutions is mixed, and it remains too early to draw any firm conclusions on their effectiveness, China's role in both initiating and sustaining these institutions, and the implications for regional and global order.

A caveat is in order in our assessment of China's institutional balancing strategies. The reasons for which Beijing has pursued these strategies may be readily recognizable, as this chapter has demonstrated, but the circumstances under which China has designed, launched, and shaped multilateral institutions are much more complex than when existing institutional constructs (e.g. the World Bank, IMF, ADB) were initiated at the behest of the United States in the 1940s and 1950s. As a result, the criteria for assessing the implications and China's role in initiating, developing, and sustaining multilateral institutions should be different as well.

Note

1 This chapter is a revised version of Yuan, Jingdong. 2018. "Beijing's Institutional-Balancing Strategies: Rationales, Implementation and Efficacy." *Australian Journal of International Affairs* 72(2): 110–28.

References

Abbott, Kenneth W., and Duncan Snidal. 1998. "Why States Act Through Formal International Organizations." *The Journal of Conflict Resolution* 42(1): 3–32.

Acharya, Amitav. 1998. "Culture, Security, Multilateralism: The 'ASEAN Way' and Regional Order." *Contemporary Security Policy* 19(1): 55–84.

Acharya, Amitav. 2001. *Constructing a Security Community in Southeast Asia: ASEAN and the Problem of Regional Order.* London: Routledge.

Acharya, Amitav. 2018. *Constructing Global Order: Agency and Change in World Politics.* Cambridge: Cambridge University Press.

ADB (Asian Development Bank). 2017. *Meeting Asia's Infrastructure Needs.* Report. February, Manila.

Allison, Graham. 2017. *Destined for War: Can America and China Escape Thucydides's Trap?* New York: Houghton Mifflin Harcourt.

Asia Europe People's Forum (AEPF). 2019. *The Belt and Road Initiative (BRI): An AEPF Framing Paper*. November. https://www.tni.org/files/publication-downloads/bri_fram ing_web_en.pdf.

Benabdallah, Lina. 2019. "Contesting the International Order by Integrating It: The Case of China's Belt and Road Initiative." *Third World Quarterly* 40(1): 92–108.

Blackwill, Robert D., and Kurt M. Campbell. 2016. *Xi Jinping on the Global Stage*. Special Report No. 74. Council on Foreign Relations, New York, February.

Blanchard, Jean-Marc F. 2017. "Probing China's Twenty-First-Century Maritime Silk Road Initiative (MSRI): An Examination of MSRI Narratives." *Geopolitics* 22(2): 246–268.

Blanchard, Jean-Marc F., and Colin Flint. 2017. "The Geopolitics of China's Maritime Silk Road Initiative." *Geopolitics* 22(2): 223–245.

Brooks, Stephen G., and William C. Wohlforth. 2008. *World Out of Balance: International Relations and the Challenge of American Primacy*. Princeton, NJ: Princeton University Press.

Brooks, Stephen G., and William C. Wohlforth. 2016. "The Once and Future Superpower: Why China Won't Overtake the United States." *Foreign Affairs* 95(3): 91–104.

Caffarena, Anna. 2017. "Diversity Management in World Politics. Reformist China and the Future of the (Liberal) Order." *The International Spectator* 52(3): 1–17.

Callaghan, Mike, and Paul Hubbard. 2016. "The Asian Infrastructure Development Bank: Multilateralism on the Silk Road." *China Economic Journal* 9(2): 116–139.

Caporaso, James A. 1992. "International Relations Theory and Multilateralism: The Search for Foundations." *International Organization* 46(3): 599–632.

Chan, Gerald, Pak K. Lee, and Lai-Ha Chan. 2011. *China Engages Global Governance: A New World Order in the Making?*London: Routledge.

Chan, Lai-Ha. 2017. "Soft Balancing against the US 'Pivot to Asia': China's Geostrategic Rationale for Establishing the Asian Infrastructure Investment Bank." *Australian Journal of International Affairs* 71(6): 568–590.

Chan, Minnie. 2014. "China to Create US$40 Billion Silk Road Fund to Upgrade Asia Links." *South China Morning Post*, November 9. https://www.scmp.com/news/china/a rticle/1635391/china-create-us40-billion-silk-road-fund-eurasian-infrastructure

Chin, Gregory T. 2016. "Asian Infrastructure Development Bank: Governance Innovation and Prospects." *Global Governance* 22(January/March): 11–25.

Chin, Gregory, and Ramesh Thakur. 2010. "Will China Change the Rules of Global Order?" *The Washington Quarterly* 33(4): 119–138.

China State Council Information Office. 2017. *White Paper: China's Policy on Asia-Pacific Security Cooperation*. January 11.

Chung, Chien-peng (C.P.). 2018. "What Are the Strategic and Economic Implications for South Asia of China's Maritime Silk Road Initiative?" *The Pacific Review* 31(3): 315–332.

CICA (Conference on Interaction and Confidence Building Measures in Asia) Secretariat. 2019. www.s-cica.org.

Clarke, Michael. 2019. "Beijing's Pivot West: The Convergence of Innenpolitik and Aussenpolitik on China's 'Belt and Road'?" *Journal of Contemporary China*, online first. http s://doi.org/10.1080/10670564.2019.1645485.

Dai, Xinyuan. 2015. "Who Defines the Rules of the Game in East Asia? The Trans-Pacific Partnership and the Strategic Use of International Institutions." *International Relations of the Asia-Pacific* 15(1): 1–15.

de Graaff, Naná, and Bastiaan van Apeldoorn. 2018. "US–China Relations and the Liberal World Order: Contending Elites, Colliding Visions?" *International Affairs* 94(1): 113–131.

de Jonge, Alice. 2017. "Perspectives on the Emerging Role of the Asian Infrastructure Investment Bank." *International Affairs* 93(5): 1061–1084.

deLisle, Jacques, and Avery Goldstein, eds. 2017. *China's Global Engagement: Cooperation, Competition, and Influence in the 21st Century*. Washington, DC: Brookings Institution Press.

Dollar, David. 2015. "China's Rise as a Global and Regional Power: The AIIB and the 'One Belt, One Road'." *Horizons*, 4(Summer): 162–172.

Economy, Elizabeth C., and Michel C. Oksenberg, eds. 1998. *China Joins the World*. New York: Council on Foreign Relations.

Emmers, Ralf. 2003. *Cooperative Security and the Balance of Power in ASEAN and the ARF*. London: Routledge.

Haas, Michael. 1965. "A Functional Approach to International Organization." *The Journal of Politics* 27(3): 498–517.

He, Kai. 2015. "Contested Regional Orders and Institutional Balancing in the Asia Pacific." *International Politics* 52(2): 208–222.

He, Hai. 2018. "Role Conceptions, Order Transition and Institutional Balancing in the Asia-Pacific: A New Theoretical Framework." *Australian Journal of International Affairs* 72 (2): 92–109.

He, Kai, and Huiyun Feng. 2013. "Xi Jinping's Operational Code Beliefs and China's Foreign Policy." *Chinese Journal of International Politics* 6(3): 209–231.

He, Kai, and Huiyun Feng. 2019. "Leadership Transition and Global Governance: Role Conception, Institutional Balancing, and the AIIB." *Chinese Journal of International Politics* 12(2): 153–178.

He, Kai, and Stephen Walker. 2015. "Role Bargaining Strategies for China's Peaceful Rise." *Chinese Journal of International Politics* 8(4): 371–388.

Hillman, Jonathan E. 2018. "China's Belt and Road Initiative: Five Years Later." Statement Before the U.S.–China Economic and Security Review Commission, January 25.

Ikenberry, G. John. 2008. "The Rise of China and the Future of the West: Can the Liberal System Survive?" *Foreign Affairs* 87(1): 23–37.

Ikenberry, G. John. 2018. "The End of Liberal International Order?" *International Affairs* 94 (1): 7–23.

Ikenberry, G. John, and Darren Lim. 2017. *China's Emerging Institutional Statecraft: The Asian Infrastructure Investment Bank and the Prospects for Counter-Hegemony*, April. Washington DC: The Brookings Institution. https://www.brookings.edu/wp-content/uploads/2017/04/chinas-emerging-institutional-statecraft.pdf.

Johnston, Alastair Iain. 2003. "Is China a Status Quo Power?" *International Security* 27(4): 5–56.

Johnston, Alastair Iain. 2008. *Social States: China in International Institutions, 1980–2000*. Princeton, NJ: Princeton University Press.

Jones, Catherine. 2013. "Understanding Multiple and Competing Roles: China's Roles in the International Order." *Pacific Focus* 28(2): 190–217.

Jones, Catherine. 2018. *China's Challenges to Liberal Norms: The Durability of International Order*. London: Palgrave Macmillan.

Jones, Catherine. 2019. "Contesting within Order? China, Socialization, and International Practice." *Cambridge Review of International Affairs*, online first. doi:10.1080/09557571.2019.1674781.

Kastner, Scott L., Margaret M. Pearson, and Chad Rector. 2016. "Invest, Hold Up, or Accept? China in Multilateral Governance." *Security Studies* 25(1): 142–179.

Kent, Ann. 2007. *Beyond Compliance: China, International Organizations, and Global Security*. Stanford, CA: Stanford University Press.

Knoerich, Jan, and Francisco Urdinez. 2019. "Contesting Contested Multilateralism: Why the West Joined the Rest in Founding the Asian Infrastructure Investment Bank." *Chinese Journal of International Politics* 12(3): 333–370.

Lake, David A. 2017. "Domination, Authority, and the Forms of Chinese Power." *Chinese Journal of International Politics* 10(4): 357–382.

Layne, Christopher. 2018. "The US–China Power Shift and the End of the *Pax Americana*." *International Affairs* 94(1): 89–111.

Leifer, Michael. 1996. "The ASEAN Regional Forum: Extending ASEAN's Model of Regional Security." Adelphi Paper 302. London and Oxford: IISS and Oxford University Press.

Liff, Adam P. 2018. "China and the US Alliance System." *The China Quarter* 233: 137–165.

Lim, Yves-Heng. 2015. "How (Dis)Satisfied Is China? A Power Transition Theory Perspective." *Journal of Contemporary China* 24(92): 280–297.

Loke, Beverley. 2018. "China's Economic Slowdown: Implications for Beijing's Institutional Power and Global Governance Role." *The Pacific Review* 31(5): 673–691.

Mastro, Oriana Skylar. 2019. "The Stealth Superpower: How China Hid Its Global Ambitions." *Foreign Affairs* 98(1): 31–39.

Mazower, Mark. 2012. *Governing the World: The History of an Idea.* London: Penguin.

McNally, Christopher A. 2012. "Sino-Capitalism: China's Reemergence and the International Political Economy." *World Politics* 64(4): 741–776.

Mearsheimer, John. 2014. *The Tragedy of Great Power Politics,* revised ed. New York: W.W. Norton.

Morse, Julia C., and Robert O. Keohane. 2014. "Contested Multilateralism." *The Review of International Organizations* 94(4): 385–412.

Müller, Harald. 2017. "The Nuclear Non-Proliferation Treaty in Jeopardy? Internal Divisions and the Impact of World Politics." *The International Spectator* 52(1): 12–27.

Nathan, Andrew J. 2016. "China's Rise and International Regimes: Does China Seek to Overthrow Global Norms?" In *China in the Era of Xi Jinping: Domestic and Foreign Policy Challenges,* edited by Robert S. Ross and Jo Inge Bekkevold, 165–195. Washington DC: Georgetown University Press.

NDRC (People's Republic of China, National Development and Reform Commission), Ministry of Foreign Affairs (MFA), and Ministry of Commerce (MOFCOM). 2015. "Vision and Actions on Jointly Building Silk Road Economic Belt and 21st-Century Maritime Silk Road." March 28. https://reconasia-production.s3.amazonaws.com/media/filer_public/e0/22/e0228017-746 3-46fc-9094 0465a6f1ca23/vision_and_actions_on_jointly_building_silk_road_economic_belt _and_21st-century_maritime_silk_road.pdf.

Newman, Edward, and Benjamin Zala. 2017. "Rising Powers and Order Contestation: Disaggregating the Normative from the Representational." *Third World Quarterly* 39(5): 871–888.

Pape, Robert A. 2005. "Soft Balancing against the United States." *International Security* 30(1): 7–45.

Parmar, Inderjeet. 2018. "The US-led Liberal Order: Imperialism by Another Name?" *International Affairs* 94(1): 151–172.

Patrick, Stewart. 2016. "World Order: What, Exactly, Are the Rules?" *The Washington Quarterly* 39(1): 7–27.

Paul, T. V. 2005. "Soft Balancing in the Age of US Primacy." *International Security* 30(1): 46–71.

Perlez, Jane. 2015. "China Creates a World Bank of Its Own, and the US Balks." *New York Times,* December 4.

Pethiyagoda, Kadira. 2017. "What's Driving China's New Silk Road, and How Should the West Respond?" Washington DC, Brookings Institution, May 17.

Pilling, David, and Josh Noble. 2015. "US Congress Pushed China into Launching AIIB, Says Bernake." *Financial Times,* June 2.

Pollack, Jonathan D. 2017. "Competing Visions: China, America, and the Asia–Pacific Security Order." In *China's Global Engagement: Cooperation, Competition, and Influence in the 21st Century*, edited by Jacques deLisle and Avery Goldstein, 155–182. Washington DC: Brookings Institute Press.

Ren, Xiao. 2016. "China as an Institution Builder: The Case of the AIIB." *The Pacific Review* 29(3): 435–442.

Roach, Stephen S., Zha Daojiong, Scott Kennedy, and Patrick Chovanek. 2015. "Washington's Big China Screw-Up." *Foreign Policy*, March 26.

Rolland, Nadège. 2017. *China's Eurasian Century? Political and Strategic Implications of the Belt and Road Initiative*. Seattle, WA: National Bureau of Asian Research.

Ruggie, John Gerard. 1992. "Multilateralism: The Anatomy of an Institution." *International Organization* 46(3): 561–598.

Shambaugh, David. 2013. *China Goes Global: The Partial Power*. New York: Oxford University Press.

Stephen, Matthew D. 2017. "Emerging Powers and Emerging Trends in Global Governance." *Global Governance* 23(3): 483–502.

Thakur, Ramesh. 2018. "The Nuclear Ban Treaty: Recasting a Normative Framework for Disarmament." *The Washington Quarterly* 40(4): 71–95.

Wang, Yi. 2015. "China's Role in the Global and Regional Order: Participant, Facilitator and Contributor." Speech at the luncheon on the Fourth World Peace Forum, June 27.

Wang, Yiwei. 2017. *The Belt & Road Initiative: What China Will Offer the World in Its Rise*. Beijing: People's Press.

Wang, Yuan-kang. 2006. "China's Grand Strategy and US Primacy: Is China Balancing American Power?" CEAP Working Papers. Washington, DC: Brookings Institution.

Wilson, Jeffrey D. 2019. "The Evolution of China's Asian Infrastructure Investment Bank: From a Revisionist to Status-Seeking Agenda." *International Relations of the Asia-Pacific* 19(1): 147–176.

Womack, Brantly. 2017. "International Crises and China's Rise: Comparing the 2008 Global Financial Crisis and the 2017 Global Political Crisis." *Chinese Journal of International Politics* 10(4): 383–401.

Wu, Guoguang, and Helen Lansdowne, eds. 2007. *China Turns to Multilateralism: Foreign Policy and Regional Security*. London: Routledge.

Wuthnow, Joel. 2012. *Chinese Diplomacy and the UN Security Council: Beyond the Veto*. London: Routledge.

Wuthnow, Joel. 2017. "Chinese Perspectives on the Belt and Road Initiative: Strategic Rationales, Risks, and Implications." *China's Strategic Perspectives* 12. Washington DC, Institute for National Strategic Studies, National Defense University, September.

Xi, Jinping. 2015. "Chinese President Xi Jinping's 2016 New Year Message." December 31. Accessed August 15, 2017. http://www.fmprc.gov.cn/mfa_eng/wjdt_665385/zyjh_665391/t1331985.shtml.

Xi, Jinping. 2017. "Full Text of President Xi's Speech at Opening of Belt and Road Forum." May 14. http://www.fmprc.gov.cn/mfa_eng/wjdt_665385/zyjh_665391/t1465819.shtml.

Xinhua. 2016. "Chinese Vice Premier Urges Closer Cooperation along Belt and Road." China. Org.cn, January 16. http://www.china.org.cn/business/2016-01/16/content_37590431.htm.

Yuan, Jing-dong. 2000. *Asia-Pacific Security: China's Conditional Multilateralism and Great-Power Entente*, January. Carlisle, PA: Strategic Studies Institute, US Army War College.

Zhang, Jiadong. 2017. "The Present Situation and Development Trend of the 'OBOR' Strategic Initiative." *Study of the Indian Ocean Economies* 2: 41–65.

Zhou, Weifeng, and Mario Esteban. 2018. "Beyond Balancing: China's Approach Towards the Belt and Road Initiative." *Journal of Contemporary China* 27(112): 487–501.

Zürn, Michael. 2018. *Theory of Global Governance*. Oxford: Oxford University Press.

7

JAPAN'S ROLE CONCEPTION IN MULTILATERAL INITIATIVES IN THE ASIA-PACIFIC

Hidetaka Yoshimatsu[1]

Introduction

Japan has been one of the key players in supporting multilateralism in the Asia-Pacific. Japan, in collaboration with Australia, took the lead in creating the Asia-Pacific Economic Cooperation (APEC) in 1989. Tokyo also sustained the creation of the Association of Southeast Asian Nations (ASEAN) Regional Forum in 1994 with the Nakayama proposal in 1991 that suggested transforming the ASEAN Post-Ministerial Conference into a multilateral forum to discuss security affairs. In implementing multilateral diplomacy, Japan has paid due attention to forging close relations with ASEAN.

After the global financial crisis in 2008, domestic conditions in Japan and external surrounding environments exhibited significant changes. In August 2009, the Democratic Party of Japan (DPJ) took power from the Liberal Democratic Party (LDP), and the Hatoyama Government was formed. In December 2012, the LDP regained power and Prime Minister Shinzo Abe has kept his government for more than seven years. On the external front, Japan's economic power has gradually declined, which has had a negative impact on maintaining political influence in the Asia-Pacific. Instead, China has steadily expanded its economic power, which it has transformed into military build-up and political clout. In particular, China has been exhibiting assertive diplomatic postures and aggressive behavior in the South China Sea and East China Sea. China's assertiveness in maritime security affairs is regarded as a major factor destabilizing the regional order. Such evolutions have significant influence on Japan's diplomatic policies toward multilateralism and the strategies of balancing and alliance.

In this chapter, I examine Japan's multilateral commitments to the Asia-Pacific after the global financial crisis in 2008. There are quite a few studies regarding Japan's regional strategies in general and multilateral commitments in particular in the Asia-Pacific after 2008. Sahashi (2011), Hosoya (2013) and Zakowski, Bochor-odycz and Socha (2017, ch. 9) have examined the Hatoyama Government's Asia policy, particularly the East Asian Community (EAC) proposal. The Abe Govern-ment's proactive diplomatic and security strategies toward Asia have attracted the growing interest of scholars (Auslin 2016; Hughes 2016; Pugliese and Insisa 2017; Suzuki 2017; Vidal and Pelegrín 2018; Koga 2018). Many of these studies have inves-tigated Japan's regional strategies in light of relations with China, seeking to characterize the nature of the strategies in terms of balancing (Hughes 2016; Pugliese and Insisa 2017; Liff 2019) or hedging (López i Vidal and Pelegrín 2018; Koga 2018).

This study seeks to deepen the understanding of Japan's regional strategies after the global financial crisis by paying special attention to its multilateral commitments to the Asia-Pacific. In so doing, it employs a theoretical framework of national role concep-tions. A role is defined as 'attitudinal and behavioral expectations that those who relate to its occupant have of the occupant and the expectations that the occupant has of himself or herself in the role' (Rosenau 1990, 220). A role, like identity, is an inter-subjective notion of holding two dimensions of an actor's understanding of what his or her behavior should be and others' expectations toward the actor's prospective beha-vior in given social settings. Role theory is based on the premise that actors' social behavior is in large part a function of the expectations attached to or associated with them on the basis of their locations or positions in social systems (Grossman 2005, 335–6). Actors define the boundaries of appropriate actions in accordance with the expectations and requirements that are produced by their perceived role in special social positions.

While role theory originally developed in social psychology and sociology, quite a few scholars have applied this theory to the study of foreign policy (Chafetz, Abramson and Grillot 1996; Grossman 2005; Holsti 1970; Walker 1987). These studies assume that national leaders and foreign policy elites are crucial players in the policy formation process, and their national role conceptions often derive from their shared beliefs about how a state should behave in the international social system (Grossman 2005, 336; Hermann 1987, 220). The leaders and elites who hold specific belief systems and unique experiences develop a particular interpretation or con-ception of their state's functions in the international arena, producing definite preferences for and approaches to foreign policy issues.

As explained in detail in the following section, Japan's position as a security ally of the US has been regarded as a key factor in defining its national role concep-tions. Japan, as a junior partner of the US, tends to play a follower role in propping up Washington's diplomatic stances or just obeying its diplomatic policies. At the same time, Japan is required to formulate delicate and careful diplomatic strategies in a period of power transition, and such a requirement is likely to urge Tokyo to develop distinguishing national role conceptions. Thus, this study takes note of the development process of role conception, exploring Japan's attempts to search for an appropriate role in evolving regional environments.

In examining Japan's commitments to regional multilateralism after 2008, this chapter pays particular attention to the two governments. The first is the Hatoyama

Government, the first substantial non-LDP government under the two-party system in post-war Japan. On the external front, the Government implemented distinctive policies, reconsidering the long-honored US-first diplomatic stance and pursuing closer political links with China and other Asian countries. In this overall diplomatic trend, the Government launched the concept of the EAC. The second is the Abe Government. This government has made serious commitments to maintaining and enhancing Japan's diplomatic position in Asia and the world, and an effective response to growing Chinese power has been a key diplomatic imperative for the Government. The initiation of and support for multilateral institutions in the Asia-Pacific has been a major pillar of the Government's diplomatic strategies.

The arguments that this chapter advances are threefold. First, the Hatoyama Government's attempt, through the advocacy of the EAC, to play a kingmaker role in creating a new order in East Asia failed due to its undue emphasis on self-reliance and distance from partnership with the US (He 2018; also Chapter 1, this volume). Second, the Abe Government sought to play a follower role in enhancing the position of the East Asia Summit (EAS) with an eye to consolidating the US-based institutional framework in the Asia-Pacific. Third, Abe's new multilateral initiative of the Free and Open Indo-Pacific (FOIP), which represented Japan's kingmaker role in maintaining a free and open regional order, has had contradictory impacts on diplomatic strategies of the US and Japan's other regional partners.

This chapter is organized as follows. The next section examines key factors defining Japan's national role conception. The third section investigates multilateral initiatives during the DPJ era by locating the EAC as the target of analysis, and the fourth section turns attention to multilateral initiatives and role conceptions under the Abe Government.

Japan's national role conception

It is difficult to define a state's national role conception because domestic political actors often develop different role conceptions for their state and a state sometimes plays contradictory roles. In the case of Japan, alliance politics is a major factor in defining the baseline of its national role conception. The relationship with the US has been the central pillar of Japan's post-war international relations and security. Japan and the US concluded the Japan–US Security Treaty in 1951, and Washington has provided security guard for Tokyo in exchange for the offer of sites for military bases in Okinawa and other areas, as well as budgets for supporting these bases. The conservative LDP regime has put stress on stable alliance relations with the US. Because of its overall importance in Japan's foreign and domestic policies, the end of the Cold War did not lead to the termination of the Japan–US Security Treaty, whose prime objective was to defend Japan from the communist threat. Tokyo and Washington sought to redefine their security relations, and the new National Defence Program Outline, formulated in November 1995, reaffirmed the centrality of the bilateral treaty to Japan's security policy (Muroyama 1997; Sakanaka 1997).

Given that tensions with China in the East China Sea escalated in the 2000s, political and security ties with the US became even more important. Japan needed a security guarantee to draw China's self-constraint on offensive actions toward Japan, particularly in the East China Sea. The Japanese government sought to get an assurance that the Senkaku Islands fell within the scope of Article V of the Japan–US Security Treaty.

The close political and security partnership with Washington has forced Tokyo to follow US's postures in international affairs, or at least establish its own diplomatic stance with due consideration to the impact on relations with this ally. A typical example is found in relation to the East Asian Economic Caucus concept that the Malaysian prime minister, Mahathir, proposed in 1991.[2] Japan's passive attitude, in addition to conceptual vagueness, constituted a major impediment to the development of the East Asian Economic Caucus. Tokyo feared that the concept would provoke opposition from Washington, which had strong political and economic stakes in the Asia-Pacific region. The constraint from the partnership with the US on Japan's Asia policy continued in the new millennium. When the ASEAN Plus Three Summit was held in October 2003, ASEAN members hoped for Japan's accession to the Treaty of Amity and Cooperation, and five out of the ten ASEAN leaders directly urged the Japanese prime minister to join the treaty. Despite the leaders' earnest encouragement, the Japanese government was, at first, reluctant to accept this encouragement. Japan was worried about the accession's negative influence on the Japan–US security alliance (Yoshimatsu 2005, 229).

Political and security links with the US basically define Japan's default national role as a follower to conform and support the external policies of the US as an order defender. Such a follower role is based on Japan's own interests in supporting the continued existence of the US-led regional/global order, but there are some specific conditions where Japan might shape and undertake a more autonomous diplomatic policy. There are at least three possibilities that Japan might change its national role conception from a passive follower to an autonomous kingmaker. The first is related to a drastic change in international environments. Japan's follower position is based on close and stable political relations with the US. If a US administration were to adopt a policy that keeps a distance from Japan or formulate a diplomatic policy that would be likely to jeopardize Japan's core diplomatic objectives, Tokyo might be forced to reconsider its follower role and pursue a more autonomous role in order to secure its diplomatic interests by positively encouraging Washington to reconsider such a policy.

The second is related to domestic power transition. An emphasis on the Japan–US alliance has been a key policy tenet for the conservative regime. This means that a liberal political circle seeks to keep a distance from the alliance, and such a policy stance is necessary for appealing to the nation that it offers a major difference in diplomatic policy from the conservative regime. When a liberal party gains power, its government seeks to reconsider Japanese diplomacy that is based on the partnership with Washington, and to pursue a more independent diplomatic style. Thus, a change in the domestic political regime might lead to a shift in the national role conception of a follower.

The third is related to the determined belief of a political leader. When a strong prime minister with solid national and in-party support has a determined political belief or diplomatic strategy, such a belief or strategy might define Japan's role conception. For instance, the basic source of Japan's follower role lies in the Yoshida Doctrine, Prime Minister Shigeru Yoshida's political belief that allows Japan to concentrate on economic development while relying on the US for its security (Catalinac 2007, 78–9; Singh 2008, 306–7). If a prime minister decisively pursues a specific diplomatic belief or strategy, such a posture might lead to a change in Japan's role conception.

Multilateral initiative under DPJ governments

The Hatoyama Government's EAC advocacy

As a consequence of a landslide victory in the Lower House general election in late August 2009, the DPJ ousted the LDP from power, and Yukio Hatoyama was appointed the ninety-third prime minister. The DPJ Government explicitly showed its willingness to search for closer and stable relations with Asian countries. The DPJ's election platform (*Manifesto*) stated that 'it would make the greatest efforts to develop relations of mutual trust with China, South Korea, and other Asian countries,' seeking to establish 'cooperative mechanisms within the Asia-Pacific region, particularly in such fields as commerce, finance, energy, the environment, disaster relief, and measures to control infectious diseases' (DPJ 2009, 22–3). Hatoyama himself expressed his desire to promote cooperation with Asia by overcoming historical animosities between Japan, on the one hand, and South Korea and China, on the other. Hatoyama selected South Korea as the destination of his first foreign trip, and explained later that this choice was because Japan and South Korea, which were the closest from an ethnic standpoint, had not established true heart-to-heart relations, and the resolution of this problem was the most crucial issue for his diplomacy (Hatoyama et al. 2014, 100–1). Hatoyama also declared that he would not visit the Yasukuni Shrine, and promised to begin talks on the construction of a secular memorial to honor Japan's war dead. This was a positive policy to remove an imperative obstacle to constructing a trusting relationship with Asian countries, especially China and South Korea, and implied a different perception of history from his LDP predecessors (Sneider 2011, 111–12).

A critical element in Hatoyama's pro-Asia diplomacy was the advocacy of an EAC. Hatoyama, who had a strong belief in the necessity of multilateral security talks in East Asia even in the 1990s, made clear the central position of the EAC in his diplomatic policy after becoming prime minister. In an article issued just after becoming prime minister, Hatoyama argued that while the Japan–US security partnership continued to be a cornerstone of Japanese diplomacy, 'we should not forget our identity as a nation located in Asia.' He then stressed the need to establish a common Asian currency and build a permanent security framework in East Asia. The EAC concept was underpinned by frameworks for stable economic cooperation and national security (Hatoyama 2009a, 139).

Role conception in the EAC initiative

What role conception led to the advocacy of the EAC? Since the DPJ had achieved a power transition for the first time in the consistent two-party system in post-war Japan, the party needed to show explicit differences from the previous LDP governance. The revision of the Japan–US alliance became a critical target for this purpose. In the 'Foreign Policy' section of the 2009 *Manifesto*, the DPJ stated that the party would pursue 'a close, *equal* Japan–US alliance relationship as a baseline for Japanese diplomacy' and 'strength in Asian diplomacy envisioning the building of an East Asian Community' (DPJ 2009, 22; my emphasis). Thus, the advocacy of the EAC was located as a critical means to articulate power transition in domestic politics.

An equally crucial factor was Hatoyama's political belief. For a long time, Hatoyama had stressed the importance of self-reliance in Japanese diplomacy. In a book written with Naoto Kan, another DPJ leader, published in 1997, Hatoyama contended that: 'we have to regret that Japanese diplomacy was the so-called America-obedient diplomacy. We need to create the diplomacy of Japan an independent nation; namely, the self-reliance diplomacy, no longer the dependent diplomacy' (Hatoyama and Kan 1997, 112). In his 2009 article, Hatoyama stated that Japan strove 'to maintain its political and economic independence and preserve national interests between the US seeking to remain a hegemonic state and China aspiring to become one' (Hatoyama 2009a, 139–40).

Such political belief encouraged Hatoyama to explore an independent and distinctive way for Japanese diplomacy in power politics between Washington and Beijing. Advocacy for the EAC derived from such strategic thinking. In the 1997 book, Hatoyama stated that: 'it is a significant diplomatic issue how Japan as a genuine leader in Asia holds together the countries in the region on the basis of the ideals of "self-reliance" and "co-existence"' (Hatoyama and Kan 1997, 113). In a 2005 book, he showed a determination that: 'I would like to regard it as one of Japan's national goals in the coming fifty years to conceptualize an Asia-Pacific version of the "EU" [European Union] and take the lead in realizing it' (Hatoyama 2005, 18). In the 2009 article, Hatoyama regarded the EAC as a foundation for regional cohesion through the building of frameworks for stable economic cooperation and national security across the region— essential for significant regional evolutions represented by the end of US unilateralism, the limit on US-led globalism and the rise of China (Hatoyama 2009a, 139–41). It seems that Hatoyama allocated a kingmaker role to Japan in creating a new order in the Asia-Pacific in evolving great-power politics.

However, such a role conception embedded in an EAC soon disappeared, largely because of criticisms of the passive perception of the Japan–US alliance in the concept. In addition to criticisms from internal politicians and bureaucrats, leaders in the Asia-Pacific countries, including the US, took a cautious stance on the exclusive nature of the EAC initiative. Within a few months, the basic character of the EAC changed into a symbol of the accumulation and assembly of functional cooperation in East Asia. When Hatoyama made a speech on Japan's Asia policy in

Singapore in November 2009, he encouraged participants to 'develop a multi-layered network of functional communities' through 'the promotion of concrete cooperation in a broad range of areas such as trade, investment, finance and education.' From such a standpoint, he referred to Japan's contributions in functional areas such as natural disasters, infectious diseases, environmental conservation, and cultural exchanges. Hatoyama did not give a special political position to Japan in leading the cooperative process, stating that 'countries with the will and the capabilities to cooperate in a particular field may choose to participate in projects initially, and as their efforts bear fruit, other countries could join later' (Hatoyama 2009b).

One day before Hatoyama's announcement of his resignation, the Cabinet Secretariat revealed the Future Efforts Regarding the East Asian Community Concept. The first two items shown in the section on the basic idea were 'to promote "open" and "transparent" regional cooperation with parties including the United States' and 'to accumulate functional cooperation under the long-term vision' (Cabinet Secretariat 2010).

The impacts of the EAC initiative

What impacts did Hatoyama's EAC idea have on regional order in the Asia-Pacific? The advocacy of the EAC, which did not necessarily presuppose Washington as a key member, invited suspicion and criticism from the US and other Asian countries. China was positioned as a major partner for creating the EAC. However, Chinese leaders were unable to understand sufficiently the real intention of the EAC and fraternity diplomacy. Thus, 'Hatoyama's original vision on an East Asian Community was unfortunately not welcomed by the Chinese Government nor by the ROK (Republic of Korea) Government, nor by ASEAN countries' (Hosoya 2013, 153). Despite Hatoyama's willingness to promote reconciliation and community building in the region, his EAC idea did not make significant contributions to stable regional order. On the contrary, Hatoyama's fraternity diplomacy contributed to unstable relations between Japan and Asian countries. When the Chinese vice-president, Xi Jinping, paid a visit to Tokyo in December 2009, the DPJ Government granted him an audience with the Emperor against the normal protocol. Chinese leaders might have had an expectation that Japan—under the DPJ with fraternity diplomacy—tended to make concessions to Chinese pressure.

Hatoyama's assumption that a new opening for stable regional order should be based on reconciliation might be correct. However, reconciliation could be realized through delicate diplomacy based on the tide of time in strategic circumstances, heads of state's leadership and diplomats' followership (Suzuki 2017, 388). For instance, reconciliation between Tokyo and Washington, which was completed with Obama's visit to Hiroshima and Abe's visit to Pearl Harbor, was realized four years after the start of the Abe Government in December 2012 (Suzuki 2017, 389–90). Although Hatoyama's ideal to create an EAC through reconciliation was sublime, his diplomacy did not necessarily take into account the subtle realities of world politics.

Subsequent DPJ governments and deteriorating Sino-Japanese relations

After Hatoyama stepped down as prime minister, two DPJ governments were formed from June 2010 to December 2012. A particularly significant diplomatic issue in this period was a sharp deterioration in diplomatic relations with China. During the Naoto Kan Government in September 2010, there occurred a crucial incident that jeopardized relations with China in the East China Sea. The Japan Coast Guard arrested the crew of a Chinese fishing boat on suspicion of operating in Japanese territorial waters and obstructing the public duties of the Coast Guard personnel by deliberately hitting patrol vessels.[3] The Chinese Government reacted to the Japanese actions decisively. The Government summoned the Japanese ambassador five times in the week after the incident, demanding the skipper's immediate, unconditional release. The Government also announced the postponement of talks with Japan over a treaty concerning joint gas field development in the East China Sea, and the suspension of ministerial and higher level exchanges with Tokyo. Moreover, the Chinese authorities detained four Japanese employees of the Fujita Corporation for allegedly entering an unauthorized area, which was regarded as an attempt to pressure Japan over the collision incident.

Sino-Japanese relations deteriorated further during the period of the Yoshihiko Noda Government, which began in September 2011. The Government adopted a policy to nationalize three of the privately owned Senkaku/Diaoyu Islands in September 2012. This policy invited China's fierce condemnation as a unilateral action to change the status quo. After the nationalization, China began to send its coastguard ships regularly to Japan-controlled waters surrounding the Senkaku/Diaoyu Islands. The number of 'incursions' into the waters by Chinese coastguard ships increased from three in January–August 2012 to 20 in September–December 2012, and 21 in January–April 2013 (MOD 2013, 173).

The Noda Government tried to discuss the issue of raising consumption tax in order to cope with the growing national debt problem. However, such efforts were unpopular, and Noda was forced to step down from his post as a consequence of his defeat in the Lower House general election of December 2012.

Multilateral initiatives under the Abe Government

Two multilateral commitments

The LDP regained power in the Lower House general election in December 2012, and Shinzo Abe began his second cabinet.[4] Abe undertook proactive diplomatic postures, pursuing diplomacy taking a panoramic perspective of the world. Under this slogan, Abe made 27 foreign visits to all parts of the world in the three years after the start of his second cabinet. In particular, Abe stressed diplomatic links with South-East Asian countries, visiting all ASEAN members in his first year in office.

Despite Abe's positive commitments to foreign affairs, his government did not necessarily demonstrate distinctive new initiatives in multilateralism. The Government put stress on economic diplomacy to sustain 'Abenomics,' which consists of aggressive monetary policy, flexible fiscal policy and a growth strategy to encourage private investment, and followed the previous DPJ Governments' pursuit of closer economic ties with the US by joining negotiations on the Trans-Pacific Partnership (TPP) agreement. In this overall context, an important commitment to multilateralism in the Asia-Pacific was support for the EAS. The Abe Government sought to enhance the position of the EAS as a prime regional forum for discussing political and security affairs. At the eighth EAS Summit in October 2013, Abe opened his remarks by stressing that the EAS was a significant forum where leaders frankly exchange views centered on political and security areas, and expressed his desire to further bolster the development of the forum (MOFA 2013).

Japan's foreign ministers have since offered concrete directions for strengthening the EAS. During the fifth EAS Foreign Ministers' Meeting in August 2015, Fumio Kishida pointed out the importance of convening regular meetings attended by permanent representatives of the EAS members, establishing an EAS unit at the ASEAN Secretariat, and enhancing links between the EAS and the ASEAN Defense Ministers' Meeting Plus (MOFA 2015a). During the seventh EAS Foreign Ministers' Meeting in August 2017, Taro Kono proposed turning the Expanded ASEAN Maritime Forum into a formal EAS maritime cooperation forum, and holding Track 1 meetings in conjunction with the Track 1.5 meetings.

Japan has striven to share the importance of the EAS with other member countries. When foreign ministers from the US, Japan and India held their first trilateral ministerial meeting in September 2015, they confirmed the importance of the EAS as a premier leaders-level forum for addressing key political and security issues in the region (MOFA 2015b). The value of the EAS as a leaders-led forum for strategic dialogue and the importance of strengthening the EAS was confirmed in the joint statements of the Japan–US–Australia Trilateral Strategic Dialogue in July 2016 and August 2017.

After 2016, Prime Minister Abe began to advance a new multilateral initiative: the FOIP. The FOIP was first revealed as the Free and Open Indo-Pacific Strategy at the Sixth Tokyo International Conference on African Development, held in Kenya in August 2016. The FOIP concept is based on an assumption that the peace and prosperity of international society is reliant on a free and open maritime order, and thereby such a maritime order should be fostered from the Pacific to the Indian Ocean. In this concept, Japan intended to promote concrete policies such as: the promotion of basic values of the rule of law, democracy, and freedom of navigation; the fostering of economic prosperity through the strength of the infra-structure of, for example, ports and railways, and enhanced economic partner-ships; and strength in cooperation in the field of maritime safety, such as maritime law-enforcement capabilities, the combating of piracy, and counter-terrorism.

The Abe Government sought to develop the FOIP as a concept to be com-monly shared by the political leaders of the states in the Asia-Pacific. During a trip to the Philippines, Indonesia, Vietnam, and Australia in January 2017, Abe explained the value of the FOIP and Japan's sincere commitments to the stability of the regional order with this concept. Abe referred to the FOIP at summit meetings with leaders from South-East Asia and South Asia, and gained their support for promoting concrete actions to realize the concept. When Abe held a summit meeting with the Australian prime minister, Malcolm Turnbull, in Manila in November 2017, he expressed his intention to coordinate closely with Australia to maintain and strengthen the free and open order in the Indo-Pacific region (MOFA 2017).

The Japanese Government sought to substantiate the creation of the FOIP with official development assistance support. From the mid-2000s, the Japanese Government intensified 'patrol boat diplomacy,' whereby it provided official development assistance funds for purchasing patrol vessels with South-East Asian countries in order to enhance their maritime patrol capabilities. The FOIP further strengthens such policy direction. In the 2018 fiscal budget, some 30 billion yen (US$265 million) were allocated as official development assistance funds for materializing the FOIP. The official development assistance projects will cover the development of the infrastructure and maritime equipment of the countries targeted in the FOIP.

Role conception in the multilateral commitments

What role conception contributed to Japan's multilateral commitments under the Abe Government? As for the strength of the EAS, it is necessary to examine Japan's policy stance toward the EAS from its establishment in 2005. There were controversies over the membership of the EAS. While China, Malaysia, Cambodia, and Vietnam opposed expanding participation in the summit beyond ASEAN Plus Three members, Japan, Singapore, Indonesia, and Thailand supported expanding the original configuration to include Australia, New Zealand, and India (Teh 2011, 349). Japan's support for Australia's membership derived from its desire to enhance the role of its partnership with the country and the US (Terada 2006, 8).

As already explained, Japan has been one of the key players that pursued the EAS's strengthened function and its higher political position. Japan attempted to achieve the higher presence with close partnership with the US. For instance, Tokyo and Washington confirmed the importance of the EAS as the premier political and security forum, and of coordination to support ASEAN and its forums, which was shown in the US–Japan Joint Statement released in April 2014. Moreover, at the Japan–US Summit in November 2015, Abe stressed his willingness to strengthen the EAS mechanisms in collaboration with the US in order to make the EAS the region's premier forum both in name and in reality. Since the US was a latecomer in the EAS, its position in the institution has not been relatively prominent. However, Japan's role perception is basically that of a follower, to raise the US presence in the EAS and pursue harmonization with the policies adopted by Washington.

Japan's role conception in the FOIP, which emerged in 2016, is more complicated. The FOIP is in line with a mid-term diplomatic strategy that Abe has developed from the period of the first cabinet in 2006–2007. Abe stressed the importance of the Indian Ocean and Pacific Ocean in his speech to the Indian Parliament in August 2007 entitled 'Confluence of the Two Seas,' pointing out that 'the Pacific and the Indian Oceans are now bringing about a dynamic coupling as seas of freedom and of prosperity' (MOFA 2007). After Abe returned to power in December 2012, he developed the idea of the confluence of the two seas into the 'Indo-Pacific.' In a speech at the Centre for Strategic and International Studies in February 2013, Abe referred to Japan's task to remain a leading promoter of rules 'when the Asia-Pacific, or the Indo-Pacific region gets more and more prosperous' (Prime Minister of Japan and His Cabinet 2013). The FOIP concept is the combination of 'Indo-Pacific' with 'free and open.' 'Free and open' reflects Abe's imperative to maintain a free and open maritime regime because the rule of law and freedom of navigation are crucial for Japan, which relies on external sources for 96 percent of its energy, and oil supply from the Middle East passes through the Indian Ocean, the Malacca Strait and the South China Sea. In order to maintain the rule of law and freedom of navigation for broader maritime areas involving the Indian Ocean, Abe pursued assent to the FOIP from the US, Australia, India, and ASEAN members. Such efforts represent Japan's kingmaker role in the specific maritime field where Japan has vital interests.

The advocacy of the FOIP is also relevant to significant evolutions in international politics. The victory of Donald Trump in the US presidential election in November 2016 and his administration's anti-multilateralism encouraged Abe to pursue a new diplomatic policy. Trump launched his 'America First' policy and exhibited a willingness to challenge the liberal trade regime by not hesitating to adopt protectionist policies. Just after the start of the Administration in January 2017, Trump signed an executive order to pull out of the 12-nation TPP, as he had promised in his election campaign. Trump also promised to renegotiate the 1994 North American Free Trade Agreement, and the negotiations began in August 2017. In contrast, China started to show its willingness to defend economic globalization, which was clearly demonstrated in Chinese President Xi Jinping's keynote speech at the World Economic Forum in Davos in January 2017.

Japan's distinctive role in maintaining the liberal economic regime in the face of the protectionist Trump Administration can be found in another multilateral commitment. Japan took the lead in reaching a final conclusion in the TPP-11 negotiations. After the Trump Administration announced its retreat from the TPP, the trade ministers of the remaining 11 members held a meeting in Vietnam in May 2017 and reaffirmed the balanced outcome and strategic and economic significance of the TPP. The senior officials undertook four rounds of negotiations, and agreed on the core elements of the Comprehensive and Progressive Agreement for Trans-Pacific Partnership in November 2017. Japan played a key role in this process. After the ministerial meeting in May 2017, the first senior officials' meeting took place at Hakone, Japan, in mid-July. After the second senior officials' meeting in Australia in late August, Japan proposed holding two more meetings before the end of October.[5] The negotiations among the senior officials were held in Japan in September and October. During these two rounds of negotiations, settlement on concrete issues was advanced. Moreover, Japan's minister in charge of economic revitalization assumed the co-chair of a ministerial meeting in Vietnam in November 2017, engaging in intensive talks with other ministers and proposing a final agreement plan.

Given the strategic uncertainties created by the Trump Administration, Japan, as a proactive secondary state, sought to play a kingmaker role in maintaining a liberal and open economic regime, and a vigor for multilateralism. This was particularly important in the transitional period when China was gaining more regional influence while the US preferred an inward-looking diplomacy, including a retreat from multilateralism.

The implications and impacts of the multilateral initiatives

Abe's support for the EAS derived from lessons learnt during his first cabinet in 2007–2008. During that time, Abe advocated a quadrilateral partnership between the US, Japan, Australia and India, all of which were democratic nations. The quadrilateral partnership was Abe's key regional strategy, which would develop into the 'Democratic Security Diamond' concept revealed during the second cabinet.[6] The partnership was partially realized in Exercise Malabar 07–2, where naval forces from the four countries, plus Singapore, gathered in the Bay of Bengal in September 2007. However, this quadrilateral-based multilateralism received a cool reception from South-East Asian countries both because this multilateralism included no ASEAN members and because it created the perception that Abe was seeking to supersede ASEAN's centrality in multilateral discussions of regional strategic affairs (Lee 2016, 40). After the emergence of the Kevin Rudd Administration in Australia, which put more importance on stable relations with China than the previous administration, the quadrilateral partnership collapsed. Partly learning from the experiences during the first cabinet, Abe stressed the ASEAN-centered multilateralism of the EAS after he returned as prime minister.

Japan's proposal to strengthen the EAS's function was realized in the Kuala Lumpur Declaration on the tenth anniversary of the EAS, which was adopted at the EAS Summit in November 2015. The declaration committed to establishing regular engagements between the Committee of Permanent Representatives to ASEAN and non-ASEAN ambassadors of the EAS, and creating a dedicated unit within the ASEAN Secretariat focusing on the EAS. This tenth-anniversary summit also adopted the EAS Statement on Enhancing Regional Maritime Cooperation, which urged members to promote peace, stability and security in the region. The establishment of the EAS as a prime regional forum and its substantial networking with other regional institutions such as ASEAN Plus Three, the ASEAN Regional Forum and the ASEAN Defence Ministers' Meeting Plus contributes to stability in regional political and security relations.

The launching of the FOIP has much to do with China's diplomatic assertiveness and practical offensive in maritime affairs. From 2014, Beijing has been engaged in building artificial islands at an unprecedented rate in order to bolster its territorial claims in the Spratly Islands in the South China Sea. China's actions included the building of harbors, radar towers and other facilities on these artificial islands, coupled with other actions comprising intensified maritime patrols and energy exploration in disputed waters. In the East China Sea, tension between Japan and China has continued as Chinese Government vessels have advanced into waters surrounding the Senkaku/Diaoyu Islands. In order to check and mitigate China's offensive actions, Japan sought to maintain a liberal, rules-based maritime order with the resolution of disputes through peaceful means not relying on unilateral actions. The FOIP is a crucial concept to achieve this goal. In order to consolidate partnership between India, Australia, the US and ASEAN members, Japan sought, under the banner of the FOIP, to promote cooperation in infrastructure development, capacity building and non-traditional security.

The FOIP concept has had contradictory impacts on diplomatic strategies of the US and Japan's other regional partners. On the one hand, the FOIP became a strategic pillar for US foreign policy. At the APEC Summit in November 2017, US President Donald Trump referred to 'Sharing our vision for a free and open Indo-Pacific.' Afterward, the key members of the Trump Administration presented concrete ideas for the FOIP in US diplomacy. For instance, James Mattis, US Secretary of Defense, developed the FOIP's strategic values at the Shangri-La Dialogue (SLD) in June 2018. Mattis regarded the dialogue as the best opportunity to 'reinforce the significance of a free and open Indo-Pacific region,' and presented four themes of the Indo-Pacific strategy: maritime space; interoperability; strength in the rule of law, civil society, and transparent governance; and the private sector-led economic development (US Department of Defense 2018). The themes 'strength in the rule of law, civil society, and transparent governance' and 'the private sector-led economic development' surely represent the US's critical perception of China's economic management, which constitutes the base for fierce US-China commercial wars.

On the other hand, ASEAN, Australia, and India—major partners for Japan in advancing the FOIP—cautioned the exclusive nature of the FOIP concept. ASEAN worried about the FOIP's strategic nature, combined with its impact on the likely deterioration of 'ASEAN centrality' in managing regional affairs. For instance, Singaporean Prime Minister Lee Hsien Loong stated in a media interview that 'We hope that the eventual outcome [of the Free and Open Indo-Pacific] will be an inclusive and open regional architecture, where all countries engage one another peacefully and constructively.'[7] ASEAN presented its own concept for the Indo-Pacific: the ASEAN Outlook on Indo-Pacific (AOIP), which was adopted in June 2019. The AOIP represents ASEAN's hope 'to strengthen and give new momentum for existing ASEAN-led mechanisms to better face challenges and seize opportunities arising from the current and future regional and global environments' by stressing 'inclusive in terms of ideas and proposals' (ASEAN 2019). Australia surely added strategic values to the 'Indo-Pacific' concept, but does not intend to exclude China by employing this concept. For instance, Australian Prime Minister Malcolm Turnbull mentioned, in a speech in August 2018, that

Australia continues to address its own interests by pursuing a relationship with China based on mutual respect and understanding. … And in doing so, we support an international order based on the rule of law, where might is not right and the sovereignty of all nations is respected by others. (Turnbull 2018)

Indian Prime Minister Narendra Modi stated, in a keynote address at SLD in June 2018, that the Indo-Pacific 'stands for a free, open, inclusive region, which embraces us all in a common pursuit of progress and prosperity' (Ministry of External Affairs (India) 2018). The addition of the term 'inclusive' intended to weaken the exclusive nature of the FOIP.

In light of the recognition of preferences among leaders in ASEAN, Australia, and India, coupled with gradual improvement in political and economic relations with China after 2017, Japan itself softened the strategic nature of the FOIP. Prime Minister Abe publicly used 'vision' instead of 'strategy' in a joint news conference with the visiting Malaysian prime minister, Mahathir Mohamad, in November 2018. Abe also stated at the EAS Summit in the same month that 'Initiatives that contribute to realizing a free and open Indo-Pacific do not exclude any countries. They benefit all countries in the region, large and small, and we will cooperate with all those who share these views' (MOFA 2018). Japan is required, in advancing the FOIP concept, to pay due attention to nuanced differences between the US that strengthens confrontational stance on China on the one hand and key regional partners that hope to maintain stable order in Asia on the basis of constructive engagement with China on the other.

Conclusion

Regional politics in the Asia-Pacific exhibited significant evolutions after the global financial crisis in 2008 and, in this overall trend, the Japanese Government made distinctive commitments to multilateralism in the region. The Hatoyama Government launched an EAC initiative, which was a new idea for multilateralism in the Asia-Pacific. Given its timing after the global financial crisis, the initiative garnered international interest. Hatoyama originally foresaw Japan assuming a kingmaker role in the creation of a new order in East Asia, but the emphasis on self-reliance and distance from its partnership with the US embedded in this initiative hindered Japan in pursuing such a role. The EAC initiative was not understood sufficiently, even by the Asian countries with which Hatoyama hoped to promote community building.

The LDP returned to power in December 2012, and Shinzo Abe formed his second cabinet. The Abe Government has made efforts to enhance the position of the EAS, seeking to make it a prime regional forum for the discussion of political, economic and security affairs, and enhance its function so it could to play a more substantial role. In its efforts to enhance the EAS's position and function, Japan pursued policy harmonization with the US, playing a follower role in consolidating the US-based institutional framework. In 2016, Abe revealed a new multilateral initiative—the FOIP—which was designed to promote the rule of law and freedom of navigation, infrastructure development and cooperation on maritime safety.

The role conception for Japan in the FOIP was as a kingmaker in maintaining a free and open regional order. The FOIP has had contradictory impacts on diplomatic strategies between the US and Japan's other regional partners.

As this study demonstrates, its political and security partnership with the US has had a significant influence on Japan's national role conceptions. However, the relative position of the US has gradually declined and both the Hatoyama and Abe governments have pursued a kingmaker role in multilateral commitments in the Asia-Pacific. A key element that urged Japan to commit to such a role was the Chinese presence. An increasingly powerful China poses a challenge to Japan relying solely on the Japan–US alliance to maintain its national interests. In this connection, Japan is required to undertake prudent diplomacy in harmonizing different policy preferences between the US and other regional partners—ASEAN, Australia, and India, which was apparent in the employment of the FOIP.

Notes

1 This chapter is a revised version of Yoshimatsu, Hidetaka. 2018. "Japan's Role Conception in Multilateral Initiatives: The Evolution from Hatoyama to Abe." *Australian Journal of International Affairs* 72(2): 129–44.
2 The East Asian Economic Caucus was to include the ASEAN countries, Japan, South Korea and China, and to exclude Australia and New Zealand, as well as the US.
3 On September 19, the Naha District Public Prosecutors Office in Okinawa Prefecture, which was investigating the detained boat skipper, decided to extend his detention. Five days later, however, the office announced its decision to release him on the grounds that the authorities were unable to prove that the captain's actions had been deliberately planned, and the collision did not result in injury or serious damage.
4 Shinzo Abe formed his first cabinet for one year from September 2006.
5 *Nihon Keizai Shimbun*, "Tsusho batoru, ajia sozatsu-sen [Trade Battle: Competition over Asia]." September 13, 2017.
6 Abe posted an article entitled 'Asia's Democratic Security Diamond' on the website of the non-profit Project Syndicate, and this article was released on December 27, 2012, the day following the launch of Abe's second cabinet (Suzuki 2017, 138).
7 *The Australian*, "Responses by Prime Minister Lee Hsien Loong to Questions from Australian Media." March 18, 2018.

References

Abe, Shinzo. 2006. *Utsukushii Kuni e[Towards a Beautiful Nation]*. Tokyo: Bungei Shunju.

ASEAN (Association of Southeast Asian Nations). 2019. "ASEAN Outlook on the Indo-Pacific." https://asean.org/storage/2019/06/ASEAN-Outlook-on-the-Indo-Pacific_FINAL_22062019.pdf.

Auslin, Michael. 2016. "Japan's New Realism: Abe Gets Tough." *Foreign Affairs* 95(2) (March/April): 125–134.

Cabinet Secretariat. 2010. "Higashi ajia kyodo tai koso ni kansuru kongo no torikumi ni tsuite [The Future Efforts Regarding the 'East Asian Community' Concept]." June 1. http://www.kantei.go.jp/jp/tyoukanpress/201006/__icsFiles/afieldfile/2010/06/01/koso_east_asia.pdf.

Catalinac, Amy L. 2007. "Identity Theory and Foreign Policy: Explaining Japan's Responses to the 1991 Gulf War and the 2003 US War in Iraq." *Politics & Policy* 35(1): 58–100.

Chafetz, Glenn, Hillel Abramson, and Suzette Grillot. 1996. "Role Theory and Foreign Policy: Belarussian and Ukrainian Compliance with the Nuclear Nonproliferation Regime." *Political Psychology* 17(4): 727–757.

DPJ (Democratic Party of Japan). 2009. *Minshuto Seiken Seisaku, Manifesto*. Tokyo: Minshuto Honbu. http://www.dpj.or.jp/special/manifesto2009/.

Grossman, Michael. 2005. "Role Theory and Foreign Policy Change: The Transformation of Russian Foreign Policy in the 1990s." *International Politics* 42(3): 334–351.

Hatoyama, Yukio. 2005. *Shin-Kenpo Shian [A Draft Proposal of New Constitution]*. Tokyo and Kyoto: PHP Kenkyujo.

Hatoyama, Yukio. 2009a. "Watashi no seiji tetsugaku: Sofu, ichiro ni mananda 'yuai' to iu tatakai no hatajirushi [My Political Philosophy: Fraternity, a Banner of Fight Learned from my Grandfather, Ichiro]." *Voice*, September, 132–141.

Hatoyama, Yukio. 2009b. "Japan's New Commitment to Asia: Toward the Realization of an East Asian Community." November 15. http://www.kantei.go.jp/foreign/hatoyama/statement/200911/15singapore_e.html.

Hatoyama, Yukio, and Naoto Kan. 1997. *Mineki-Ron [Theory of Private Interest]*. Tokyo and Kyoto: PHP Kenkyujo.

Hatoyama, Yukio, et al. 2014. "Hatoyama seiken to minshu-to seiji no kaishi [The Hatoyama Government and the Start of DPJ Politics]." In *Minshuto Seiken towa Nandattanoka [What the DPJ Government Left]*, edited by Jiro Yamaguchi and Koji Nakakita. Tokyo: Iwanami Shoten.

He, Kai. 2018. "Role Conceptions, Order Transition and Institutional Balancing in the Asia-Pacific: a New Theoretical Framework." *Australian Journal of International Affairs* 72(2): 92–109.

Hermann, Charles F. 1987. "Superpower Involvement with Others: Alternative Role Relationships." In *Role Theory and Foreign Policy Analysis*, edited by Stephen G. Walker. Durham, NC: Duke University Press.

Holsti, K. J. 1970. "National Role Conceptions in the Study of Foreign Policy." *International Studies Quarterly* 14(3): 233–309.

Hosoya, Yuichi. 2013. "Japan's Two Strategies for East Asia: The Evolution of Japan's Diplomatic Strategy." *Asia-Pacific Review* 20(2): 146–156.

Hughes, Christopher W. 2016. "Japan's 'Resentful Realism' and Balancing China's Rise." *Chinese Journal of International Politics* 9(2): 109–150.

Koga, Kei. 2018. "The Concept of 'Hedging' Revisited: The Case of Japan's Foreign Policy Strategy in East Asia's Power Shift." *International Studies Review* 20(4): 633–660.

Lee, John. 2016. "In Defense of the East Asian Regional Order: Explaining Japan's Newfound Interest in Southeast Asia." *Geopolitics, History, and International Relations* 8(1): 30–53.

Liff, Adam P. 2019. "Unambivalent Alignment: Japan's China Strategy, the US Alliance, and the 'Hedging' Fallacy." *International Relations of the Asia-Pacific* 19(3): 453–491.

Ministry of External Affairs (India). 2018. "Prime Minister's Keynote Address at Shangri La Dialogue (June 01, 2018)." June 1. https://www.mea.gov.in/Speeches-Statements.htm?dtl/29943/Prime+Ministers+Keynote+Address+at+Shangri+La+Dialogue+June+01+2018.

MOD (Ministry of Defence, Japan). 2013. *Heisei 25-nen Boei Hakusho [White Paper on Japan's Defence Policy, 2013]*. Tokyo: Nikkei Insatsu.

MOFA (Ministry of Foreign Affairs, Japan). 2007. "'Confluence of the Two Seas', Speech by H.E. Mr. Shinzo Abe, Prime Minister of Japan at the Parliament of the Republic of India." August 22. http://www.mofa.go.jp/region/asia-paci/pmv0708/speech-2.html.

MOFA (Ministry of Foreign Affairs, Japan). 2013. "The Eighth East Asian Summit (EAS): Summary." October 10. http://www.mofa.go.jp/mofaj/area/page3_000488.html.

MOFA (Ministry of Foreign Affairs, Japan). 2015a. "The Fifth East Asia Summit (EAS) Foreign Ministers' Meeting." August 7. http://www.mofa.go.jp/a_o/rp/page3e_000361.html.

MOFA (Ministry of Foreign Affairs, Japan). 2015b. "Inaugural US–India–Japan Trilateral Ministerial Dialogue." September 30. http://www.mofa.go.jp/s_sa/sw/page4e_000325.html.

MOFA (Ministry of Foreign Affairs, Japan). 2017. "Japan–Australia Summit Meeting." November 13. http://www.mofa.go.jp/a_o/ocn/au/page4e_000710.html.

MOFA (Ministry of Foreign Affairs, Japan). 2018. "The 13th East Asia Summit." November 15. https://www.mofa.go.jp/a_o/rp/page4e_000945.html.

Muroyama, Yoshimasa. 1997. "Reisengo no nichibei anzen hosho taisei [Japan–US Security Structure after the Cold War]." *Kokusai Seiji* 115: 126–145.

Prime Minister of Japan and His Cabinet. 2013. "'Japan Is Back', Policy Speech by Prime Minister Shinzo Abe." February 22. http://japan.kantei.go.jp/96_abe/statement/201302/22speech_e.html.

Pugliese, Giulio, and Aurelio Insisa. 2017. *Sino-Japanese Power Politics: Might, Money and Minds*. London: Palgrave Macmillan.

Rosenau, James. 1990. *Turbulence in World Politics*. Princeton, NJ: Princeton University Press.

Sahashi, Ryo. 2011. "Hatoyama Yukio Seiken ni okeru ajia gaiko [Asian Diplomacy under the Yukio Hatoyama Government]." *Mondai to Kenkyu* 40(2): 93–131.

Sakanaka, Tomohisa. 1997. "Reisen no shuen to anzen hosho seisaku no sai hensei [The End of the Cold War and the Reformulation of the Security Policy]." In *Gendai Nihon no Kokusai Seisaku [External Policy of Contemporary Japan]*, edited by Akio Watanabe. Tokyo: Uhikaku.

Singh, Bhubhindar. 2008. "Japan's Security Policy: From a Peace State to an International State." *Pacific Review* 21(3): 303–325.

Sneider, Daniel. 2011. "The New Asianism: Japanese Foreign Policy under the Democratic Party of Japan." *Asia Policy* 12(July): 111–112.

Suzuki, Yoshikatsu. 2017. *Nihon no Senryaku Gaiko [Japan's Strategic Diplomacy]*. Tokyo: Chokuma Shobo.

Teh, Benny Cheng Guan. 2011. "Japan–China Rivalry: What Role Does the East Asia Summit Play?" *Asia Pacific Viewpoint* 52(3): 347–360.

Terada, Takashi. 2006. "Forming an East Asian Community: A Site for Japan–China Power Struggles." *Japanese Studies* 26(1): 5–17.

Turnbull, Malcolm. 2018. "Speech at the University of New South Wales, Sydney—7 August 2018." August 7. https://www.malcolmturnbull.com.au/media/speech-at-the-university-of-new-south-wales-sydney-7-august-2018.

US Department of Defense. 2018. "Remarks by Secretary Mattis at Plenary Session of the 2018 Shangri-La Dialogue." June 2. https://www.defense.gov/Newsroom/Transcripts/Transcript/Article/1538599/remarks-by-secretary-mattis-at-plenary-session-of-the-2018-shangri-la-dialogue/.

Vidal, Ll López i, and Àngels Pelegrín. 2018. "Hedging against China: Japanese Strategy Towards a Rising Power." *Asian Security* 14(2): 193–211.

Walker, Stephen G., ed. 1987. *Role Theory and Foreign Policy Analysis*. Durham, NC: Duke University Press.

Yoshimatsu, Hidetaka. 2005. "ASEAN Plus Three: Political Leadership, Informality, and Regional Integration in East Asia." *European Journal of East Asian Studies* 4(2): 205–232.

Zakowski, Karol, Beata Bochorodycz, and Marcin Socha. 2017. *Japan's Foreign Policy Making: Central Government Reforms, Decision-Making Processes, and Diplomacy*. Cham, Switzerland: Springer.

8

SOUTH KOREA'S ROLE CONCEPTION AND STRATEGIES FOR MULTILATERALISM

A 'balance of role' analysis

Jaechun Kim and William Kang

Introduction

The alliance with the US has been the centerpiece of South Korea's strategy to protect and promote its security and economic interests for over six decades. Nonetheless, South Korea has become quite active in participating in the region's multilateral institutions and proposing its initiatives for multilateralism, as the nation has acquired the unique status of 'middle power' in the region. Kai He (2018) argues that a state's role conception shapes its institutional balancing strategy. The objective of this research is two-fold. First, it attempts to investigate factors that have shaped South Korea's role conception. Since the government's conception of a proper role of the state is most relevant to the making of institutional strategies, this research examines different role conceptions starting from the Rhee Syngman Government to the present Moon Jae-in Government in South Korea. In doing so, the research attempts to identify some of the more salient variables that have contributed to the shaping of role conceptions of different South Korean governments. In South Korea, four variables seemed to have made important contributions in shaping the role conceptions of different governments. Those four variables are 'political ideologies of South Korean governments,' 'South Korea's diplomatic profiles (middle power status),' 'perceived North Korean threats,' and 'order transition from the US to China.'

Second, this research traces how different role conceptions of South Korean governments have affected the nation's inter-institutional strategies for multilateralism. This research conducts in-depth case studies starting from Syngman Rhee's multilateral initiative to the current Moon Jae-in Government's inter-institutional strategy of the Northeast Asia Plus Community of Responsibility (NAPCOR). Kai He (2018) claims that the impact of role conception on institutional strategy is more salient during the period of 'order transition'—he identifies the period after the global financial crisis

(GFC) of 2008 as the starting point. By analyzing the motives, achievements, and limits of South Korea's multilateral initiatives, the research intends to investigate the way the role conceptions of South Korea have affected inter-institutional strategies for multilateralism before and after GFC. This research adopts the 'balance of roles' theoretical framework and offers a nuanced analysis of South Korea's varied inter-institutional strategies throughout its history.

The framework of South Korea's role conceptions and institutional strategies

Role theory first gained traction in the international relations literature from K. J. Holsti's (1970) work on national role conceptions (NRCs). When a state develops its NRC, the political elites are motivated by norms, national identity, and cultural values (Aggestam 2006), along with structural and material factors, which are based on the policy makers' perceptions of how the state can act in the international arena given its capabilities and opportunities (Breuning 2011). Role theory is a useful analytical tool that not only elucidates states' foreign policy behaviors, but can also incorporate different levels of analysis and other theoretical approaches (Thies and Breuning 2012). According to Kai He (2015, 2018), his 'balance of roles' framework integrates role theory with institutional balancing theory to explain how states' role conceptions shape diverse institutional strategies during an order transition period. An order defender utilizes exclusive institutional balancing to exclude a target state from a multilateral institution, while the order challenger uses inclusive institutional balancing to include a target state in a multilateral institution and exclusive institutional balancing, and the kingmaker opts for inter-institutional balancing by initiating a new institution to supplant an existing institution (He 2018).

Before investigating the way a role conception affects one country's institutional strategy, it is important to find out where that particular role conception comes from. In South Korea, four factors seemed to have played important parts in determining the role conceptions of different governments. Those four factors are 'political ideologies of South Korean governments,' 'South Korea's diplomatic profiles,' 'perceived North Korean threats,' and 'order transition from the US to China.' These four factors do not constitute the exhaustive list of variables that have determined role conceptions of South Korea, but they do appear to be the more salient variables. Furthermore, role conception comprises the two interacting mechanisms of the ego and the alter (Holsti 1970). The ego part is composed of a domestic source, where such a source could be grounded in changes in the domestic political constellations (Cantir and Kaarbo 2012), while the alter is the external source. The political ideological preferences, diplomatic profiles, and perception about North Korea fit with the ego, where the domestic sources of ideology, capabilities, and location could be comprised in the NRC (Holsti 1970, 246), while order transition is the external source that emanates from the international system structure (Holsti 1970, 246). South Korea's inter-institutional strategy as a middle power is noteworthy considering that Robert Keohane believes a middle power can 'have a system impact in a small group or through an international institution' (Keohane 1969, 296).

Formative years: 'junior partner' of the US 'hub-and-spokes' and inclusive institutional strategy

The first South Korean proposal for multilateralism came from the Rhee Syngman Government after the country gained independent statehood from Japan's colonial rule. In the aftermath of the Korean War (1950–1953), President Rhee called for the 'Pacific Union' to establish a NATO-like multilateral alliance network against communism in Asia and the Pacific. Rhee's proposal was motivated solely by the security concern of ensuring the country's survival from the communist North. President Rhee's proposal failed to attract serious attention, as the US Cold War security strategy toward Asia and the Pacific took the form of the 'hub-and-spokes' bilateral alliances rather than a multilateral one. In the 1960s, President Park Chung-hee called for an 'Asia Pacific Council (ASPAC),' the motivation of which was quite similar to Rhee's call for the Pacific Union. It was driven by the security concern to establish a network of free nations against communism. But unlike Rhee, Park thought that South Korea could play a more assertive role in creating ASPAC as a key alliance partner of the US since the Park Government made the politically difficult decision to dispatch South Korean troops in the US-led war in Vietnam (Kim 2003, 2010). As with Rhee's proposal, however, the US did not pay serious attention to Park's proposal. President Chun Doo-hwan, who came into power through a military coup after Park's assassination, proposed a 'Pacific Summit' that would regularize summits in Asia and the Pacific, but the proposal was too vague to be considered seriously by other countries.

The Presidencies of Rhee Syngman, Park Chung-hee, and Chun Doo-hwan coincided with the entire life-span of the Cold War. Communist North posed an existential threat to the South during most of the Cold War era. It made all the sense to three conservative and staunchly anti-communist governments of South Korea (i.e., Rhee, Park, and Chun) to rely heavily on the powerful Americans to secure the survival of the fledgling republic. Since South Korea's survival depended on the US role as 'order defender' in the region, the nation was more than content to play the role of 'junior security partner' to the American 'hub-and-spokes' system during the formative years. As such, South Korea's role conception of junior security partner to the US also shaped its inter-institutional strategy for multilateralism. South Korea's notion of multilateralism was to complement the ROK (Republic of Korea)–US bilateral security partnership with a multilateral security network of anti-communist countries in the region. South Korea during this period had been supportive of American institutional building efforts to establish the UN and Bretton Woods System in the world and to institute the bilateral US alliance system in the region because these efforts were seen as indispensable to order and security on the Korean peninsula. South Korea's inter-institutional strategy during this period was 'inclusive' in nature as it strove to keep the US committed to Asian and Korean peninsular affairs. Due to the nation's low diplomatic profile, however, specific proposals of South Korea during this period failed to attract the attention of the US and neighboring countries (Lee and Kwon 2015).

The demise of the Cold War order and a more proactive institutional strategy

South Korea's venture with multilateralism entered a different phase after the demise of the Cold War international order. During the 1970s and 1980s, South Korea experienced rapid economic growth, and after the 1987 presidential election, it transitioned to liberal democracy. As South Korea's diplomatic capital began to increase as a newly-industrialized country and burgeoning liberal democracy, Roh Tae-woo, who took the presidential office in 1988 after winning the popular democratic election, grew more confident of participating in the region's dialogues on multilateralism. The Roh Government proactively embraced the call for the Asia-Pacific Economic Cooperation (APEC), a multilateral institution between Asia and the Pacific countries driven in large part by economic interests. Accordingly, South Korea became a founding member of APEC and hosted the third APEC Summit in 1991. With the end of the Cold War, South Korea's diplomatic horizon expanded through the initiatives of *Nord-politik* of the Roh Government, as it normalized diplomatic relations with Russia and China in 1990 and 1992, respectively. A growing number of South Koreans began to develop positive images of the two former communist foes in the country (Chung 1991; Kim 1994). However, the Roh Government retained the role conception of junior security partner to the US. Despite the collapse of the Soviet Union, North Korea's threats remained largely intact. Roh Tae-woo was a former four-star army general whose political outlook was conservative like his predecessor and classmate of the Korea Military Academy, Chun Doo-hwan.

Kim Young-sam, the first civilian president since 1962, promoted 'internationalization' as his diplomatic slogan and attempted to broaden the scope of South Korea's diplomatic landscape. Both Roh Tae-woo and Kim Young-sam governments exerted considerable efforts to move beyond bilateral relations with the US to diversify South Korea's diplomatic portfolio and to expand the nation's diplomatic horizon, but both governments retained the 'junior partner' role conception and were explicit in accepting the role of the US as the region's 'order defender.' Kim Young-sam was a political conservative who lost his mother to North Korea's armed guerilla attack in his hometown of *Geoje* in 1960. As with Roh Tae-woo, Kim viewed the North as the archenemy of the South. The Cold War was over, but the communist North remained unaffected by the disintegration of the Cold War order. On the contrary, the first North Korea nuclear crisis erupted in the early 1990s when the American reconnaissance satellite discovered secret nuclear activities in *Yongbyon* facilities, ratcheting up tension over the Korean peninsula. To cope with the North Korean nuclear threat, Kim attempted to strengthen the alliance partnership with the US, the sole superpower after the Cold War. The enhanced diplomatic profile of South Korea indeed enabled both Roh and Kim governments to participate in the region's discussion on multilateralism more proactively, but they retained the role conception of American junior security partner. Their inter-institutional strategies for multilateralism were inclusive in that they supported broader membership, including countries in the Pacific, to reassure the American role as order defender in the region.

The era of progressive governments: South Korea's role conception as 'balancer' in the region

South Korea's view toward multilateralism took a different turn as Kim Dae-jung, a former dissident and prominent progressive politician, took the presidential office in 1998. Before the presidency of Kim Dae-jung, South Korea's vision of multilateralism had been quite broad; it was termed by academics as 'Pacifist' in that the vision supported inclusive multilateralism incorporating countries beyond the traditional Asian countries to the Pacific (Hundt and Kim 2011, 252). The arrival of the Kim Dae-jung Government signaled an abrupt departure from that tradition. The governments that preceded Kim Dae-jung had been content with South Korea's role as an American junior partner, but the Kim Dae-jung Government envisioned a diplomatic role for South Korea that was rather independent of the US. Kim's role conception of South Korea had to do with his ideological predilection as a political progressive in South Korea known for anti-Americanism, but it also had to do with the changing international environment in the region.

The inauguration of the Kim Government coincided with the period of the Asian financial crisis. The Asian financial crisis worked as a catalyst to stimulate the region's discussion on a more specific multilateral cooperation *between* Asian countries. Countries in the region came to share the understanding that a multilateral approach was indispensable to prevent another regional crisis and that the initiative should come from *within* and not from the West. For instance, Japan proposed the Asian Monetary Fund (AMF) to enhance financial stability in the Asian region (Lipscy 2003). The proposal for the AMF drew significant support from ASEAN countries and South Korea that were hit hard by the Asian financial crisis, but it was rejected by the US and IMF as they wanted to protect the existing financial institution (Lipscy 2003; Lee 2006). ASEAN + 3 (APT) states entered into the 'Chiang Mai Initiative (CMI)' that allowed currency swap agreements between ten member states of APT in 2000 (Simon 2008). CMI started as a series of bilateral swap arrangements, but it evolved into 'Chiang Mai Initiative Multilateralization (CMIM)' in 2009. The advent of APT and a series of regional initiatives that came out from it were part of an 'exclusive' institutional balancing act by Asian countries to exclude the West in efforts to institutionalize cooperation in Asia (Beeson 2003).

In the aftermath of the Asian financial crisis, the Kim Dae-jung Government realized South Korea should also play an important part in the region's discussion on multilateralism that emphasized the importance of cooperation among Asian countries. President Kim Dae-jung proposed the East Asian Vision Group (EAVG) during the APT summit meeting in 1998, and the proposal for EAVG was accepted in 1999 (He 2010). As a result, a group of intellectuals from APT countries 'was commissioned to provide a blueprint for the development of East Asian regional cooperation' (Hundt and Kim 2011, 257). To evaluate recommendations of EAVG, Kim Dae-jung proposed the East Asian Study Group (EASG) that would consist of government officials of APT countries. This proposal was also accepted by the APT, and EASG began operating in 2001. EAVG and EASG contributed to the establishment of annual summits between APT states and also laid the foundation for the East Asian Summit (EAS) (Cai 2010, 124). Kim's achievement in APT venues was a testament that South Korea, with growing diplomatic capital as an emerging middle-power country, could make important contributions to the region's discussion on institutional cooperation.

North Korea still posed a significant threat to the South, but Kim Dae-jung's threat perception toward the North began to diverge from that of the previous conservative South Korean presidents. Kim believed that North Korea's threat was manageable, if not ready to be eliminated altogether, by engaging the North Korean regime in economic and cultural exchanges. The *Sunshine* policy to engage the North Korean regime succeeded in drawing support from a significant portion of the Korean population in the early 2000s, who also grew to view North Korea as the same brethren, not as archrivals. This brotherly perception toward the North reached its peak when Kim Dae-jung met with the then North Korean leader, Kim Jong-il, for the first inter-Korean summit in 2000. The Kim Government went as far as to remove North Korea from the list of South Korea's archenemies in the 2004 Defense White Paper. Many South Koreans saw the junior Bush Administration's harsh policy response toward the North as more of a danger to the nation than North Korea (Armacost 2004; C. Lee 2004). The perception of China also improved dramatically in the early 2000s. The Kim Dae-jung Government expected that China would play an honest role of arbiter in inter-Korean relations, while the US was a waning hegemon that could get in the way of inter-Korean cooperation and ultimately Korean reunification. In 2004, about 55 percent of the members in South Korea's national assembly responded that China was the most important foreign policy partner of the nation, not the US (H. Lee 2004). It was not just the ruling elites but the country as a whole that was attracted to China, hence the term 'China fever' (Kim 2015).

Under such circumstances, Kim Dae-jung was not content with South Korea's role as a junior partner of the US. Although Kim was not explicit in rejecting South Korea's role as a junior partner of the US, it was obvious that he was looking for a more independent diplomatic role from the US. Kim's independent role conception reflected his exclusive inter-institutional strategy for multilateralism. Kim's inter-institutional strategy for multilateralism was exclusive and 'Asianist' in nature in that he supported Asian multilateralism, but not an Asia-Pacific one (Shin 2005). Kim's penchant for Asian multilateralism reflected his view that Asia needed an independent strategic space from the US. Kim's view elicited support from many Asian countries, but understandably not from the US. Kim's role conception and inter-institutional strategy created a big stir in South Korea's domestic politics as well. Many conservatives in South Korea became concerned that Kim's independent role conception and ensuing inter-institutional strategy could do irreparable damage to the nation's security relations with the US, thereby endangering the security of the nation.

South Korea's vision for multilateralism became even narrower, as another progressive politician Roh Moo-hyun succeeded Kim. Kim was interested in multilateralism for East Asia, but the scope of Roh's vision of multilateralism and South Korea's diplomatic role focused on Northeast Asia (Kim 2005). Roh said, 'the power equation in Northeast Asia will change depending on the choices we make' (Roh 2005). Unlike his predecessor, Kim Dae-jung, Roh Moo-hyun was explicit in envisioning South Korea as playing the role of 'balancer' in Northeast Asia's security affairs (Pastreich 2005). Likewise, Roh presented South Korea as a 'hub' country in Northeast Asia's economy. Roh's role conception of South Korea as 'balancer' and 'hub' in Northeast Asia shaped his inter-institutional balancing strategy, which was not well received by the US and was vehemently opposed by the conservatives in South Korea (Shin 2009). Both Kim and Roh viewed China's rise as a sign of 'order transition' in the region, which calls for a different role conception of South Korea as a 'balancer' between the US and China. To both progressive governments of South Korea, the power balance between the US and China had already shifted in favor of China to a substantial extent. As such, the US no longer occupied the central stage in the nation's grand strategy. They believed that, with the rise of China and the ensuing shift in the region's balance of power, South Korea's inter-institutional strategy would have to be more accommodating toward China's strategic concerns. But the role conception of 'balancer' was highly contested during the 2000s in South Korea, thereby confirming the observation that role contestation can become more salient during the period of perceived order transition (He 2018). The Roh Moo-hyun Government eventually had to back down from the role conception of 'balancer' to 'mediator' or 'facilitator,' but the damage was already done.

South Korea's role as 'facilitator' and the Northeast Asia Peace and Cooperation Initiative

Lee Myung-bak, who ended a ten-year-long progressive government, took great pains to portray South Korea as a responsible 'middle power' country that should contribute to the 'international community' (Lee 2016; Robertson 2017). It made sense to promote the image of South Korea as a middle power or 'Global Korea,' not just because of the growing hard power of the country, but because soft power represented by *Hallyu* (Korean cultural wave) began to have great appeal to many parts of the world. But unlike his two progressive predecessor presidents, Lee favored the inter-institutional strategy of expanding the scope of the region's multilateralism to 'Asia *and* the Pacific,' and sought to improve ties with countries outside Northeast Asia. Lee supported the proposal for ASEAN + 5 that included Australia and New Zealand to the existing ASEAN + 3. Lee also extended support for the Australian Prime Minister Kevin Rudd's call for an 'Asia-Pacific Community' (Frost 2009). Lee believed that Roh's role conception of South Korea as Northeast Asia's 'balancer' did damage to the relationship with the US. After all, despite the skeptics, the US retained its sole superpower position well into the late 2000s. Contrary to the expectations of many, the US economy quickly recovered from the subprime mortgage crisis of 2008 and the ensuing global economic recession. Subsequently, China's attempt to build the 'Beijing Consensus' to replace the 'Washington Consensus' elicited a lukewarm response from Asian countries and was countered by the 'American rebalancing' strategy toward Asia. It seemed that the US was once again poised to lead Asia. Besides, despite the 'sunshine policy' of the preceding progressive governments, North Korea's nuclear and missile threats escalated. North Korea conducted its first nuclear weapons test in 2006, two years before Lee took the presidential office, and conducted the second test in 2009, one year after his inauguration. Under such circumstances, it made more sense to the conservative Lee Government to embrace the role of 'junior partner' of the US rather than 'balancer.' President Lee accordingly took great pains to restore that relationship by seeking a broader vision of multilateralism with the US as a core member (Sohn 2015).

President Park Geun-hye also supported a broader vision of multilateralism that was open to the US and other Pacific countries. The Park Government proposed a multilateral institution known as the 'Northeast Asia Peace and Cooperation Initiative (NAPCI).' Despite the expression 'Northeast Asia' in its label, NAPCI envisioned inclusive and open regional cooperation. NAPCI's membership was initially offered to Northeast Asian countries such as South Korea, China, Russia, Japan, and Mongolia, as well as to the US, a Pacific country, in the realization that the US is an important stakeholder country in the region. North Korea was invited to participate in the NAPCI venues, but it declined the invitation. Aside from five original members, NAPCI soon extended membership invitations to ASEAN and the Pacific countries and also sought cooperative and complementary relations with existing multilateral venues such as ARF, EAS, and Six-Party Talks. In this sense, NAPCI was not an inter-institutional balancing strategy to replace or compete with the existing multilateral institutions in the region. Rather, it was an inclusive and open institutional strategy to complement the existing institutional mechanisms.

NAPCI was launched to cope with the deteriorating security environment in the region, which Park termed as 'Asia Paradox' (Pollack 2016; Lee 2017). Asia has become one of the most dynamic and prosperous regions in the world, but significant security challenges have been plaguing the region. Geopolitics has returned to the region in full force, because the region's balance of power, which had been dominated by the US, has been shifting gradually in favor of China. The shifting balance of power from the US to China has fostered strategic uncertainties in this very volatile region of the world. In 2013, President Xi Jinping suggested that the Sino-US relations should be rooted in a 'New Type of Great Power Relations,' the Obama Administration, from its part, declared the strategy of 'Rebalancing toward Asia,' reorganizing the importance of Asia in prioritizing US foreign policy agendas (Saunders 2013; Campbell 2016). Japan's foreign and security policy has become increasingly militant and aggressive. In addition, Russia's foreign relations with the US have been under strain (Cossa 2015). It is paradoxical for economically interdependent countries to maintain such belligerent security policies toward each other, hence the term 'Asia Paradox.'

South Korea has grown to be an important middle-power country in the world, but President Park realized that South Korea's status as 'geopolitical lightweight' in the region's power dynamics makes it difficult to play the role of 'balancer' in Northeast Asia. More importantly, the US interpreted Roh Moo-hyun's conception of the 'balancer' role as an act of balancing *against* the US and leaning toward the China bandwagon (Kang 2009; Zhao 2015). Therefore, the Park Government rejected South Korea's role as 'balancer'; rather, it embraced the role of 'facilitator' or 'mediator' that could initiate open and inclusive multilateralism in discussing the region's security affairs. Although Park was a political conservative, Park's role conception of South Korea as 'facilitator' was a meaningful departure from the 'junior partner' role conception of the previous conservative governments. Although there is no denying that, during the presidency of Park Geun-hye, the US occupied the central place in South Korea's foreign and security policies, it is worth noting that President Park adopted a more balanced approach to the US and China in comparison to her conservative predecessors (Kim 2016). At the risk of estranging relations with the US, Park attended China's 70th war victory ceremony, joined the Asian Infrastructure Investment Bank (AIIB), and expressed support for the Belt and Road Initiative (BRI). She even refused the American proposal to discuss the deployment of the Terminal High Altitude Area Defense (THAAD) for fear of angering the Chinese Government. A series of Park's peace gestures toward China raised many eyebrows in the US. When the North conducted the fourth nuclear testing in January 2016, Park Geun-hye finally called it quits with her strategic flirtation with China and made an abrupt decision to deploy THAAD, which prompted China's petty retaliatory measures against South Korea. Although Park was fairly accommodating toward China's strategic concerns, the Park Government was critical of Shanghai Cooperation Organization (SCO) from the very onset for fear that SCO would destabilize the US 'hub-and-spokes' system in the region.

President Park figured that, given its historical record as a 'non-aggressor' and its peculiar status as a middle power without hegemonic ambition, South Korea seemed to be well suited to play the role of facilitator or mediator. With escalating Sino-US rivalry, South Korea has been increasingly asked by the two great powers to pick a side. NAPCI was an inter-institutional balancing strategy to cope with the volatilities associated with the escalating geopolitical rivalry in the region in this era of order transition. The introduction of NAPCI was expected to bring about changes in perception and attitudes toward the pursuit of cooperation, as well as common awareness of multilateral security cooperation by identifying sources of shared conflicts and threats (MOFA 2016, 4–5). To induce cooperation in the Asian region, NAPCI intended to take a gradual path that was agreeable to all participating countries, allowing them to experience the benefits of the voluntary cooperation (MOFA 2016, 8). NAPCI proposed that the countries in the region cooperate on non-traditional security issues first rather than tackling seemingly intractable traditional security issues such as territorial disputes or North Korean nuclear problems (Smith 2010). Accordingly, agendas for NAPCI were not overly demanding. The idea was that, by cooperating on such non-traditional security issues as environmental degradation, new forms of epidemics, disaster reliefs, anti-drug and human trafficking, anti-piracy, anti-terrorism, and so forth, countries would cultivate the habit of cooperation (MOFA 2016). Continuous cooperation on resolving non-traditional security issues was expected to generate trust and other-regarding norms among member states, which in turn would prove instrumental in coping with more intractable traditional security issues (Katsumata 2010). Critics later claimed that the neo-functionalist bottom-up approach should be complemented by the top-down approach, noting that mobilizing the political will of the top leadership is critical in moving NAPCI forward.

Roh Moo-hyun presented South Korea's role as 'balancer' in Northeast Asia's security affairs and 'hub' in Northeast Asia's economy, but he did not propose to establish a regional institution where South Korea could play such pivotal roles. The EAVG and EASG, which Kim proposed, laid the basis for a regular summit between APT and later EAS, but EAVG and EASG were to strengthen APT and operated on an ad hoc basis. In comparison, NAPCI was a more ambitious plan to establish an overarching multilateral institution for the region's security dialogues and cooperation. NAPCI succeeded in eliciting official support from 29 countries and eight multilateral bodies and provided several venues where the representatives of countries in the region gathered together to cooperate on non-traditional security issues. Based on the gradualist approach from the non-traditional security issue, the NAPCI has achieved progress in high-level intergovernmental meetings for consecutive years since 2014 (MOFA 2016, 13). Nonetheless, the institutionalization of the NAPCI initiatives was not successful.

First, despite the official pledge to support NAPCI, stakeholder countries in the region remained skeptical. The US was the most skeptical of NAPCI. The US was uncertain about the 'ownership' of NAPCI; it was worried that, if the institutionalization of NAPCI moved forward in earnest, China might take the initiative, in which case the US role as an order defender could become marginalized. The Park Government went to great lengths to explain to the US how NAPCI and the US 'Asia rebalancing' strategy could be complementary, but with limited success. China and Japan welcomed the NAPCI proposal in principle but doubted whether NAPCI would generate a positive spillover effect on hard security issues (Goh 2004). Second, the Park Government spent most of its foreign policy capital in dealing with the North Korean nuclear and missile problems. The *trustpolitik* of Park Geun-hye toward North Korea to build trust was met by the North's testing of nuclear weapons three times during her short-lived presidency. Third, a political scandal that cost the presidency of Park also adversely affected most foreign policy initiatives of the Park Government, including NAPCI.

The Moon Jae-in Government: 'Northeast Asia Plus Community of Responsibility' and the Indo-Pacific dilemma

After the impeachment of Park Geun-hye in December 2016, South Korea held a snap presidential election in May 2017 that inaugurated the progressive Moon Jae-in

Government. Moon Jae-in was a former chief of staff for president Roh Moo-hyun and the leader of a very cohesive progressive 'pro-Roh' faction in South Korean politics. Moon had been the closest friend and political ally of Roh since the early 1980s, when they fought concertedly against the Chun Doo-hwan military regime, until 2009 when Roh committed suicide; it was quite natural to associate the Moon Government with that of Roh's. In fact, many people suspected that the Moon Government would turn out to be the 'Roh Government 2.0' (Choe 2017a; Choi and Kim 2017). In making foreign and security policies, there was an expectation that the Moon Government would emulate the Roh Government. During an interview with the *New York Times*, Moon was reported to have said that South Korea should be able to say 'no' to the US (Choe 2017b). He was also reported to have said that he hoped to visit North Korea first before the US (Choe and Motoko 2017). Since taking office, Moon has taken great pains to mend fences with Beijing by delaying the deployment of THAAD, the decision made by the previous Park Government. Escalation of North Korean nuclear and missile threats forced the Moon Government to complete the 'temporary' deployment of one battery of THAAD in September 2017. But to improve the deteriorated relations with China, the Moon Government went as far as to make three public promises to Beijing in October 2017 that South Korea would not deploy another battery of THAAD, would not participate in the American Missile Defense (MD), and would refuse the trilateral security alliance between South Korea, the US, and Japan. The Moon Government also made a series of peace overtures toward the North in the hope that its friendly gesture would reinstate the now-defunct 'sunshine' engagement policy toward the North.

Much to the disappointment of the Moon Government, South Korea's call for rapprochement fell on deaf ears in North Korea. North Korea reciprocated Moon's peace gesture with multiple testing of scud and *Hwasong* ballistic missiles, eventually testing the hydrogen bomb (or at least a boosted fission bomb) in 2017. Escalation of North Korean threats forced President Moon to visit the US first, not North Korea. But since nuclear negotiation with the North began in early 2018, the Moon Government claimed that South Korea, along with the North, should take the driver's seat in Korean peninsular affairs. The Moon Government has exerted good faith efforts to reinforce the relationship with the Trump Administration, but at the same time, it began to mention 'balanced' foreign relations, which is seen by conservatives as a threat to the country's security alliance with the US. The US and conservatives in South Korea are allergic to 'balancer' or 'balanced' foreign relations, which reminds them of the Roh Moo-hyun Government's role conception of South Korea as a balancer in Northeast Asia.

During the presidential campaign period, Moon proposed the 'Northeast Asia Plus Community of Responsibility (NAPCOR)' as South Korea's inter-institutional strategy for multilateralism. The Moon Government has clarified that NAPCOR is not to supplant NAPCI, but to continue and expand from it. Arguably, NAPCOR comprises NAPCI, New Nord-politik, and New Sud-politik (J. Kim 2017). The New Nord-politik is expected to offer the possibility of inter-Korean reconciliation and to create a synergy effect with China's BRI. The New Sud-politik is to broaden South

Korea's diplomatic horizon to ASEAN and further to India, but most of NAPCOR initiatives are at a deadlock, as all the NAPCI initiatives came to a halt. On the surface, NAPCOR appears to be an inclusive inter-institutional strategy, but the role of the US appears relatively insignificant in NAPCOR. So far, the Moon Government has been more enthusiastic about Nord-politik than Sud-politik. It established the Presidential Committee on Northern Economic Cooperation and appointed a minister-level president for the Committee. The Moon Government had not been active in reaching out to India for fear of estranging relations with China. Moon's enthusiasm with Nord-politik reflects his desire to connect South Korea to North Korea, as well as China and Russia.

The Indo-Pacific is an overarching regional concept, as well as a new US strategy toward Asia, that has been on the rise in recent years (Bhatia and Vijay 2014; Medcalf 2014), but the Moon Government has expressed qualms about this emerging regional concept and the Indo-Pacific strategy, and it has been hesitant to embrace them. In November 2017, President Trump recommended to President Moon Jae-in that the ROK–US alliance should be an indispensable entity in the Indo-Pacific strategy and that South Korea should participate in this strategic framework. The Moon Government was taken aback by Trump's recommendation. The Ministry of Foreign Affairs (MOFA) welcomed the strategy claiming that it was compatible with South Korea's strategy of diversifying foreign relations, but the MOFA's response met a rebuff by the Blue House. The Blue House responded that the Indo-Pacific is a Japanese strategic initiative that includes the Quadrilateral Security Dialogue members of Japan, the US, Australia, and India, where it would leave South Korea in the sidelines. A Blue House official later confirmed during the Trump–Moon summit that South Korea declined to participate in the Indo-Pacific strategy, stating that it was 'President Trump' who 'highlighted that the ROK–US alliance remains a linchpin for security, stability, and prosperity in the Indo-Pacific,' not both Trump and Moon (Kim 2018). Only recently has the Moon Government allayed the anxiety of the US, making a public statement that the Sud-politik and Indo-Pacific strategy share commonalities in reaching out to and engaging Southeast Asia.

Professor Moon Chung-in is a top adviser to President Moon Jae-in regarding foreign relations and national security. It is believed that Professor Moon exerts great influence on President Moon's foreign and security strategies. In an interview with the *Atlantic*, Professor Moon expressed his views about the ROK–US alliance and the region's multilateral institutions. He is reported to have said the following:

> [Alliances are a] very unnatural state of international relations … for me, the best thing is to really get rid of alliance … in the short to medium term, it might be inevitable for us to rely on the alliance … But in the longer term, I personally hope that we can make a transformation from an alliance system into some form of a multilateral security cooperation regime. (Friedman 2018)

He also mentioned that if South Korea and North Korea sign a peace treaty, then an alliance is no longer justified on the Korean peninsula. Professor Moon's remarks suggest that the Moon Government is not content with the US as order defender in the region and believes a multilateral institution should be an *alternative* to the alliance rather than a supplement to it. President Moon's decision to withdraw from GSOMIA (General Security of Military Information Agreement) with Japan also testifies that the Moon Government is not satisfied with the traditional role that South Korea played in the region. In case North Korean threats scale down, and China's status improves in South Korea, it should not come as a surprise for the Moon Government's role conception to converge with that of the Roh Government.

The link between role conception and inter-institutional strategy

The case analyses suggest that role conception has been an important factor driving South Korea's inter-institutional strategy for multilateralism. It seems that, by and large, four factors have affected South Korea's role conception (Figure 1). During most of the Cold War era, when North Korea posed an existential threat to the South, South Korean governments embraced the US 'junior partner' role identity that largely determined the inter-institutional strategy of reassuring the US of its role as 'order defender' in the region's security affairs. South Korea's increasingly enhanced diplomatic profile and the unique middle power status that the nation obtained toward the turn of the 20th century have enabled the nation to envision a more proactive diplomatic role in regional affairs (K'ng and Hinata-Yamaguchi 2011). The political ideological predilection of the South Korea governments mattered as well. The conservative governments have tended to envision their roles as the US' 'junior security partner' or 'facilitator' (in the case of the Park Geun-hye Government), whereas progressive governments have preferred their role identities as 'balancer.' As a result, South Korea's vision for multilateralism has oscillated from broader multilateralism with inclusive membership to a narrower version with limited membership. Conservative governments have tended to adopt an inter-institutional strategy to embrace the US' role as order defender, whereas progressive governments have tended to view multilateralism as a possible alternative to bilateral relations with the US (Table 8.1).

Oscillation of role conceptions and ensuing inter-institutional strategies from conservative to progressive governments have been visible in the region's other middle power countries such as Australia and Japan. In Australia, while Kevin Rudd had been actively plunging himself into the task of promoting the Asia Pacific Community (APC), John Howard had been content with the role of the US' 'deputy sheriff.' In Japan, Yukio Hatoyama envisioned East Asian Community (EAC) for Asian countries, while some media has criticized Shinzo Abe for trying to be Trump's poodle (H. Kim 2017). In the case of South Korea, role contestation has been more conspicuous because of the North Korea factor and the nation's geographical proximity to China. Measurements for the four variables in Table 8.1 are admittedly arbitrary to a certain extent, but a simplification of measurements highlights the salience of such categories.

Conclusion: South Korea's strategy for multilateralism in the future

As a middle power country, South Korea thinks that it could take the lead in the region's discussion on multilateralism, but it also understands that its inherent limitation as a 'geopolitical lightweight' in the region's power dynamics makes it difficult to do so, and its future strategy for multilateralism will remain modest in its objective. Consequently, South Korean inter-institutional strategies for multilateralism have sought close cooperation with the region's existing multilateral institutions. But South Korea also realizes that with the return of geopolitics and a growing rivalry between great powers in the region, the nation's strategic interests would be better protected under the multilateral institutional security frameworks, and by it taking a more active part in the region's discussion on multilateralism. In order not to be marginalized in the region's geopolitical games, South Korea has continuously exerted efforts to rein in the uneasy nature of 'great power politics' within the framework of inter-institutional balancing, as South Korea ventured with NAPCI to complement other existing multilateral institutions, not to *supplant* them. At surface level, NAPCOR appears to be an inclusive inter-institutional strategy, but the role of the US appears relatively negligible as the Moon Government is unenthusiastic about the Indo-Pacific strategy. If the balance of power shifts further in favor of China and the North Korean threat diminishes, South Korea may as well seek a more exclusive inter-institutional balancing strategy that would be compliant with China's strategic concerns.

References

Aggestam, Lisbeth. 2006. "Role Theory and European Foreign Policy: A Framework of Analysis." In *The European Union's Roles in International Politics: Concepts and Analysis*, edited by Ole Elgstrom and Michael Smith, 11–29. London: Routledge.

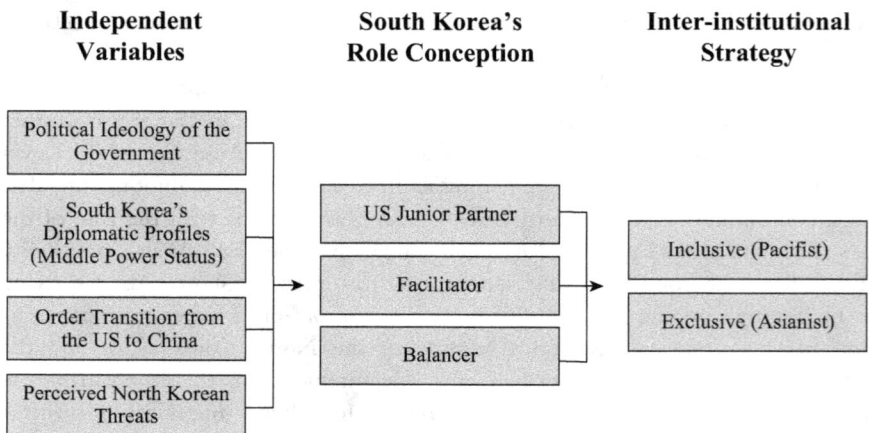

FIGURE 8.1 Link between the role conception and inter-institutional strategy

TABLE 8.1 Inter-institutional strategies of South Korean governments

Government	Political ideology	South Korea's diplomatic profiles (middle power status)	Order transition (the US →China)	Perceived North Korean threats	Role conception	Inter-institutional strategy
Rhee Syngman (1948–1960)	Conservative	Low	X	High	US Junior Partner	Inclusive
Park Chung-hee (1962–1979)	Conservative	Low	X	High	US Junior Partner	Inclusive
Chun Doo-hwan (1980–1988)	Conservative	Low	X	High	US Junior Partner	Inclusive
Roh Tae-woo (1988–1993)	Conservative	Increasing	X	High	US Junior Partner	Inclusive
Kim Young-sam (1993–1998)	Conservative	Increasing	△	High	US Junior Partner	Inclusive
Kim Dae-jung (1998–2003)	Progressive	Increasing	△	Low	Balancer	Exclusive
Roh Moo-hyun (2003–2008)	Progressive	Increasing	△	Low	Balancer	Exclusive
Lee Myung-bak (2008–2013)	Conservative	Increased	△	High	US Junior Partner	Inclusive
Park Geun-hye (2013–2016)	Conservative	Increased	O	High	Facilitator	Inclusive
Moon Jae-in (2017–)	Progressive	Increased	O	High	Balancer (?)	Inclusive (?)

Armacost, Michael H. 2004. "The Future of America's Alliances in Northeast Asia." In *The Future of America's Alliances in Northeast Asia*, edited by Michael H. Armacost and Daniel I. Okimoto, 16–17. Washington, DC: Asia-Pacific Research Center.

Beeson, Mark. 2003. "ASEAN Plus Three and the Rise of Reactional Regionalism." *Contemporary Southeast Asia: A Journal of International and Strategic Affairs* 25(2): 251–268.

Bhatia, Rajiv K., and Sakhuja Vijay. 2014. *Indo Pacific Region: Political and Strategic Prospects*. New Delhi: Publication of Indian Council of World Affairs.

Breuning, Marijke. 2011. "Role Research: Genesis and Blind Spots." In *Role Theory in International Relations: Approaches and Analyses*, edited by Sebastian Harnisch, Cornelia Frank, and Hanns W. Maull, 16–35. London: Routledge.

Cai, Kevin G. 2010. *The Politics of Economic Regionalism Explaining Regional Economic Integration in East Asia*. Basingstoke: Palgrave Macmillan.

Campbell, Kurt M. 2016. *The Pivot: The Future of American Statecraft in Asia*. New York: Hachette.

Cantir, Cristian, and Juliet Kaarbo. 2012. "Contested Roles and Domestic Politics: Reflections on Role Theory in Foreign Policy Analysis and IR Theory." *Foreign Policy Analysis* 8(1): 5–24.

Choe, Sang Hun. 2017a. "Allies for 67 Years, US and South Korea Split Over North Korea." *New York Times*, September 4. http://www.nytimes.com/2017/09/04/world/asia north-korea-nuclear-south-us-alliance.html.

Choe, Sang Hun. 2017b. "Ouster of South Korean President Could Return Liberals to Power." *The New York Times*, March 10. https://www.nytimes.com/2017/03/10/world/asia/south-korea-liberals-impeachment.html.

Choe, Sang Hun, and Rich Motoko. 2017. "South Korean Leader Boxed in as Trump Threatens North Korea." *The New York Times*, November 3. https://www.nytimes.com/2017/11/03/world/asia/south-korea-trump-nuclear.html.

Choi, Kang, and James Kim. 2017. "The ROK–US Summit and Prospective Problems: Half Success and its Beginning." Issue Brief. Seoul: The ASAN Institute for Policy Studies.

Chung, Tae Dong. 1991. "Korea's Nordpolitik: Achievements and Prospects." *Asian Perspective* 15(2): 149–178.

Cossa, Ralph A. 2015. "Regional Overview: The Rebalance Picks up Steam." *Comparative Connections* 17(2): 1–16.

Friedman, Uri. 2018. "A Top Advisor to the South Korean President Questions the U.S. Alliance." *The Atlantic*, May 17. https://www.theatlantic.com/international/archive/2018/05/moon-south-korea-us-alliance/560501/.

Frost, Frank. 2009. "Australia's Proposal for an 'Asia Pacific Community': Issues and Prospects." Research Paper. Department of Parliamentary Services, Parliament of Australia, Canberra.

Goh, Evelyn. 2004. "The ASEAN Regional Forum in United States East Asian Strategy." *The Pacific Review* 17(1): 47–69.

He, Baogang. 2010. "East Asian Ideas of Regionalism: A Normative Critique." *Australian Journal of International Affairs* 58(1): 105–125.

He, Kai. 2015. "Contested Regional Orders and Institutional Balancing in the Asia Pacific." *International Politics* 52(2): 208–222.

He, Kai. 2018. "Role Conceptions, Order Transition and Institutional Balancing in the Asia-Pacific: A New Theoretical Framework." *Australian Journal of International Affairs* 72(2): 92–109.

Holsti, K. J. 1970. "National Role Conceptions in the Study of Foreign Policy." *International Studies Quarterly* 14(3): 233–309.

Hundt, David, and Jaechun Kim. 2011. "Competing Notions of Regionalism in South Korean Politics." *Japanese Journal of Political Science* 12(2): 251–266.

K'ng, Yee Pei, and Ryo Hinata-Yamaguchi. 2011. "South Korea as a Rising Middle Power: The Leading Shrimp amongst Whales." Paper presented at the International Studies Association, Montreal, Quebec, Canada, March 16.

Kang, David C. 2009. "Between Balancing and Bandwagoning: South Korea's Response to China." *Journal of East Asian Studies* 9(1): 1–28.

Katsumata, Hiro. 2010. *ASEAN's Cooperative Security Enterprise: Norms and Interests in the ASEAN Regional Forum*. Basingstoke: Springer.

Keohane, Robert O. 1969. "Liliputians' Dilemmas: Small States in International Politics." *International Organization* 23(2): 291–310.

Kim, Choong Nam. 2005. "The Roh Moo Hyun Government's Policy Toward North Korea." East-West Center Working Papers, Honolulu.

Kim, Hak Joon. 1994. "The Establishment of South Korean–Chinese Diplomatic Relations: A South Korean Perspective." *Journal of Northeast Asian Studies* 13(2): 31–48.

Kim, Hyun-ki. 2017. "A Left Out Feeling." *Joong Ang Ilbo*, October 17.

Kim, Hyung-A. 2003. *Korea's Development under Park Chung Hee*. London: Routledge.

Kim, Jaechun. 2015. "Alliance Adjustment in the Post-Cold War Era: Convergence of Strategic Perceptions and Revitalization of the ROK–US Alliance." *Pacific Focus* 30(1): 33–58.

Kim, Jaechun. 2018. "South Korea's Free and Open Indo-Pacific Dilemma." *The Diplomat*, April 27. https://thediplomat.com/2018/05/south-koreas-free-and-open-indo-pacific-dilemma.

Kim, Joon Hyung. 2017. "The Moon Administration's Multilateral Regional Diplomacy: An Initiative of Northeast Asia Plus Community of Responsibility." *Korea Institute for Defense Analyses* 165: 1–4.

Kim, Kee Seok. 2010. "How Has Korea Imagined Its Region? Asia-Pacific, Northeast Asia, and East Asia." *The Korean Journal of International Relations* 50(3): 73–110.

Kim, Sung-mi. 2016. "South Korea's Middle-Power Diplomacy: Changes and Challenges." Asia Programme Research Paper, Chatham House, London.

Lee, Chung Min. 2004. "Domestic Politics and Changing Contours of the ROK–US Alliance: The End of the Status Quo." In *The Future of America's Alliances in Northeast Asia*, edited by Michael H. Armacost, and Daniel I. Okimoto, 199–200. Palo Alto, CA: Stanford University Press.

Lee, Chung Min. 2017. "Asia's New Long March: Bottling Conflicts and Managing Political Turbulences." *The Pacific Review* 30(6): 843–856.

Lee, Hoon. 2004. "Special Feature Series Part 1: Dangseonja eenyum-goa seonghyang [The Political Ideology and Orientation of the Elected]." *Donga Ilbo*, April 16. http://news.donga.com/3//20040416/8051641/1.

Lee, Kyung Suk. 2016. "New Approach of South Korea's Middle Power Diplomacy: Focusing on Global Agenda Setting." *Global Politics Review* 2(2): 40–57.

Lee, Shin-wha, and Bo Ram Kwon. 2015. "The Pursuit of Multilateral Security Cooperation Amidst Growing Political and Economic Divides in Northeast Asia." *The Korean Journal of International Studies* 13(2): 353–381.

Lee, Yong Wook. 2006. "Japan and the Asian Monetary Fund: An Identity–Intention Approach." *International Studies Quarterly* 50(2): 339–366.

Lipscy, Phillip Y. 2003. "Japan's Asian Monetary Fund Proposal." *Journal of East Asian Affairs* 3(1): 93–104.

Medcalf, Rory. 2014. "In Defense of the Indo-Pacific: Australia's New Strategic Map." *Australian Journal of International Affairs* 68(4): 470–483.

MOFA (Ministry of Foreign Affairs, South Korea). 2016. *Northeast Asia Peace and Cooperation Initiative*. Policy Planning and Coordination Division of the Ministry of Foreign Affairs, Seoul.

Pastreich, Emanuel. 2005. "The Balancer: Roh Moo-hyun's Vision of Korean Politics and the Future of Northeast Asia." *The Asia-Pacific Journal* 3(8): 1–14.

Pollack, Jonathan D. 2016. "Order at Risk: Japan, Korea and the Northeast Asian Paradox." Asia Working Group Paper5. Brookings Institution, Washington, DC.

Robertson, Jeffrey. 2017. "Middle Power Definitions: Confusion Reigns Supreme." *Australian Journal of International Affairs* 71(4): 355–370.

Roh, Moo-hyun. 2005. "Address at the 40th Commencement and Commisioning Ceremony of the Korea Third Military Academy." *Cheong Wa Dae Presidential Archive*, March 1.

Saunders, Phillip C. 2013. "The Rebalance to Asia: US–China Relations and Regional Security." *Strategic Forum* 281: 1–16.

Shin, Gi Wook. 2005. "Asianism in Korea's Politics of Identity." *Inter-Asia Cultural Studies* 6 (4): 616–630.

Shin, Soon Ok. 2009. "A Failed 'Regional Balancer': South Korea's Self-Promoted Middle Power Identity." Paper presented at the International Studies Association, New York City, NY, USA, February 15.

Simon, Sheldon. 2008. "ASEAN and Multilateralism: The Long, Bumpy Road to Community." *Contemporary Southeast Asia: A Journal of International and Strategic Affairs* 30(2): 264–292.

Smith, Sheila A. 2010. "New Impulses for Security Cooperation in Northeast Asia." Paper, International Institutions and Global Governance Program. Council on Foreign Relations, New York.

Sohn, Yul. 2015. "Searching for a New Identity: South Korea's Middle Power Diplomacy." *FRIDE Policy Brief* 212: 1–6.

Thies, Cameron G., and Marijke Breuning. 2012. "Integrating Foreign Policy Analysis and International Relations through Role Theory." *Foreign Policy Analysis* 8(1): 1–4.

Zhao, Suisheng. 2015. "A New Model of Big Power Relations? China–US Strategic Rivalry and Balance of Power in the Asia–Pacific." *Journal of Contemporary China* 24(93): 377–397.

9

MIKTA

A case study of Australian multilateralism

Melissa Conley Tyler[1]

Kai He's 'balance of roles' argument proposes that a new wave of multilateralism in Asia has emerged: contested multilateralism 2.0 (He, Chapter 1, this volume). This new multilateralism is characterized by states engaging in institutional balancing strategies in accordance with their perceived role identity as an order defender, an order challenger or a kingmaker. According to He's account, Australia—which he sees as a kingmaker—should be adopting inter-institutional balancing strategies in its multilateral behavior. He gives the example of former Australian Prime Minister Kevin Rudd's 2009 proposal for an Asia Pacific community where Australia tried to supplant the existing dominance of the Association of Southeast Asian Nations (ASEAN) institutions in the regional order.

This chapter looks at a case study of a recent multilateral initiative—MIKTA—to determine whether it fits within this paradigm. In He's model, one would expect to see MIKTA used to challenge existing institutions and any increased influence used to provide support for either the US or China. By contrast, if MIKTA does not fit this framework, it suggests that this is not the only impetus for institution building and that other role orientations may be at play.

First, a detailed case study of MIKTA will be provided. Brought to life in late 2013, MIKTA is a fairly recent institution. As such, both knowledge and academic literature on it is still nascent, though growing. A detailed summary of MIKTA is provided for increased awareness of MIKTA's aims and what it has done to date. Second, Australia's approach to foreign policy will be analyzed through the lens of role theory. Because He's theory uses a role identity, it is appropriate to compare it with other potential role orientations for Australian foreign policy. This enables a conclusion to be reached on whether Australia is acting as a kingmaker through MIKTA, or if instead it is more in line with Australia's traditional middle power mode.

MIKTA

What is MIKTA?

MIKTA is an acronym for the grouping of Mexico, Indonesia, Korea, Turkey and Australia. This grouping was created on the sidelines of the September 2013 UN General Assembly meeting in New York and has been meeting at foreign minister, senior officials and other levels since then.

At first glance the nature of the grouping is not obvious: there is no shared language, geography or culture and no strong historical ties. The five do not all fit into the conventional conception of middle powers (Jeong 2019; Lee and Park 2017). Instead the MIKTA countries define themselves as 'democracies that benefit from open economies with robust growth rates and a significant level of economic power' (MIKTA 2015). (Whether this is still accurate is debatable.) They see themselves as strategically located and strongly linked to their surrounding regions in all aspects. These are all assets which provide the grouping a strong foundation (Sukma 2013).

Most importantly, the MIKTA countries define themselves as 'like-minded on many of the global challenges of our time' (MIKTA 2015), which appears to be borne out by MIKTA diplomats who report a shared assumption that the member countries are like-minded and share similar viewpoints on world affairs (Kim, Haug and Rimmer 2018, 479).

All of the MIKTA nations are G20 members, which is where their relationship is rooted.

Why has MIKTA been created?

MIKTA is a direct analogue to the BRICS grouping: Brazil, Russia, India, China and South Africa (McDonald-Seaton and Conley Tyler 2014). Made up of five of the seven G20 nations belonging to neither the BRICS nor the G7, MIKTA is sometimes explicitly referred to as a 'middle power' grouping (Colakoglu 2017) although others dislike this moniker (Bergin 2013). As Alex Oliver suggests, 'Calling such a group "middle powers" is beside the point. It's what they do, not what they're called, that counts' (Oliver 2013).

MIKTA can be seen as a vehicle to increase its members' influence in the international sphere through a group of their own. MIKTA nations are able to pool their resources, exchange points of view, consult and promote coordination on issues of common interest. They also possess the potential to establish a block of 'swing vote shareholders' within international fora (Toloraya 2013). Together, MIKTA members ought to have the potential for more serious impact in international fora than they would have alone (Conley Tyler and McDonald-Seaton 2014). In the words of the MIKTA vision statement, 'Working together, MIKTA can play a constructive role in the international agenda and exert greater influence' (MIKTA 2015).

Recent research summarizing 70 interviews with MIKTA diplomats shows that MIKTA is seen as a low-cost toolkit to diversify traditional diplomatic channels and increase global visibility in various multilateral forums (Kim et al. 2018, 480). Importantly, there's no indication from these interviews that forming MIKTA was seen as a way of siding with one or another great power. As an interviewed Turkish diplomat put it, there was 'no compelling need for MIKTA to appear when it did …. MIKTA was not created in the context of hostility or an urgent problem' (Kim et al. 2018, 478). Instead it is a value-for-money minilateral mechanism that provides capacity building and network-sharing benefits at a limited cost (Kim et al. 2018, 480).

While not determining any formal program, the Joint Communiqués released by MIKTA identify many areas for increased collective effort including counter-terrorism, resisting protectionism, aiding effectiveness, the post-2015 development agenda, cyberspace security, climate change, human rights and migration (MIKTA 2019). On these issues MIKTA can act as a counter-balance to potential domination by G7 and BRICS, and therefore as an attempt to increase its member nations' international influence. In the 2014 Joint Communiqué, MIKTA foreign ministers noted that 'the gradual transformation of the international system opens a window of opportunity for their countries to further develop their constructive and conciliatory role in tackling pressing international issues' (MIKTA 2019). Most recently MIKTA has described itself 'as a bridge builder and consensus-maker … working to facilitate dialogue and constructively contribute to debate in a range of forums' (Aspe et al. 2018).

What has MIKTA achieved so far?

MIKTA has not set itself overly ambitious goals; its focus has been on regular and consistent engagement at both foreign minister level and below. When setting up MIKTA, member countries did not frame it as a mechanism to address a specific problem, rather as a platform for a wide range of issue areas; this means there have been no pressing expectations attached to it (Kim et al. 2018). In celebrating MIKTA's fifth anniversary in September 2018, foreign ministers focused more on the success of the process rather than on concrete achievements:

> We have made strong progress in advancing MIKTA's objectives over the past five years. Our achievements include increasing mutual understanding, deepening bilateral ties and finding common ground for cooperation. We have held regular consultations aimed at advancing multilateral discussions on common issues and have successfully bridged polarized policy positions with creative solutions to global and regional challenges. (MIKTA 2019)

Since its inception, MIKTA has convened 15 meetings at foreign minister level, four for senior officials (including via videoconference), four consultations for speakers of parliament and one meeting of ministers responsible for trade (MIKTA 2019). It has also released 42 joint statements on issues such as disaster relief, climate change, development, North Korean nuclear testing, terrorism, human rights, gender equality, and good governance (MIKTA 2019). Instead of aiming to focus on one particular issue area, MIKTA has looked to increase its role in global governance to give the grouping greater clout in the international community.

MIKTA has been able to engage outside diplomatic channels including with academics, the private sector and youth. During Australia's term as chair in 2016 for example, MIKTA held several dialogues on issues including: counter-terrorism and security, trade and economy, gender equality, goods governance, sustainable development, and international energy governance (DFAT 2016).

MIKTA has hosted exchanges for young professionals, journalists and diplomats and has created an academic network (MIKTA 2019). It has held workshops on issues such as trade and investment, e-commerce, development cooperation, disaster risk reduction, narcotic drug abuse, policy planning, and gas security. In addition to this, it has also hosted outreach events including an International Women's Day event in Canberra, an interfaith and intercultural dialogue in Yogyakarta and briefings in Brussels.

What can MIKTA achieve?

It can be argued that MIKTA's relatively low profile in its initial years is linked to the lack of a specific focus. For example, Andrew Carr (2015) has characterized MIKTA as 'cooperating without a purpose.'

Andrew Cooper illustrates this point through IBSA: the India, Brazil and South Africa Dialogue Forum. He argues that after IBSA's initial purpose—securing permanent UN Security Council membership—failed to materialize, the group's momentum slowed down and they have not met at the leaders' level since 2011 (2015, 99). MIKTA may face a similar scenario of slowing momentum (Green 2019). Cooper suggests that, in order to avoid this outcome, MIKTA nations must meet at the leader level in order to amplify their role and to ensure that their presence in the hub of global governance is maintained (Cooper 2015, 95). To date MIKTA has rejected this idea. MIKTA sees itself as more of a tool of diplomacy as opposed to a coalition of nations centered on themselves; as such it believes that it is appropriately centered at the foreign ministry level (Flake and Wang 2017, 28.)

MIKTA can arguably best be understood through soft power and 'the practice of a broader model of international statecraft' (Douglas and Flake 2014, 5). From Mexico's perspective, a great proportion of the project is around public diplomacy and soft power (Rivas 2018, 797).

There is no lack of suggestions as to how MIKTA can achieve its goals including: making a common stand on important international issues, instituting common agencies, offering services for dispute mediation, sharing lessons with developing countries and acting together to build global governance (Conley Tyler 2016).

One possible role for MIKTA is to focus on creating solutions for shared problems and leveraging its soft power to encourage others to adopt these solutions. MIKTA has made efforts to do exactly that, such as at the UN in May 2017 on the

2030 Agenda for Sustainable Development (MIKTA 2017). MIKTA's potential for powerful advocacy derives from its 'genuine combination of such geographical diversity with an abundance of common interests … [that] enables member countries to build cultural, social, geographical, and economic bridges in its multilateral debates' (Colakoglu 2016, 274).

Most recently, there are indications that MIKTA is finding a focus as a bulwark of the rules-based order in line with MIKTA's vision statement on 'protecting public goods and strengthening global governance' (MIKTA 2015).

In 2018, five MIKTA ambassadors (Aspe et al. 2018) penned a statement reformulating MIKTA as defending 'the rules-based global order that we all depend on' and noting the five members' common interest in promoting the global trading system and making the multilateral system work for the many. It cited the examples of the MIKTA Workshop on Trade and Investment at the World Trade Organization (WTO) and the two-year modernization agenda of the International Energy Agency (IEA). Another indication of the focus on the global trading system is the first meeting of Ministers Responsible for Trade of MIKTA Countries in December 2017 (MIKTA 2019).

Shifts in the language used to define MIKTA suggest a greater focus on defending rules and order as a key MIKTA goal. Australia's Department of Foreign Affairs and Trade now describes MIKTA as a group that 'works to bridge divides in the multilateral system and build consensus on complex and challenging issues, drawing on the diverse perspectives of its members and their shared interest in an effective, rules-based global order' (DFAT 2019) while Indonesia's Ministry of Foreign Affairs says that MIKTA has become not only a place to share ideas and experience, but also a forum to find an innovative and breakthrough strategy in the management of global order (Pramono 2018). The MIKTA official website has developed a tagline: 'Fulfilling the Role of a Responsible Middle Power in the Service of World Peace and Prosperity' (MIKTA 2019). Rules-based language appears again in the MIKTA Foreign Ministers' Statement on MIKTA's Fifth Anniversary:

> As we move forward towards MIKTA's consolidation, we reassert our commitment to a rules-based international system, anchored in the purposes and principles of the UN Charter and other universally recognized norms governing international relations. We will continue to support peace, stability, prosperity and sustainable development in our regions and across the world. (MIKTA 2019)

This fits very comfortably in the ideal of middle power behavior to strengthen international institutions in the preservation of order (Gök and Karadeniz 2018).

What are the limitations of MIKTA?

MIKTA's limitations include its membership, the level it meets and divergent views on some issues.

The MIKTA countries have some sway in international affairs but are by no means great powers. As a grouping it is necessarily limited by the ambitions and commitment of its members. Sung-Mi Kim, Sebastian Haug and Susan Harris Rimmer characterize it as suffering from weak member commitment, resource constraints, forum-shopping risks and a leadership vacuum (Kim et al. 2018, 486).

As an initiative personalized to foreign ministers, it is vulnerable to domestic political cycles, budget cuts and the changing whims of political leaders (Kim et al. 2018, 486). In some cases, it has been viewed as a personal pet project of specific ministers, making it harder to maintain commitment over time.

Finally, the key limitation for MIKTA is that it can only function where there is a commonality of interest on a particular issue. Interviews with MIKTA diplomats suggest that this is not a problem in most areas—according to a Turkish diplomat, 'It happens only very rarely that anyone of us is opposed to what another member country suggests'—but it can be a problem for issues of strategic significance.

An example of this is the issue of nuclear non-proliferation. Selcuk Colakoglu (2016, 276) argues that this is one area where MIKTA nations can act successfully, since no MIKTA nation is a nuclear power. However, in practice MIKTA countries have not formed a united front on this issue. When faced with UN General Assembly Resolution L.41 in 2017 on negotiating a legally binding instrument to prohibit nuclear weapons leading toward their total elimination, Indonesia and Mexico voted in favor of the resolution while Australia, South Korea, and Turkey all voted against it (International Campaign to Abolish Nuclear Weapons 2016). Australia cited several reasons for opposing the resolution including that the measure would be premature, ineffective and would potentially have adverse consequences for regional and global security (Tanter 2017; Rublee, Hanson and Burke 2017). In essence, Australia's position is that its commitment to its national security under the US nuclear umbrella takes precedence over its commitment, as a responsible global citizen, to a world free of nuclear weapons. Similar arguments apply for South Korea and for Turkey, but do not for Indonesia and Mexico.

As Michael Green puts it,

> Geopolitics also constrain the members of MIKTA, since the diplomatic strategies of several members are more defined by their regional alignments than their global contributions—Australia and Korea by alliance with the United States, and Indonesia by membership in ASEAN, for example. (Green 2019, 10)

Australia's approach to MIKTA

Julie Bishop served as Australia's Minister for Foreign Affairs from the formation of MIKTA until 2018 and showed enthusiasm for the initiative. After hosting the eighth MIKTA foreign ministers' meeting in Sydney in November 2016, Bishop praised MIKTA's 'informality and its agility' and pointed to MIKTA's ability to deal with any regional or global challenges—as opposed to being limited to a narrow agenda—as a key strength (Bishop 2016). Australia took on the role of chair in 2016, hosting the 2nd Senior Officials' Meeting in Canberra in January, the 2nd MIKTA Speakers'

Consultation in Hobart in October and the 8th MIKTA Foreign Ministers' Meeting in Sydney in November. The Department of Foreign Affairs and Trade has identified achievements in multiple arenas, including counter-terrorism and security, trade, gender equality, and sustainable development (DFAT 2016).

Australia has displayed a willingness to be involved in and a high level of commitment toward MIKTA. Observers see Australia's active involvement as in line with its initial decision to become part of MIKTA to increase its 'weight and reputation as a competent, creative and active member of the international community' (Engin and Baba 2015, 19). If, as Andrew Cooper (2018) argues, global reach is equated with national ambition, it makes sense that ambitious states prioritize their inclusion and influence in global summits. Australia fits with his model of self-aware actors operationalizing their 'globality' given that it, like the other members of MIKTA, is more 'regionally entrapped' than global. One of the major benefits identified by diplomats involved in MIKTA is its contribution to global visibility and weight for countries that often have to act alone to exercise global influence (Kim et al. 2018, 481).

Importantly, involvement in MIKTA does not require a significant investment of resources. MIKTA adds some leverage to its members' foreign policy playbook and some modest contribution to global governance for relatively little investment and is good for networking and branding (Green 2019, 10). It is viewed as a 'low-maintenance diplomatic instrument' (Kim et al. 2018, 481) which is ideal for Australia given continuing cuts to its investment in foreign affairs (Conley Tyler 2019).

Characterizing Australia's approach to foreign policy using role theory

Before assessing whether or not MIKTA is a case of Australia engaging in institutional balancing, it is useful to identify other potential role orientations for Australia's approach to foreign policy.

Underpinning role theory[2] is the assumption that actors adopt certain roles according to prescribed identities (Aggestam 2006, 12). Here, roles refer not to a position but rather the expected and appropriate action and behaviors of an actor (Turner 1956, 316). Role theory in foreign policy analysis was initially made popular by K. J. Holsti's 1970s study, within which he saw role theory as composed of four elements: role performance, role conceptions, role prescriptions and role positions (Holsti 1970, 240). Role performance refers to the attitudes and decisions of a government; role conceptions are the ways in which an actor conceptualizes of itself (for example as a good international citizen); role prescriptions are those external forces at work on an actor such as the expectations of the public as well as from its membership of institutions; and role positions are the outcome of the combined forces of the role prescriptions.

Role theory plays out in a circular fashion. A nation's material attributes determine its national role conception; its national role conceptions determine its foreign policy behavior; and a nation's foreign policy behavior, in turn, determines its national material attributes (Wish 1987, 96). These role orientations are the driving force behind how states interact with each other; they provide an overarching rationale and pattern for this interaction (Hermann 1987, 134).

Within the MIKTA group, there have been attempts to apply role theory to Indonesia (Thies and Sari 2018) and to Turkey by conducting a discourse analysis of statements by Turkey and the other MIKTA countries at the opening sessions of the United Nations General Assembly from 2001–2017 to see how they define their roles in global governance, attitude toward international order and the nexus between their global and regional roles (Gök and Karadeniz 2018). Some of the ways Turkey presented its role included as 'donor state,' 'humanitarian actor,' 'bridge,' 'responsible state,' 'promoter of harmony among civilizations,' and 'promoter of peace' (Gök and Karadeniz 2018, 144).

Applying role theory to Australia's approach to multilateralism shows that a number of potential role orientations can be in play. Adapting Jamie Gaskarth's six role orientations, presented in the context of the UK, Table 9.1 sets out their applicability to Australia (Gaskarth 2014).

The isolationist and great power orientations have not been part of Australia's role identity. Australia does not engage in isolationist role performance—including neutrality, minimal defense spending, withdrawal from treaty commitments—nor

TABLE 9.1 Applicability of Gaskarth's role orientations to Australia

Role orientation	Definition	Applicable to Australia	Examples
Isolationist	Solely concerned with domestic issues	No	
Regional partner	Active in regional institutions; regional defence cooperation	Yes	Involvement with ASEAN Regional Forum, IORA, RCEP; involvement in regional conflicts
Influential rule of law state	Possesses a respectable amount of power, but also seeks to uphold international law	Yes	Spearheaded INTER-FET; significant role in Arms Trade Treaty.
Thought leader	Identifying and addressing issues that affect the international community	Yes	Cairns Group; elevation of G20 to leaders' level
Opportunist-interventionist	Exploits situations to advance liberalism and democracy	Yes (by proxy through the US alliance)	Participation in Iraq and Afghanistan invasions at behest of the US
Great power	Military preponderance and global policeman	No	

does it adopt the role of a great power, which entails being a global policeman, a regional protector and a military power. Discarding these two orientations leaves four useful archetypes that can be applied to Australian foreign policy. The role orientations of regional partner and opportunist-interventionist, while accurate, are not relevant to the MIKTA case study, as MIKTA is neither a regional institution nor an example of Australia being an opportunist.

The two remaining role orientations—influential rule of law state and thought leader—both arguably apply to Australia's approach to multilateralism.

Australia as an influential rule of law state

Figure 9.1 shows the role orientation, conception and performance of an influential rule of law state.

There is evidence for this role orientation in Australia's strong history of upholding and contributing to international law.

Australia has a strong history of diplomatic efforts within the UN. As Peter Nadin argues, 'UN leadership is in Australia's foreign policy DNA' (Nadin 2017). As Minister for External Affairs, H. V. Evatt played a very influential role in drafting the UN Charter and was president of the UN General Assembly from 1948–1949. Some outside observers see this a crucial period for forming Australia's ideational role: 'Australia's middle power identity explicitly referring to its middle power role of preserving order emerged immediately following the WWII' (Gök and Karadeniz 2018, 152).

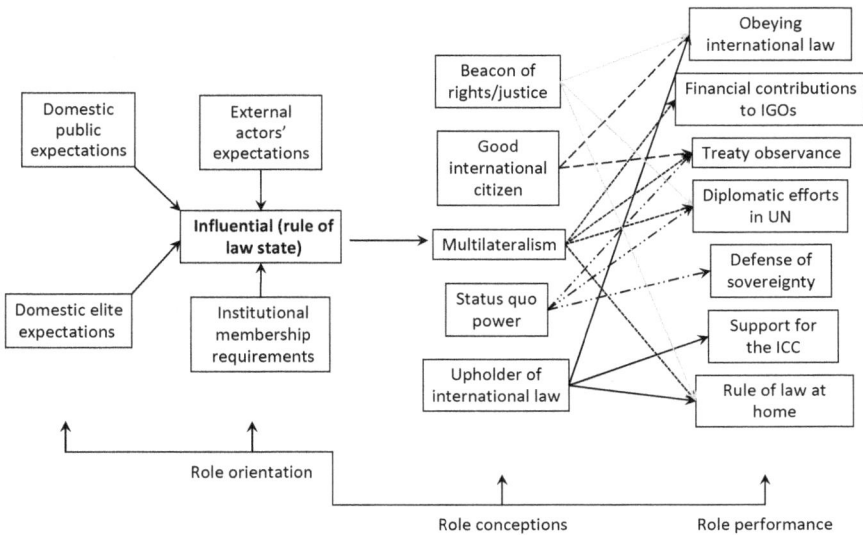

FIGURE 9.1 Gaskarth's (2014, 574) influential (rule of law state) role play
Note: IGO, inter-governmental organization; ICC, International Criminal Court.

In 1999 under the Howard government Australia led the International Force in East Timor (INTERFET) mission, a peacekeeping mission in response to the violence that broke out in East Timor following a vote of independence from Indonesia. In more recent times, Australia has held the presidency of the UN Security Council in 2013–2014. Richard Gowan points out that, during Australia's time as president, 'Australia's advocacy for human rights, humanitarian causes and more effective sanctions has had a positive impact on both the Council and attitudes to Australia across the United Nations' (Gowan 2014). Australia has announced that it will be seeking the presidency again in 2029–2030.

Australia has been credited with playing a critical role in the adoption of the Arms Trade Treaty and has led the development within the Convention for the Conservation of Antarctic Marine Living Resources (CCAMLR) of an agreement that established a system of marine protected areas in the Southern Ocean (Conley Tyler, Scott and Dao 2017, 67).

While Australia fits the role orientation of an influential rule of law state, this does not mean Australia is always a good international citizen or welcomes international scrutiny of its own behavior. As Holsti frames it,

> [j]ust as designating persons as judge, professor, or politician does not indicate adequately all the tasks these individuals fulfil within their formal positions and casual relationships, [specific role orientations] do not reveal all the behavioral variations observable in the different sets of relationships into which states enter. (Holsti 1970, 235)

The issue is whether this conception of its role has influenced Australia's approach to multilateralism.

Australia as a thought leader

Figure 9.2 shows the role orientation, conception and performance of a thought leader. This also fits Australia's approach to foreign policy.

Australia plays regular host to multilateral conferences and consistently pursues leadership roles in those institutions. In recent times, the most prominent example of this is Australia's hosting of the G20 summit in Brisbane in 2014. Australia—particularly then-Prime Minister Kevin Rudd—played a very important role in the G20's evolution. After the global financial crisis, Rudd was the driving force behind turning the G20 from a meeting of finance ministers to a leaders' level summit where heads of government could steer economic governance (Yi-Chong 2011, 12). Australia's willingness to hold conferences and summits is not limited to the G20. A few other examples include hosting the Asia Pacific Economic Cooperation (APEC) summit in Sydney in 2007; hosting the Commonwealth Heads of Government Meeting in Perth in 2011; or, in 2013–2015 taking on the role of chair in the Indian Ocean Rim Association (IORA).

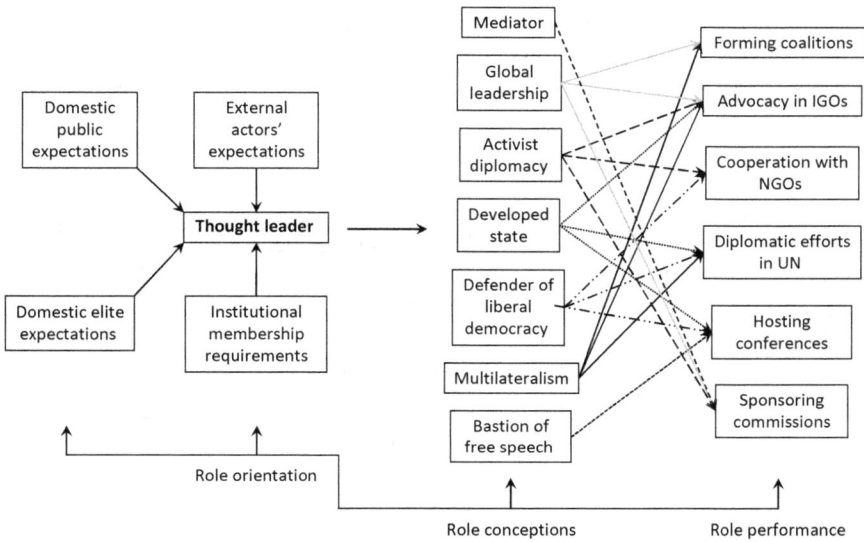

FIGURE 9.2 Gaskarth's (2014, 576) thought leader role play
Note: IGO, inter-governmental organization.

Australia's willingness to form coalitions can be seen in the formation of the Cairns Group in 1986. The Cairns Group was spearheaded by the Hawke government and its purpose was to push for the General Agreement on Tariffs and Trade (GATT) to cover agricultural trade in its process. After being frustrated by failed attempts to reform the GATT directly, it was realized by Australian policy makers that collective action was necessary (Higgott and Cooper 1990, 609). The Cairns Group was ultimately successful when, after seven years of 'torturous negotiations' (Firth 2011, 35), GATT rules were extended to cover agricultural trade. This is an example of Australia pursuing multilateral solutions to national problems through a strong leadership role. Higgott and Cooper (1990, 615) point out that 'it is not an overstatement to say that Australia took on the functions as well as the burdens of being the manager of the group with relish'.

Australia has regularly supported international commissions. For example, during his time as prime minister, Kevin Rudd proposed the International Commission on Nuclear Non-Proliferation and Disarmament (ICNND) in 2008, which was co-chaired by former Australian Foreign Minister Gareth Evans.

The role orientation of thought leader is thus also apt for Australia, showing that it can have multiple orientations concurrently. The examples drawn from a long time period demonstrate that Australia has used multilateralism as a tool within its conception of itself as both an influential rule of law state and a thought leader. They also accord with Australia's current practice in how it presents itself in international forums, with a detailed analysis of Australian leaders' discourse at the United Nations General Assembly (UNGA) between 2000–2017 showing terms used such as 'good international citizenship,' 'strong democracy,' 'responsible nation,' 'a voice for small and medium nations,' and 'creative middle power' (Gök and Karadeniz 2018, 150).

Australia as a middle power

It is impossible to avoid mentioning another potential role orientation for Australian foreign policy, that of a 'middle power.' A debate on defining 'middle powers' has raged through Australia's international relations scholarship for decades (Robertson 2017; Patience 2014; Carr 2013; Beeson 2011; Sussex 2011; Ravenhill 1998). While the definition of 'middle power' remains contested, it is clearly a role definition that has often been used to describe Australia's foreign policy (Cotton and Ravenhill 2011). Carl Ungerer points out that, while the concept of Australia as a 'middle power' has been both inconsistent and malleable, the concept 'has provided the one and perhaps only consistent framework for the conduct of Australian diplomacy' (Ungerer 2007, 539).

Arguably both the role orientations of influential rule of law state and thought leader fit within the conception of the 'middle power' role. Multilateral initiatives fitting within these roles can thus be seen as part of a wider Australia's role conception of 'middle power'.

Is MIKTA a case of Australia being a 'kingmaker'?

According to contested multilateralism 2.0, if Australia was attempting to become a kingmaker, then its engagement with MIKTA should be a form of inter-institutional balancing. The purpose of MIKTA would then be to challenge existing institutions, such as BRICS or the G7, by creating its own set of norms and rules to challenge those of these groups. The increased influence gained through this inter-institutional balancing could then be used to act as a 'kingmaker' in providing support for the US or China in their respective aims as order defender and order challenger.

MIKTA, however, does not fit within this paradigm. While the member nations have aimed to increase their international standing through their engagement with MIKTA, the purpose has not been to become a kingmaker. There is no evidence of MIKTA as a bloc using its collective influence to provide consistent support for the US or China. The example of the nuclear ban negotiations shows that member nations' decisions are not all in the interest of the US. Similarly, Indonesia, South Korea, Turkey, and Australia all signed on to the Asian Infrastructure Investment Bank (AIIB) despite direct US opposition. Even if MIKTA tried to turn its hand to kingmaking, it is doubtful that as a grouping it would have the power or leverage to be successful. Ultimately, there are very few institutions that can restrict and balance other nations; even the longest-standing and most powerful institutions can be ignored by powerful states when inconvenient.

Instead of viewing MIKTA in this light, a better characterization of MIKTA is to see it as a case of five nations working together as classic 'constructive middle powers,' meaning that they 'firmly believe in institutional frameworks to solve disputes and reach consensus on different areas of the international agenda' (Schiavon and Domínguez 2016, 498). MIKTA's vision statement, which demonstrates a focus on tackling global challenges through the frameworks of the UN and international law, strongly supports this (MIKTA 2015).

That is not to say that MIKTA has been immune from the geopolitical situation. There are arguably two ways that MIKTA has been affected by contestation in Asia.

First, it is possible that MIKTA may have achieved more in an easier environment for international cooperation. Michael Green (2019, 10) believes that MIKTA has yet to offer concrete public goods with one of the reasons being the broader geopolitical environment where its members' capacity 'to shape the security environment through multilateralism is waning in the face of increased geopolitical rivalry in Asia' (Green 2019, 3). He sees middle power strategies 'based on convening and bridging' as vulnerable whilst geopolitical competition increases (Green 2019, 1).

Second, MIKTA may be developing in response to the environment of contestation precisely to be a more explicit defender of global rules. MIKTA countries appear to be concerned about threats to the rules-based global order by both the hegemonic and challenging power. As such, it makes sense for them to take an active role shoring up international order: 'middle power diplomacy through informal venues presents a new road for cooperation under the post-hegemonic world order' (Gök and Karadeniz 2018, 152). This accords with the characterization of MIKTA as a mechanism for the world's lesser powers grappling with heightened global uncertainty and deepening interdependency (Kim et al. 2018, 475).

An acute scholar of middle powers, Tanguy Struye de Swielande (2019, 192), suggests that 'when leadership topples or tensions emerge between great powers … the initiative to guarantee the status quo (i.e. a liberal order) can be provided by middle powers'. Using this approach, it makes sense that at a time of geopolitical rivalry, middle powers reinforce their relationships with other middle powers into what he describes as a 'community of practice' (at least among the Indo-Pacific MIKTA members) and a 'leading from the middle' approach.

This suggests it is not so strange to launch an old-fashioned middle power initiative at a time of contestation:

> The current distribution of power grants middle powers a window of opportunity to advance their political, economic, and security goals—provided they work collectively. The intensive cooperation between them illustrates how they do not want to be passive bystanders, but active stakeholders …. The more middle powers interact with each other, the more they will be able to influence agenda-setting in the region and fulfil the roles of facilitator, mediator, and bridge-builder. Middle powers, by counterbalancing the United States and China and exploiting their rivalry, can be a driving force for the future of the international system. (de Swielande 2019, 203)

The MIKTA case thus fits well within Australia's long history of engaging in multi-lateralism with the motive of increasing its influence in the international system. Role theory might characterize it as an 'influential rule of law state' or 'thought leader' while other wording used in Australian discourse is 'good international citizen,' which has been described as one of Australia's 'primary foreign policy identities' (Conley Tyler, Scott and Dao 2017, 56). Being a good international citizen involves pursuing Australia's 'own political and economic interests with maximum effectiveness, but in a way that makes as positive a contribution as possible to a more peaceful and prosperous world' (Evans and Grant 1995, 343). Australia's engagement with MIKTA fits this role conception. As a member of MIKTA, Australia can contribute to global issues while still pursuing its own economic and political interest as a primary goal.

These role orientations more accurately reflect the characteristics of Australia's foray into multilateralism through MIKTA than does the kingmaker role. MIKTA thus poses a problem for He's model of the balance of roles and suggests that Australia's policy of multilateralism is at least in part motivated by other factors and role definitions.

This is not to dispute He's entire model. It may very well be the case that the US is the order defender and that China is the order challenger and their multi-lateral diplomacy accords with this. However, in the case of Australia, this model does not fully explain Australia's multilateral behavior. MIKTA is better explained as an example of Australia using multilateral diplomacy to increase its relevance and international influence very much in traditional 'middle power' mode as a 'influential rule of law state' and 'thought leader.' These role orientations better explain Australia's engagement with MIKTA than the kingmaker role.

Notes

1 This chapter was prepared while the author was National Executive Director of the Australian Institute of International Affairs. She thanks Evan Keeble for his research assistance on this project. An edited version of the MIKTA case study material was published in Wilson 2018.
2 For important contributions to role theory see: Holsti (1970); Walker (1981); Hollis and Smith (1986); Hermann (1987); Walker and Simon (1987); Wish (1987); Aggestam (2006); Thies and Breuning (2012).

References

Aggestam, Lisbeth. 2006. "Role Theory and European Foreign Policy: A Framework of Analysis." In *The European Union's Roles in International Politics*, edited by Ole Elgstrom and Michael Smith, 11–29. London: Routledge.

Aspe, Monica, Jong-Won Yoon, Erdem Başçı, Brian Pontifex, and Hotmangaradja Pand-jaitan. 2018. "Creative Multilateralism: Stronger Collaboration for All." *OECD Observer*, March. Accessed November 28, 2019. http://oecdobserver.org/news/fullstory.php/aid/6025/Creative_multilateralism:_Stronger_collaboration_for_all.html.

Beeson, Mark. 2011. "Can Australia Save the World? The Limits and Possibilities of Middle Power Diplomacy." *Australian Journal of International Affairs* 65(5): 563–577.

Bergin, Anthony. 2013. "Dump Middle-Power Tag: Australia Carries Bigger Stick than That." *Sydney Morning Herald*, October 10. http://www.smh.com.au/comment/dump -middlepower-tag–australia-carries-bigger-stick-than-that-20131009-2v8hr.html.

Bishop, Julie. 2016. "Press Conference at MIKTA Ministerial Meeting." Minister for Foreign Affairs, November 25. https://www.foreignminister.gov.au/minister/julie-bishop/tra nscript-eoe/press-conference-mikta-ministerial-meeting.

Carr, Andrew. 2013. "Is Australia a Middle Power? A Systemic Impact Approach." *Australian Journal of International Affairs* 68(1): 70–84.

Carr, Andrew. 2015. "MIKTA, Middle Powers, and New Dynamics of Global Governance: The G20's Evolving Agenda." http://andrewcarr.org/?p=2468.

Colakoglu, Selcuk. 2016. "The Role of MIKTA in Global Governance: Assessments & Shortcomings." *Korea Observer* 47(2): 267–290.

Colakoglu, Selcuk. 2017. "Is MIKTA Sustainable as a Middle Power Grouping in Global Governance?" *Diplo Blog*, July 11. https://www.diplomacy.edu/blog/mikta-sustainable-m iddle-power-grouping-global-governance.

Conley Tyler, Melissa. 2016. "MIKTA: An Acronym in Search of Meaning." *Australian Outlook*, Australian Institute of International Affairs, November 26. http://www.interna tionalaffairs.org.au/australian_outlook/mikta-an-acronym-in-search-of-meaning/.

Conley Tyler, Melissa. 2019. "How to Rebuild Australia's Diplomatic Capacity." *Australian Foreign Affairs* 7: 109–115.

Conley Tyler, Melissa, and Doris McDonald-Seaton. 2014. "MIKTA: The Middle Child of International Cooperation." *El Blog de Comexi: Consejo Mexico de Asuntos Internationales*, April 24.

Conley Tyler, Melissa, Shirley V. Scott, and Duc Dao. 2017. "Australia's Engagement with the UN, G20 and International Law." In *Navigating the New International Disorder: Australia in World Affairs 2011–2015*, edited by Mark Beeson and Shahar Hameiri, 56–74. South Melbourne: Oxford University Press.

Cooper, Andrew F. 2015. "MIKTA and the Global Projection of Middle Powers: Toward a Summit of Their Own?" *Global Summitry* 1(1): 95–114.

Cooper, Andrew F. 2018. "'Rising' States and Global Reach: Measuring 'Globality' among BRICS/MIKTA Countries." *Global Summitry* 4(1): 64–80.

Cotton, James, and John Ravenhill. 2011. "Middle Power Dreaming: Australian Foreign Policy During the Rudd-Gillard Governments." In *Middle Power Dreaming: Australia in World Affairs*, edited by James Cotton and John Ravenhill, 1–12. Melbourne: Oxford University Press and Australian Institute of International Affairs.

de Swielande, Tanguy Struye. 2019. "Middle Powers in the Indo-Pacific: Potential Pacifiers Guaranteeing Stability in the Indo-Pacific?" *Asian Politics & Policy* 11(2): 190–207.

DFAT (Department of Foreign Affairs and Trade). 2016. "Australia's Term as Chair 2015–2016: Key Achievements." Australian Government. http://dfat.gov.au/international-rela tions/international-organisations/mikta/Pages/australias-term-as-chair-2015-16-key-achie vements.aspx.

DFAT (Department of Foreign Affairs and Trade). 2019. "MIKTA: Mexico, Indonesia, the Republic of Korea, Turkey, Australia." Australian Government. Accessed December 5, 2019. https://dfat.gov.au/international-relations/international-organisations/mikta/Pages/mikta.aspx.

Douglas, Elena, and Gordon Flake. 2014. "Smart Power Vol 2: MIKTA Narratives." *Data Stories*, vol. 2. Perth USAsia Centre and the University of Western Australia. http:// perthusasia.edu.au/getattachment/82b83df7-1add-47dd-945c-1d4857367f3c/Smart-Pow er-Vol-2-MIKTA-Narratives.pdf.aspx?lang=en-AU.

Engin, Belma, and Gurol Baba. 2015. "MIKTA, A Functioning Product of 'New' Middle Power-ism?" *Uluslararasi Hukuk ve Politika* 11(42): 1–40.

Evans, Gareth, and Bruce Grant. 1995. *Australia's Foreign Relations: In the World of the 1990s.* Melbourne: Melbourne University Press.

Firth, Stewart. 2011. *Australia in International Politics: An Introduction to Australian Foreign Policy*, 3rd ed. Crows Nest: Allen & Unwin.

Flake, Gordon, and Xu Wang. 2017. "MIKTA: The Search for a Strategic Rationale." Perth USAsia Centre, January. http://perthusasia.edu.au/getattachment/2e8754a3-8e76-4e16-ade3-18bcf9f6131e/PUAC-MIKTA-Flake-Xu-Jan2017.pdf.aspx?lang=en-AU.

Gaskarth, Jamie. 2014. "Strategizing Britain's Role in the World." *International Affairs* 90(3): 559–581.

Gök, Gonca Oğuz, and Radiye Funda Karadeniz. 2018. "Analyzing 'T' in MIKTA: Turkey's Changing Middle Power Role in the United Nations." In *Middle Powers in Global Governance: The Rise of Turkey*, edited by Emel Parlar Dal, 133–161. Cham, Switzerland: Palgrave Macmillan.

Gowan, Richard. 2014. "Australia in the UN Security Council." Lowy Institute, June 12. https://www.lowyinstitute.org/publications/australia-un-security-council.

Green, Michael J. 2019. "Is the Era of Korean Middle Power Diplomacy Over? A Realist Perspective." *Korean Journal of Defense Analysis* 31(1): 1–20.

Hermann, Margaret G. 1987. "Foreign Policy Role Orientations and the Quality of Foreign Policy Decisions." In *Role Theory and Foreign Policy Analysis*, edited by Stephen G. Walker, 123–140. Durham, NC: Duke University Press.

Higgott, Richard A., and Andrew Fenton Cooper. 1990. "Middle Power Leadership and Coalition Building: Australia, the Cairns Group, and the Uruguay Round of Trade Negotiations." *International Organization* 44(4): 589–632.

Hollis, Martin, and Steve Smith. 1986. "Roles and Reasons in Foreign Policy Decision Making." *British Journal of Political Science* 16(3): 269–286.

Holsti, Kal. 1970. "National Role Conceptions in the Study of Foreign Policy." *International Studies Quarterly* 14(3): 233–309.

International Campaign to Abolish Nuclear Weapons. 2016. "Full Voting Result on UN Resolution L.41." October 27. http://www.icanw.org/campaign-news/results/.

Jeong, Monica S. 2019. "Critical Realism: A Better Way to Think about Middle Powers." *International Journal: Canada's Journal of Global Policy Analysis* 74(2): 240–257.

Kim, Sung-Mi, Sebastian Haug, and Susan Harris Rimmer. 2018. "Minilateralism Revisited: MIKTA as Slender Diplomacy in a Multiplex World." *Global Governance: A Review of Multilateralism and International Organizations* 24(4): 475–489.

Lee, Shin-wha, and Chun Young Park. 2017. "Korea's Middle Power Diplomacy for Human Security: A Global and Regional Approach." *Journal of International and Area Studies* 24(1): 21–44.

McDonald-Seaton, Doris, and Melissa Conley Tyler. 2014. "Mixing with the MIKTAS." *Australian Outlook*, Australian Institute of International Affairs, April 24. http://www.internationalaffairs.org.au/australian_outlook/mixing-with-the-miktas/.

MIKTA. 2015. "MIKTA Vision Statement." May 22. Accessed December 5, 2019. http://www.mikta.org/about/vision.php.

MIKTA. 2017. "MIKTA Statement for the 2017 ECOSOC Integration Segment: Making Eradication of Poverty an Integral Objective of All Policies: What Will it Take?" Accessed December 5, 2019. http://www.mikta.org/document/others.php.

MIKTA. 2019. "About MIKTA," "MIKTA Projects," "MIKTA Documents," "MIKTA News." Accessed December 5, 2019. www.mikta.org.

Nadin, Peter. 2017. "The Shape of Australia's Future Engagement with the United Nations." Policy Brief, Lowy Institute for International Policy, March 31. https://www.lowyinstitute.org/publications/shape-australia-s-future-engagement-united-nations.

Oliver, Alex. 2013. "MIKTA: Where Middle Powers Proudly Meet." *The Interpreter*, Lowy Institute, November 28. https://www.lowyinstitute.org/the-interpreter/mikta-where-middle-powers-proudly-meet.

Patience, Allan. 2014. "Imagining Middle Powers." *Australian Journal of International Affairs* 68(2): 210–224.

Pramono, Siswo. 2018. *MIKTA: Current Situation and the Way Forward*. Jakarta: Policy Analysis and Development Agency, Ministry of Foreign Affairs, Republic of Indonesia.

Ravenhill, John. 1998. "Cycles of Middle Power Activism: Constraint and Choice in Australian and Canadian Foreign Policies." *Australian Journal of International Affairs* 52(3): 309–327.

Rivas, César Villanueva. 2018. "Mexico's Public Diplomacy Approach to the Indo-Pacific: A Thin Soft Power?" *Politics & Policy* 45(5): 793–812.

Robertson, Jeffrey. 2017. "Middle-Power Definitions: Confusion Reigns Supreme." *Australian Journal of International Affairs* 71(4): 355–370.

Rublee, Maria Rost, Marianne Hanson, and Anthony Burke. 2017. "Australia's Misstep on Nuclear Weapons Treaty." *Australian Outlook*, Australian Institute of International Affairs, February 20. http://www.internationalaffairs.org.au/australian_outlook/australias-misstep-nuclear-weapons-treaty/.

Schiavon, Jorge A., and Diego Domínguez. 2016. "Mexico, Indonesia, South Korea, Turkey, and Australia (MIKTA): Middle, Regional, and Constructive Powers Providing Global Governance." *Asia & the Pacific Policy Studies* 3(3): 495–504.

Sukma, Rizal. 2013. "MIKTA: What Does It Want?" *The Jakarta Post*, October 24. http://www.thejakartapost.com/news/2013/10/24/mikta-what-does-it-want.html

Sussex, Matthew. 2011. "The Impotence of Being Earnest? Avoiding the Pitfalls of 'Creative Middle Power Diplomacy'." *Australian Journal of International Affairs* 65(5): 545–562.

Tanter, Richard. 2017. "A Global Nuclear Weapons Ban? Ready or Not, Here It Comes." *Australian Outlook*, Australian Institute of International Affairs, June 19. http://www.internationalaffairs.org.au/australian_outlook/global-nuclear-weapons-ban/.

Thies, Cameron G., and Marijke Breuning. 2012. "Integrating Foreign Policy Analysis and International Relations through Role Theory." *Foreign Policy Analysis* 8(1): 1–4.

Thies, Cameron G., and Angguntari C. Sari. 2018. "A Role Theory Approach to Middle Powers: Making Sense of Indonesia's Place in the International System." *Contemporary Southeast Asia* 40(3): 397–421.

Toloraya, Georgy. 2013. "MIKTA: Is It a New Element of the Global Governance Structure?" *Russian International Affairs Council Analysis*, December 23. http://russiancouncil.ru/en/analytics-and-comments/analytics/mikta-is-it-a-new-element-of-the-global-governance-structure/.

Turner, Ralph H. 1956. "Role-Taking, Role Standpoint, and Reference Group Behavior." *American Journal of Sociology* 61(4): 316–328.

Ungerer, Carl. 2007. "The 'Middle Power' Concept in Australian Foreign Policy." *Australian Journal of Politics and History* 53(4): 538–551.

Walker, Stephen G. 1981. "The Correspondence between Foreign Policy Rhetoric and Behavior: Insights from Role Theory and Exchange Theory." *Systems Research and Behavioural Science* 26(3): 272–280.

Walker, Stephen G., and Sheldon W. Simon. 1987. "Role Sets and Foreign Policy Analysis in Southeast Asia." In *Role Theory and Foreign Policy Analysis*, edited by Stephen G. Walker, 141–159. Durham, NC: Duke University Press.

Wilson, Jeffrey, ed. 2018. *Expanding Horizons: Indonesia's Regional Engagement in the Indo-Pacific Era*. Report. Perth: Perth USAsia Centre.

Wish, Naomi B. 1987. "National Attributes as Sources of National Role Conceptions." In *Role Theory and Foreign Policy Analysis*, edited by Stephen G. Walker, 94–108. Durham, NC: Duke University Press.

Yi-Chong, Xu. 2011. "Australian Participation in the G20." In *G20 Perceptions and Perspectives for Global Governance*, edited by Wilhelm Hofmeister, 11–19. Singapore: Konrad Adenauer Stiftung.

10

ASEAN AND MULTILATERALISM 2.0

Locating ASEAN centrality within the FOIP and the BRI

See Seng Tan

This chapter examines the responses of the Association of Southeast Asian Nations (ASEAN) to 'multilateralism 2.0'—which, insofar as it concerns the contemporary Asia Pacific, refers to new regional economic and security architectures initiated and/or championed by non-ASEAN powers (He 2019). The chapter contends that against an unsettled regional backdrop of strategic rivalry and rising tensions over trade and security concerns between the United States and China, ASEAN-led multilateralism continues to perform critical functions in maintaining the stability of the region. In this respect, the idea or the principle of 'ASEAN centrality' advanced by ASEAN has become a policy catch-all for actions undertaken by that regional grouping to mitigate against the region's increasing instability from great power discord and to ensure its own institutional relevance. Thus understood, ASEAN's institutional interest and preservation strategy in response to the destabilizing impact of US–China competition on the region can be explained in terms of its role perception as an 'order stabilizer.' This is not to suggest that the conduct of all ten member countries of ASEAN always contributes positively to their grouping's role realization, especially not when each of them is susceptible—highly so in the case of some—to pressure from external actors to side with one great power over another. Indeed, differences among its members have at times caused ASEAN to lose its unity, focus and effectiveness. That said, regional stability is a precondition sought after and upheld generally by all member states in pursuit of their respective national goals.

In a sense, nowhere is ASEAN's regional role as a stabilizer more pronounced today than in the way it has been responding to two key ideational cum institutional expressions of multilateralism 2.0 initiated and led by the United States and China respectively, namely, the Free and Open Indo-Pacific (FOIP) and the Belt and Road Initiative (BRI). It has been suggested that ASEAN conceivably serves as a sort of 'balancer,' arguably a third pole, between the US-led group of 'Quad' members (Australia, India, Japan, and the United States), on the one hand, and China on the other (Wagle 2018). However, as a grouping of relatively weak states, ASEAN does not, indeed cannot, act as a balancing force as traditionally understood in the literature, not just because it lacks military power but also because it is not a singular military actor. Rather than countervailing against the FOIP and the BRI as conventionally conceived, this chapter argues that what ASEAN has been doing is simultaneous engagement and hedging on both fronts with and against those two expressions. Thus understood, attempts by ASEAN to garner American and Chinese concessions to the putative 'centrality' of ASEAN within the FOIP and the BRI—as well as in defense diplomacy engagements with the United States and China—could be explained as a key part of the regional grouping's broader effort to stabilize a regional order threatened by great power rivalry and discord.

Superpower rivalry and institutional balancing

The Asia-Pacific in the post-Cold War period has been referred to as a multipolar region owing to the emergence of China, Japan, and India as prospective challengers to American hegemony (see, for example, Friedberg 1993–1994; Kupchan 1998, 62–6; Stuart and Tow 1995). Of late, this conventional wisdom has been challenged in the light of compelling evidence that among those three ascending powers, only China possesses the combination of power and aspiration to become a possible peer competitor and revisionist power to the United States, whose standing and resolve as the world's undisputed global power increasingly invites questions. That said, the fact remains that the Chinese and Americans still stand head and shoulders above everyone else. According to the '2019 Asia Power Index' published by Australia's Lowy Institute—which rank-ordered Asia-Pacific countries in terms of not only their economic and military power, but also paid equal attention to their policy choices and initiatives, the networks and alliances of which they are part, and the level of influence they wield over other countries all competing in a context of shifting relativities—the United States and China, identified in the index as 'super powers,' are clearly in a league of their own (Lemahieu 2019). These findings are corroborated by a recent study by Oystein Tunsjo (2018), who persuasively argues the Asia-Pacific and indeed the world has experienced a return to bipolarity as a consequence of the enormity of the US–China rivalry over other sets of competitive relationships.

Kai He has raised an intriguing proposition regarding the emergence of new regional institutional arrangements in the Asia-Pacific region in the aftermath of the 2008 global financial crisis (GFC) (He 2019). In response to the strategic uncertainty posed by the GFC, He proposes that those new arrangements—most if not all initiated by non-ASEAN powers—represent a new generation in Asia-Pacific multilateralism. For our purposes, a major outcome of the bipolar competition between the Americans and the Chinese highlighted above has therefore been the rise of multilateralism 2.0 in the Asia-Pacific region, where regional visions and their accompanying architectures have been initiated and erected by strategic rivals and their partners. This has led to balances of power and influence played out between Washington and Beijing within and across Asia-Pacific institutional arrangements. The notion that countries balance one another within as well as across institutional settings is well established (see He 2008a, 2008b; Lee 2012). By and large, proponents of institutional balancing accept that countries balance one another under specific conditions and pursue cooperation with one another under other conditions.[1] It is not impossible, therefore, that balancing can and will take place among countries that are linked together through economic and other forms of collaboration. In short, economic interdependence does not preclude balancing (Khong 2004). It may be recalled that one plausible reason behind the inclusion of Australia and India as founding members of the East Asia Summit (EAS) in 2005 was so they could help 'balance' against China's dominance in East Asian regionalism, albeit not in such a way as to contain China's rise and arguably destabilize the region (Goh 2013). That Beijing arguably understood and even accepted situations—as it appeared to have done vis-à-vis the founding of the EAS—implies the existence of a mutually consensual form of institutional balancing that has been referred to in the past as 'associational' and 'cooperative' balancing (see Little 1989; Zhang 2011).

However, whether the current form of assertive balancing in which the United States and China have been engaging bilaterally under Presidents Donald Trump and Xi Jinping respectively can still be considered associational or cooperative is questionable (Tan 2018a). Indeed, their strategic rivalry, in the view of some analysts, has escalated to the point where war in the Asia-Pacific region is presumably not as unimaginable as some might think (Gady 2017). Specifically, it is the state of the region's maritime domain—which has witnessed frequent clashes among naval, coast guard, and paramilitary vessels and civilian actors—that worries most observers (Bowers 2018). According to Tunsjo, direct superpower confrontation and proxy wars are less likely compared with the time of the Cold War, not least because China's security concerns are primarily regional rather than global. However, he believes the risk of conflict in maritime East Asia, where both superpowers have vital interests, remains high (Tunsjo 2018). But even if war is not inevitable, regional instability clearly is. All this makes ASEAN's efforts as regional stabilizer even more complicated and challenging.

Stabilizing the Asia/Indo-Pacific order

As noted earlier, the prospect of ASEAN as a balancing force between the two superpowers has been suggested (Wagle 2018). It has also been suggested that ASEAN's ability to play a balancing role between the major powers is in fact the foundation for ASEAN's centrality in Asia-Pacific regionalism (Huang 2014, 10). For this to make sense at all, ASEAN must possess the requisite economic, military and political heft with which to balance the United States and China. The grouping has been described as a potential 'middle power' given the combined economic and political weight of its ten members (see Gilley and O'Neil 2014; Ryu 2013). However, in order for ASEAN to take advantage of its supposed heft, its members have to think and act in concert and with coherence—a potential strength that has not yet been translated into reality, at least not in any sustainable fashion. Yet this does not mean ASEAN has not been an inconsequent regional actor (Asia Society n.d.). Far from passive, ASEAN states—and, by extension, the grouping as a whole—do what they can to stabilize their regional order from the negative impact of great power discord. They predominantly rely on a combination of hedging and limited alignments in their ties with great powers (Tan 2020). Neither outright balancing nor bandwagoning as conventionally understood in the literature, their conduct toward the big powers can be described as accommodation (Kang 2009, 1). As David Shambaugh has put it, 'ASEAN is not a completely passive party; it has proven itself adroit at flexible manoeuvring and hedging behaviour' (Shambaugh 2018, 99). Needless to say, ASEAN's efforts to that end have not always worked; indeed, given the reliance by its member countries on external incentives, ASEAN has at times failed to think, act and speak consistently and clearly for its own interests owing to the primacy of narrow national concerns among its members (Lee 2018). That said, whenever they have sought proactively to collaborate toward realizing common regional aims—as they have collectively done in disaster relief, counter-terrorism and the like through ASEAN-based platforms such as the ASEAN Defense Ministers' Meeting (ADMM) and the ADMM+ —the outcomes have been impressive by Asia-Pacific standards (see Tan 2019a).

In doing so, ASEAN has, less by design than default, sought to contribute to security by engaging the United States and China and stabilizing the regional order. No scholar has done more to understand Southeast Asia and the wider Asia-Pacific from the viewpoint of interstate order than the late Michael Leifer. We may recall that Leifer's yardstick of choice for assessing the international relations of the region was regional order (see Tan 2012). Yet the portrait Leifer painted of the region was one devoid of order. Yuen Foong Khong has argued that Leifer's notion of order is theoretically underdeveloped and methodologically imprecise, which thereby allows the analyst to see disorder in every minor perturbation in the region (Khong 2005). In place of regional order, Khong suggests going with 'peace and stability,' the preferred terms of the discourse by ASEAN's policy elites. By those latter criteria, he concludes that ASEAN and the Asia-Pacific, contrary to the sceptics, have in fact made impressive progress in the post-Cold War years. More plausibly, rather than the questionable proposition of ASEAN as a collective regional actor balancing against the great powers, ASEAN has sought to cultivate a complex balance of influence between the United States and China partly through a process of institutionally enmeshing the two superpowers within the ASEAN-based multilateral architecture (Goh 2008). Ironically, that ASEAN has been able to achieve this is due to its relative weakness, which has enhanced its legitimacy as a regional leader for the reason that it is perceived by external players as non-threatening to their aspirations and interests (Stubbs 2014)—by being 'hugely imperfect,' so to speak (Asia Society n.d.).

Engaging the FOIP

For ASEAN, the United States' FOIP strategy and China's BRI constitute developments which, in a time of growing rivalry between the major powers, are forcibly reviving an era of bilateralism. This poses a key challenge to ASEAN centrality, which is predicated upon the multilateral house of post-Cold War Asia built by ASEAN and its dialogue partners (that is, the '1.0' version of multilateralism of which ASEAN serves as the appointed custodian) (Tan 2015, 4–17). As Ian Storey and Malcolm Cook have argued in reference to the Indo-Pacific strategies of the Quad countries,

> The crystalizing of the overlapping Indo-Pacific concepts of the US, Japan, Australia and India may well mean that ASEAN has lost the ability to lead the development of this concept and use it—as they did with the idea of the Asia-Pacific—to tie major powers more closely to the ASEAN-led regional architecture. (Storey and Cook 2018, 6)

On the other hand, a chorus of assurances have been voiced by the Quad countries over ASEAN's concerns about the former's respective Indo-Pacific strategies. At the Shangri-La Dialogue (SLD) in June 2018, the Indian premier Narendra Modi emphasized that Southeast Asia is at the centre of Delhi's view of the Indo-Pacific and that ASEAN has been and would remain central to the future of the Indo-Pacific. India's support for ASEAN has since been echoed by its fellow Quad countries. At the ASEAN meetings in August 2018 in Singapore, US Secretary of State Mike Pompeo reassured his fellow ministers that the United States remains committed to ASEAN centrality and emphasized his own expectation and eagerness for US engagement with the region on that basis (Hussain 2018). Pompeo's assurance came in the wake of similar remarks issued in July by the Japanese foreign minister Taro Kono about ASEAN as being equally at the heart of Japan's vision of the Indo Pacific (Sim 2018). As a Japanese foreign ministry official reportedly insisted, 'There has been some misunderstanding about the [Indo-Pacific] strategy but I can assure you that ASEAN sits right in the centre of the Indo-Pacific and ASEAN is centre to this concept' (cited in Sim 2018). In response, ASEAN has welcomed Japan's promotion of international law and focus on building 'high-quality infrastructure' as the core elements of its Indo-Pacific strategy (Yi 2018).

After a pregnant pause where some (but not all) ASEAN countries publicly expressed their views on the Indo-Pacific—with most adopting a 'wait and see' attitude, despite their shared concern over China's growing power and its assertiveness in the South China Sea—ASEAN eventually if belatedly issued its 'Outlook on the Indo Pacific' in June 2019. Recognizing that the Indo-Pacific region constitutes arguably the most economically dynamic yet geopolitically unsettled part of the world today, the Outlook document pointedly notes 'the rise of material powers'—notably, without identifying who they are—and cautions against 'the deepening of mistrust, miscalculation, and patterns of behaviour based on a zero-sum game' that could and presumably has accompanied that power shift (ASEAN 2019a, 1). The Outlook left little doubt as to how ASEAN sees its role and place in the Indo-Pacific. Whether or not the assurances given ASEAN by the Quad countries were mere afterthoughts, it is evident that viewing the Asia-Pacific and Indian Ocean regions not as contiguous territorial spaces but as a closely integrated and interconnected region, 'with ASEAN playing a central and strategic role' (ASEAN 2019a, 2)[2] was intended to enhance ASEAN's community building process and to strengthen and give new momentum to existing ASEAN-led mechanisms to better face challenges and seize opportunities arising from the current and future regional and global environments.

Ultimately, what could prove problematic, as some have pointed out, is the host of thorny issues—the stubborn nature of illiberalism in Southeast Asia, ASEAN's apparent impotence amid the South China Sea conflicts, ASEAN's inability to deliver on its own promised regional integration and community formation, among others—which potentially undermine ASEAN's case for centrality in the Indo-Pacific and make it difficult for non-ASEAN powers to accept this proposition (Parameswaran 2018a). As Singapore's prime minister Lee Hsien Loong has cautioned, ASEAN centrality is by no means a given because the organization, in Lee's view, has 'no automatic right' to be at centre of regional architecture, but must prove its worth through greater institutional cohesion and deeper regional commitment among its members.[3]

Engaging the BRI

Southeast Asia's geographical proximity to China has served the ASEAN economies well (Xilian 2019). There is no question that China's BRI, seen by many as China's key contribution to multilateralism 2.0, has much to offer Southeast Asia. It shares major goals with the ASEAN Master Plan on ASEAN Connectivity (MPAC)—which China and the ASEAN states have formally agreed to 'synergise' with the BRI (ASEAN 2019b)—since both initiatives envisage transport connectivity as a way of bringing countries closer together and improving access to trade, investment and tourism. At the China-ASEAN Expo in Nanning, China in September 2019, participating ASEAN dignitaries spoke of the BRI—and the China-ASEAN strategic partnership as it relates to the BRI—in glowing terms. The Cambodian deputy prime minister Hor Nam Hong averred that the BRI provides momentum for regional economic integration and connectivity, helping China and ASEAN forge a closer community of shared future, while the Thai deputy prime minister Jurin Laksanawisit offered the view that the BRI accelerates regional connectivity and improves people's livelihoods (Xinhuanet 2019). Singapore, Vietnam, Thailand, Malaysia, Cambodia, and Myanmar are all ranked among the top ten countries most connected to China via trade and BRI-related capital flows.[4] Opportunities thereby exist for even greater mutual benefit for both China and the ASEAN region through regional connectivity wrought through BRI-MPAC connectivity (Hamzah 2018, 19).

But the BRI has also prompted questions over the political and strategic ramifications of their increasing economic reliance if not overdependence on China. Notwithstanding Southeast Asia's general positivity toward the BRI when it was launched in 2013 as the 'Silk Road Economic Belt' and the '21st Century Maritime Silk Road,' the reception to the BRI in the ensuing years has been decidedly mixed among ASEAN participants. On the one hand, all of them recognize the opportunities that come with engaging with China, even if the extent of their participation hitherto comprises a mix of old and new projects, not all of which are fully implemented. For example, despite the Chinese Government's claim at the 2019 Belt and Road Forum (BRF) in Beijing that the BRI has reportedly delivered '283 concrete results in six categories,' it is uncertain how many of those agreements are actually new or implementable. As Prashanth Parameswaran has observed, several of the agreements 'constitute either the repackaging of older initiatives or limited new convergences, as evidenced by the diversity of mechanisms beyond more binding memorandums of understanding such as declarations of intent' (Parameswaran 2019a). On the other hand, these countries have also grown more aware of the challenges—the oft-mentioned debt diplomacy being but the most obvious—that involvement in the BRI are likely to bring, directly and indirectly. The example of the Hambantota port in Sri Lanka has gained wide attention as a stark illustration of not only the dual-use potential for BRI-financed infrastructural facilities, but, crucially, China's creeping control of such (Abi-Habib 2018). Arguably, some BRI-related projects in Southeast Asia could also go the same way, as evidenced by Chinese investments and involvement in Koh Kong province and Ream naval base in Cambodia (see Page, Lubold and Taylor 2019; Parameswaran 2018b).

Crucially, there is concern among ASEAN states over China's apparent readiness to use the BRI to advance its global influence and military presence and, more specifically, assert its claims over the South China Sea (see Smith 2018; *South China Morning Post* 2019). In this regard, it is telling that Malaysian leader Mahathir Mohamad, in a primarily laudatory speech on the BRI, nonetheless took the opportunity afforded him at the 2019 BRF to remind his Chinese hosts that freedom of navigation was an important concern for all involved (Lo 2019). On the part of Beijing, at the same BRF meeting, the Chinese leadership acknowledged international concerns over how the BRI had hitherto been implemented. At the BRF, Chinese president Xi Jinping gave the assurance that the BRI would reportedly adopt multilateral rules and international best practices in implementing the projects (Vineles 2019). As Jinny Yan has argued, the BRI ought to serve as a catalyst for regional and global growth and not as an excuse for China to seek further leverage (Yan 2018, 7). Beijing's assurances are unlikely to assuage the region's angst over Chinese strategic ambitions. While the process in negotiating the code of conduct in the South China Sea has moved forward with agreement over a single draft text for the code and a deadline for delivering the finalized code within three years from 2019 onward, the Chinese demand for 'foreign powers' to be kept out of the South China Sea as a precondition for concluding the code underscore Beijing's intention to complicate ASEAN's hedging strategy (*The Standard* 2019).

On the other hand, it could be argued that because ASEAN stays committed to engaging China, it has earned for itself the 'right' to assert its centrality—and, by implication, its declared commitment to hedge—in what is supposedly a non-ASEAN initiative and framework. According to the ASEAN-China Joint Statement on Synergising the MPAC 2025 and the BRI, both sides reaffirmed the maintenance of 'ASEAN centrality in the evolving regional architecture,' while also acknowledging the ASEAN Outlook on the Indo-Pacific and reaffirming the principles of openness, transparency, inclusiveness and ASEAN centrality presented therein (ASEAN 2019a, 2). Indeed, precisely because the ASEAN Outlook on Indo-Pacific highlights the notion of 'connecting the connectivities' as a priority area of cooperation—language reminiscent of the BRI and MPAC—ASEAN has essentially ensured that it is ASEAN's version of the Indo-Pacific—not those of the Quad countries—that China supports, if only nominally.

ASEAN's maritime exercises

Inasmuch as persistent US–China competition is clearly going to pose a serious challenge to ASEAN's centrality in cooperative multilateralism, there are indications that suggest some ASEAN members have sought to redefine and reinterpret ASEAN centrality in a way more appropriate to developments in the region. Nowhere was this more evident than in ASEAN's pursuit of regional security cooperation separately with the Chinese in 2018 and the Americans in 2019. Under the 'ASEAN plus one' format, ASEAN and China jointly conducted a maritime exercise involving over a thousand personnel and eight ships off the coast of Zhanjiang city in Guangdong province in October 2018. The exercise, which allowed naval elements from China and the ASEAN member states to practise search and rescue operations and apply the code of unplanned encounters at sea (CUES), followed a table-top exercise held in Singapore two months earlier (Beng 2018). But even before the start of this exercise, the defense ministers of Singapore and the United States were already confirming on the sidelines of the ASEAN-led defense ministers' meetings that October that ASEAN and the United States would conduct their version of a joint maritime exercise some time in 2019, likely in conjunction with the US-led exercise Southeast Asia Cooperation and Training (SEACAT) (Ministry of Defence 2018).

Coming just under a year after the ASEAN-China exercise off Zhanjiang, the ASEAN–US maritime exercise took place off the coast of Vietnam's Ca Mau province and focused on aspects of maritime security—including search and seizure, maritime domain awareness and maritime asset tracking, capabilities critical in checking illegal fishing and monitoring grey zone actors and non-innocent forays—in the wake of the 2019 edition of SEACAT. Brunei, Philippines, Singapore, Thailand, and Vietnam participated by sending vessels and troops for their respective joint exercises, whereas the rest of the ASEAN members—including Indonesia and Malaysia, both significant regional maritime actors—opted against deploying assets in the two exercises but sent observers instead (Pitlo III 2019).

Apart from the operational value this exercise holds and its contribution to building the capacity of ASEAN maritime forces and coordination among them, the initiative can arguably be seen as an effort by the United States to advance its defense ties with ASEAN countries under the security dimension of its FOIP strategy (Parameswaran 2019b).

In themselves, these joint exercises, significant as they are for various reasons—for instance, the ASEAN-China maritime exercise was the first ever between both sides—might not seem extraordinary in that they are treated as dimensions of the ADMM-Plus (see Tan 2019b). Arguably, the ADMM-Plus, an 18-member arrangement centred upon ASEAN—comprising the ten ASEAN member states and the 'Plus' countries, Australia, China, India, Japan, New Zealand, Russia, South Korea, and the United States—has achieved a level of success in regional cooperation hitherto unattained by other ASEAN-led forms of institutionalized multilateral mechanisms in the Asia-Pacific (see Tan 2017a). However, whether the ADMM-Plus represents effective security multilateralism is still unclear. This is because the ADMM-Plus shares many of the institutional qualities of weaker counterparts like the ASEAN Regional Forum (ARF). That said, at a time where multilateralism as a whole appears to be on the wane (Laidi 2018), the ADMM-Plus has not only kept afloat but flown high because of its willingness, for pragmatic reasons stemming from its stakeholders' collective quest for effective regional cooperation, to (quietly) test some of ASEAN-led multilateralism's most cherished conventions.

What is interesting is the way ASEAN states have sought to redefine such engagements with the Chinese and the Americans at the 'ASEAN plus one' level as evidence, fairly or otherwise, of ASEAN's continued relevance as well as the significance of its centrality in the region's multilateral architecture[5]—including, presumably, aspects of multilateralism 2.0, even though technically ASEAN is not a part of that. ASEAN's ability to collaborate separately with China and the United States on maritime security is arguably an indication that the grouping has regained the regional initiative in the region, not least where maritime security cooperation is concerned. Crucially, they are not meant to replace the ADMM-Plus multilateral exercises—which include American and Chinese troops and equipment, often working together—that have continually grown in size and sophistication, but rather to supplement them. Together, both multilateral and bilateral efforts reflect ASEAN's belief that both the ADMM—comprising just the ten ASEAN members—and the ADMM-Plus are vital elements of the region's architecture. They provide platforms that are open and inclusive, and bring together all-important regional stakeholders for dialogue and cooperation (see Tan 2018b). That said, while these exercises display a regional desire for inclusivity and balanced security ties with the two great powers, their conduct in successive order and undertaken against a backdrop of incidents in the South China Sea is no coincidence and is arguably indicative of intensifying major power contestation playing out in the context of defense diplomacy (see, for example, Chang and Chong 2016; Chong and Lee 2018).

What the above developments conceivably imply, at least in the context of regional security cooperation, is a readiness by ASEAN—through activities deemed useful by both the Chinese as well as the Americans—to position itself as still the regional actor of consequence in an era of growing great power discord where its centrality in cooperative multilateralism is increasingly in question. Furthermore, what is notable of ASEAN's conduct in this instance is an effort to demonstrate its relevance to the major powers in concrete ways, rather than relying on rhetorical declarations alone. More broadly, it also reflects ASEAN's persistent commitment to hedging and nonalignment in the face of increasing pressures from China and the United States on its member states to choose sides in the strategic rivalry between the Chinese and the Americans. In other words, ASEAN's initiatives with China and the United States in maritime security cooperation are reflective of its continued propensity to hedge.

Conclusion

This chapter has briefly looked at how ASEAN, the trustee of the Asia-Pacific multilateralism centred upon itself, has responded to the new forms of multilateralism in the region introduced and implemented by non-ASEAN powers, especially the United States and China. In the face of the growing strategic rivalry between these two superpowers and the competing regional visions and architectures they respectively offer—the Free and Open Indo-Pacific (FOIP) and the Belt and Road Initiative (BRI), respectively—and the instability that these have brought to the region, ASEAN has responded with efforts to stabilize the regional order. It has done so through a strategy of hedging and engagement with the two big powers that is less about balancing—as conventionally understood—and more about accommodation, but importantly without choosing sides.

Notes

1 This argument is elaborated in He (2008b).
2 Emphasis added.
3 Urging his fellow Southeast Asian leaders to 'look beyond their domestic concerns (and) put emphasis on ASEAN,' Lee furnished a stark appraisal of the situation back in March 2018, 'There is nothing to prevent other groupings or regional cooperation projects from being launched. Some will compete with ASEAN, others will contribute in complementary ways to regional cooperation and stability ... Amidst this Darwinian process, ASEAN members must come together to maintain ASEAN's relevance and cohesion ... Governing a country internally is already an all-consuming business, but ASEAN governments need to look beyond their domestic concerns ... Invest political capital in the ASEAN project, and make a conscious effort to think regionally, not just nationally. Only with this commitment by member states, can we deepen our partnership and make progress on ASEAN': cited in Ng (2018).
4 Among ASEAN member countries, Indonesia (US$171bn), Vietnam (US$152bn), Cambodia (US$104bn), Malaysia (US$98bn), and Singapore (US$70bn) are the countries seeing the largest BRI-related capital flow.
5 Redefining ASEAN's centrality is perhaps not difficult since ASEAN centrality is itself an ambiguous concept or principle to begin with: Tan (2017b).

References

Abi-Habib, Maria. 2018. "How China Got Sri Lanka to Cough Up a Port." *The New York Times*, June 25. https://www.nytimes.com/2018/06/25/world/asia/china-sri-lanka-port.

ASEAN (Association of Southeast Asian Nations). 2019a. "ASEAN Outlook on the Indo Pacific." June 23, pp. 1–5. https://asean.org/storage/2019/06/ASEAN-Outlook-on-the-Indo-Pacific_FINAL_22062019.pdf.

ASEAN (Association of Southeast Asian Nations). 2019b. "ASEAN-China Joint Statement on Synergising the Master Plan on ASEAN Connectivity (MPAC) 2025 and the Belt and Road Initiative (BRI)." November 3. https://asean.org/storage/2019/11/Final-ASEAN-China-Joint-Statement-Synergising-the-MPAC-2025-and-the-BRI.pdf.

Asia Society. n.d. "Why Being 'Hugely Imperfect' Is the Secret to ASEAN's Success." https://asiasociety.org/new-york/why-being-hugely-imperfect-secret-aseans-success.

Beng, Koh Eng. 2018. "ASEAN–China Maritime Exercise Helps Boost Regional Stability: Dr Ng." *Pioneer*, October 23. www.mindef.gov.sg/web/portal/pioneer/article/regular-article-detail/ops-and-training/2018-Q4/23oct18_news.

Bowers, Ian. 2018. "Escalation at Sea: Stability and Instability in Maritime East Asia." *Naval War College Review* 71(4, Autumn): 1–21. https://digital-commons.usnwc.edu/cgi/viewcontent.cgi?article=7672&context=nwc-review.

Chang, Jun Yan, and Alan Chong. 2016. "Security Competition by Proxy: Asia Pacific Interstate Rivalry in the Aftermath of the MH370 Incident." *Global Change, Peace & Security* 28(1): 75–98.

Chong, Alan, and Il-woo Lee. 2018. "Asia's Security Competition by Proxy: Competitive HADR as a Respectable Arena?" In *International Security in the Asia-Pacific: Transcending ASEAN Towards Transitional Polycentrism*, edited by Alan Chong, 377–400. Cham, Switzerland: Palgrave Macmillan.

Friedberg, Aaron L. 1993–1994. "Ripe for Rivalry: Prospects for Peace in a Multipolar Asia." *International Security* 18(1, Winter): 5–33.

Gady, Franz-Stefan. 2017. "The Coming War in Asia: Why It Is Hard to Imagine the Unimaginable." *The Diplomat*, August 3. https://thediplomat.com/2017/08/the-coming-war-in-asia-why-it-is-hard-to-imagine-the-unimaginable/.

Gilley, Bruce, and Andrew O'Neil. 2014. *Middle Powers and the Rise of China*. Washington DC: Georgetown University Press.

Goh, Evelyn. 2008. "Great Powers and Hierarchical Order in Southeast Asia: Analyzing Regional Security Strategies." *International Security* 32(3): 113–157.

Goh, Sui Noi. 2013. "Asean Eyes India as a Soft Balancer." *The Straits Times*, March 22. http://www.nationmultimedia.com/news/opinion/aec/30202528

Hamzah, Hanim. 2018. "Legal Issues and Implications of the BRI." In *China's Belt and Road Initiative (BRI) and Southeast Asia*, Special report, October, 19–25. London and Kuala Lumpur: IDEAS, London School of Economics and CIMB ASEAN Research Institute.

He, Kai. 2008a. *Institutional Balancing in the Asia Pacific: Economic Interdependence and China's Rise*. London: Routledge.

He, Kai. 2008b. "Institutional Balancing and International Relations Theory: Economic Interdependence and Balance of Power Strategies in Southeast Asia." *European Journal of International Relations* 14(3): 489–518.

He, Kai. 2019. "Contested Multilateralism 2.0 and Regional Order Transition: Causes and Implications." *The Pacific Review* 32(2): 210–220.

Huang, Xiaoming. 2014. "The Emerging Security Landscape in the Asia-Pacific: Where ASEAN Fits." Paper presented at the Goh Keng Swee Command and Staff College (GKSCSC) Seminar, October 9–10, Singapore.

Hussain, Zakir. 2018. "US Remains Committed to Asean Centrality, Mike Pompeo Tells Foreign Ministers." *The Straits Times*, August 3. www.straitstimes.com/politics/us-rema ins-committed-to-asean-centrality-mike-pompeo-tells-foreign-ministers.

Kang, David C. 2009. "Between Balancing and Bandwagoning: South Korea's Response to China." *Journal of East Asian Studies* 9(1): 1–28.

Khong, Yuen Foong. 2004. "Coping with Strategic Uncertainty: The Role of Institutions and Soft Balancing in Southeast Asia's Post-Cold War Strategy." In *Rethinking Security in East Asia: Identity, Power, and Efficiency*, edited by J. J. Suh, Peter J. Katzenstein, and Allen Carlson, 172–208. Stanford, CA: Stanford University Press.

Khong, Yuen Foong, 2005. "The Elusiveness of Regional Order: Leifer, the English school and Southeast Asia." *The Pacific Review* 18(1): 23–41.

Kupchan, Charles A. 1998. "After *Pax Americana*: Benign Power, Regional Integration, and the Sources of Multipolarity." *International Security* 23(2, Fall): 40–79.

Laidi, Zaki. 2018. "Is Multilateralism Finished?" *Project Syndicate*, May 18. https://www.pro ject-syndicate.org/onpoint/is-multilateralism-finished-by-zaki-laidi-2018-05?barrier=acce sspaylog.

Lee, John. 2018. "ASEAN Must Choose: America or China?" *The National Interest*, December 28. https://nationalinterest.org/feature/asean-must-choose-america-or-china-39067.

Lee, Seungjoo. 2012. "The Evolutionary Dynamics of Institutional Balancing in East Asia." EAI Asia Security Initiative Working Paper, February, East Asia Institute, Seoul.

Lemahieu, Herve. "Five Big Takeaways from the 2019 Asia Power Index." *Lowy Interpreter*, May 29. https://www.lowyinstitute.org/the-interpreter/power-shifts-fevered-times-2019-a sia-power-index.

Little, Richard. 1989. "Deconstructing the Balance of Power: Two Traditions of Thought." *Review of International Studies* 15(2): 87–100.

Lo, Kinling. 2019. "Malaysia's Mahathir Backs China's Belt and Road but Insists on Open Trade Routes." *South China Morning Post*, April 26. https://www.scmp.com/news/china/ diplomacy/article/3007874/malaysias-mahathir-backs-chinas-belt-and-road-insists-open.

Ministry of Defence (Singapore). 2018. "ASEAN and US to Conduct Joint Maritime Exercise in 2019." October 19. https://www.mindef.gov.sg/web/portal/mindef/news-a nd-events/latest-releases/article-detail/2018/october/19oct18_nr2/!ut/p/z0/fY27DsIwFEO _hSFjdNOKRxkLDIAoXQoKWVBoLxAoN31EBf6egBiY2GzLxwYFEhTpzpy0M5Z06f 1ODfejdDadi364TgdZIOJtlq0Gk_ViMxrCEtT_gl8wl7pWMajcksOHA3kzVOCRfzw5Js7 2hkwQ3luuqeDY-bRlotQOW8cbLFG36INQBBETNnf2gA0TwdjLINpTE75vwia ZJidQlXZnbuhoQb4BkF8A5C9QXdXheY97L8LD9Tw!/

Ng, Kelly. 2018. "Asean Has 'No Automatic Right' to Be at Centre of Regional Architecture: PM Lee." *Today*, March 13. www.todayonline.com/singapore/asean-has-no-automatic-right-be-centre-regional-architecture-pm-lee.

Page, Jeremy, Gordon Lubold, and Rob Taylor. 2019. "Deal for Naval Outpost in Cambodia Furthers China's Quest for Military Network." *The Wall Street Journal*, July 29. http s://www.wsj.com/articles/secret-deal-for-chinese-naval-outpost-in-cambodia-raise s-u-s-fears-of-beijings-ambitions-11563732482.

Parameswaran, Prashanth. 2018a. "Trump's Indo-Pacific Strategy Challenge in the Spotlight at 2018 Shangri-La Dialogue." *The Diplomat*, June 5. https://thediplomat. com/2018/06/trumps-indo-pacific-strategy-challenge-in-the-spotlight-at-2018-shangri -la-dialogue/.

Parameswaran, Prashanth. 2018b. "What's in the China–Cambodia Military Base Hype?" *The Diplomat*, November 24. https://thediplomat.com/2018/11/whats-in-the-china-cam bodia-military-base-hype/.

Parameswaran, Prashanth. 2019a. "Southeast Asia and China's Belt and Road Initiative." *The Diplomat*, May 15. https://thediplomat.com/2019/05/southeast-asia-and-chinas-belt-and-road-initiative/.

Parameswaran, Prashanth. 2019b. "Why the First US–ASEAN Maritime Exercise Matters." *The Diplomat*, August 29. https://thediplomat.com/2019/08/why-the-first-us-asean-maritime-exercise-matters/.

Pitlo III, Lucio B. 2019. "The ASEAN–US Maritime Exercises Are More Important than Ever." *The National Interest*, October 27. https://nationalinterest.org/feature/asean-us-maritime-exercises-are-more-important-ever-90956.

Ryu, Yongwook. 2013. "ASEAN's Middle Power Diplomacy toward China." EAI Issue Briefing MPDI no. 2013–2012, October 10. East Asia Institute, Seoul.

Shambaugh, David. 2018. "US–China Rivalry in Southeast Asia: Power Shift or Competitive Coexistence?" *International Security* 42(4, Spring): 85–127.

Sim, Walter. 2018. "Asean at Heart of Japan's Free and Open Indo-Pacific Strategy: Kono." *The Straits Times*, July 27. www.straitstimes.com/asia/east-asia/asean-at-heart-of-japans-free-and-open-indo-pacific-strategy-kono.

Smith, Jeff. 2018. *China's Belt and Road Initiative: Strategic Implications and International Opposition*. Report, The Heritage Foundation, August 9. https://www.heritage.org/asia/report/chinas-belt-and-road-initiative-strategic-implications-and-international-opposition

South China Morning Post. 2019. "Belt and Road's Real Aims? Expanding China's Global Influence and Military Presence, US Study Says." April 18. https://www.scmp.com/news/china/diplomacy-defence/article/2142266/belt-and-roads-aim-promote-chinese-interests-and.

Storey, Ian, and Malcolm Cook. 2018. "The Trump Administration and Southeast Asia: America's Asia Policy Crystalizes." *Perspective* 77, November 2. ISEAS Yusof Ishak Institute, Singapore.

Stuart, Douglas T., and William Tow. 1995. "A US Strategy for the Asia-Pacific: Building a Multipolar Balance-of-Power System in Asia." Adelphi Papers, No. 22. International Institute for Strategic Studies, London.

Stubbs, Richard, 2014. "ASEAN's Leadership in East Asian Region-Building: Strength in Weakness." *The Pacific Review* 27(4): 523–541.

Tan, See Seng. 2012. "Spectres of Leifer: Insights on Regional Order and Security for Southeast Asia Today." *Contemporary Southeast Asia* 34(3): 309–337.

Tan, See Seng. 2015. *Multilateral Asian Security Architecture: Non-ASEAN Stakeholders*. London: Routledge.

Tan, See Seng. 2017a. "A Tale of Two Institutions: The ARF, ADMM-Plus and Security Regionalism in the Asia Pacific." *Contemporary Southeast Asia* 39(2): 259–264.

Tan, See Seng. 2017b. "Rethinking 'ASEAN Centrality' in the Regional Governance of East Asia." *Singapore Economic Review* 62(3, June): 721–740.

Tan, See Seng. 2018a. "When Giants Vie: China–US Competition, Institutional Balancing, and East Asian Multilateralism." In *US–China Competition and the South China Sea Disputes*, edited by Huiyun Feng and Kai He, 116–133. London: Routledge.

Tan, See Seng. 2018b. "Singapore Paving the Way for Greater Regional Security." *The Straits Times*, February 23, p. A21.

Tan, See Seng. 2019a. *The Responsibility to Provide in Southeast Asia: Towards an Ethical Explanation*. Bristol: Bristol University Press.

Tan, See Seng. 2019b. "The ADMM and ADMM-Plus: Regional Security Mechanisms That Work?" In *Asia-Pacific Regional Security Assessment 2018*, edited by Tim Huxley and William Choong, 165–175. London: International Institute for Strategic Studies.

Tan, See Seng. 2020. "Consigned to Hedge: Southeast Asia and America's 'Free and Open Indo-Pacific' Strategy." *International Affairs* 96(1): 131–148.

The Standard. 2019. "Beijing Insisted on Keeping Foreign Powers Out in South China Sea, Manila Says." September 11. http://www.thestandard.com.hk/breaking-news.php?id=134450&sid=6.

Tunsjo, Oystein. 2018. *The Return of Bipolarity in World Politics: China, the United States, and Geostructural Realism.* New York: Columbia University Press.

Vineles, Phidel. 2019. "Making the Belt and Road Work for Southeast Asia." *East Asia Forum,* July 13. https://www.eastasiaforum.org/2019/07/13/making-the-belt-and-road-work-for-southeast-asia/.

Wagle, Ankush A. 2018. "How Will ASEAN Balance a Tug of Power between China and US-led 'Quad' in the Indo-Pacific?" *The Jakarta Post,* October 24. https://www.thejakartapost.com/academia/2018/10/24/how-will-asean-balance-a-tug-of-power-between-china-and-us-led-quad-in-the-indo-pacific.html.

Xilian, Huang. 2019. "China and ASEAN Doing Well on Economic, Trade Cooperation." *The Jakarta Post,* January 31. https://www.thejakartapost.com/academia/2019/01/31/china-and-asean-doing-well-on-economic-trade-cooperation.html.

Xinhuanet. 2019. "China Focus: China, ASEAN Embrace Shared Future along Belt and Road." September 23. http://www.xinhuanet.com/english/2019-09/23/c_138415949.htm.

Yan, Jinny. 2018. "The Belt and Road Initiative in Southeast Asia." In *China's Belt and Road Initiative (BRI) and Southeast Asia.* Special report, October, pp. 4–9. London and Kuala Lumpur: IDEAS, London School of Economics and CIMB ASEAN Research Institute.

Yi, Seow Bei. 2018. "Japan's Indo-Pacific Strategy Aligns Well with Singapore, Asean Priorities: PM Lee." *The Straits Times,* November 15. https://www.straitstimes.com/singapore/japans-indo-pacific-strategy-aligns-well-with-spore-asean-priorities-pm-lee.

Zhang, Feng. 2011. "Reconceiving the Balance of Power: A Review Essay." *Review of International Studies* 37(2): 641–651.

INDEX

For Product Safety Concerns and Information please contact our EU
representative GPSR@taylorandfrancis.com
Taylor & Francis Verlag GmbH, Kaufingerstraße 24, 80331 München, Germany

www.ingramcontent.com/pod-product-compliance
Lightning Source LLC
Chambersburg PA
CBHW050713280326
41926CB00088B/3006

* 9 7 8 0 3 6 7 8 9 3 3 8 5 *